For the Record

**_28:50_ - A journey toward self-discovery
and the Cannonball Run Record**

Ed Bolian

ISBN: 9781520341033 - Copyright 2017

For the Record
Table of Content

Introduction from Brock Yates Jr.		4
Foreword by Alex Roy, Previous Record Holder		5
Dedication		10
1	All Roads Lead to Cannonball	11
2	The Interview	29
3	Finding My Flaw	36
4	$1 million in Debt at 20	53
5	Two Lightning Bolts in the Darkness	56
6	Lawyers, Politicians, & Used Car Salesmen	81
7	A Prostitute and a Lamborghini	96
8	Finalizing the Playbook	104
9	Becoming a Christian Outlaw	122
	Remarks from Forrest Sibley	129
	Countermeasure Expert	
10	The Criminal in the Mirror	133
	Remarks from Dave Black	139
	Co-Outlaw	
11	Assembling the Bomb	148
	Remarks from Charles Carden	151
	Lambo Tech & Fuel Cell Engineer	
12	The Nine Thousand Dollar Tune Up	156

Remarks from David "Klink" Kalinkiewicz 166

Master Mercedes Technician

13 The Co-Driver Draft   180

14 You're Leaking Gas   196

Remarks from Nick Reid   210

Los Angeles Scout

15 Pulled over in NYC   212

Remarks from Dan Huang   225

Navigator & Support Passenger

16 Down the Hot Wheels Track   229

Remarks from Danny Landoni   235

Pennsylvania Scout

17 Roadside Urination and Driver Changes   237

Remarks from Chris Staschiak   242

Ohio Scout

18 Surely we can't keep this up   246

Remarks from Dave Black   249

19 Excessive Oil Consumption   256

Remarks from Adam Kochanski   274

GPS Witness, Eye in the Sky

20 Beating the AMEX Algorithm   280

21 The Final Push   299

22 Catharsis   309

Epilogue: Now Find Yours!   322

Photo Archive   328

An introduction
from Brock Yates Jr.

One of my favorite memories with my father was riding along on the first Cannonball in our Moon Trash van in 1971 when I was just 14 years old. The thing I will probably never forgive him for is intentionally not telling me about the 1979 running until it was impossible for me to get to the starting line in time. Regardless of your engagement with the actual running, the folklore of the Cannonball Baker Sea to Shining Sea Memorial Trophy Dash holds a special place in the heart of any gearhead. Perhaps no modern passion for Cannonball burns brighter than that of Ed Bolian.

Ed called me for the first time a few days after his 2013 run. He told me about the discussion he had with my father nearly a decade prior and told me for the first of many times what my father meant to him. These modern interpretations of an idea going on fifty years old leave me with mixed feelings but I am happy to congratulate Ed on adding himself to the annals of Cannonball lore and thank him for another safe outcome in a coast to coast drive. Condone is not the right word now that most of us from 1970s runs have aged but I believe that "respect" is right way to put it. Fortunately that respect was clearly mutual. Ed exhibits a respect for my father, the history, and the craft that makes me happy to enjoy the rest of this fascinating story of personal growth and to call him a fellow Cannonballer.

A foreword by Alex Roy
Previous Record Holder

This is a terrible book, written by a terrible person about terrible people inspired by terrible people, all of whom have done terrible things for no damn good reason at all. Or, as an FBI agent once told me, "never have so few accomplished so much on behalf of so few." He was wrong, of course, as proven by the fact that you're reading this now, and hopefully paid for it. Those terrible people aren't to be feared or reviled, but thanked, for in a world where you can pay a guide to carry your luggage up Mount Everest, there are still things that money can't buy.

That's just one of the reasons the Cannonball Run still matters.

All the money in the world won't get you across the United States in a car under 30 hours. It takes intelligence, character and skill. I should know, because I led the team whose record was broken by Ed Bolian, David Black, and Dan Huang in 2013.

Ed Bolian didn't participate in the actual Cannonball Run, nor did I, or anyone since 1979. But we came close. While the punks, "street racers," cowards, charlatans and liars upload YouTube videos of donuts, drag times and rallies "inspired" by the real thing, Ed joins a short list of people with the nerve to actually get out and drive, rather than hashtag some pretty stills.

5

And not just drive. Go after the big one. The Cannonball Record. New York to California, non-stop except for gas. One can quibble over routes and details, but you either went, or you didn't. Bolian went, joining a list of no more than a few hundred people who've even tried, let alone done it in under 34 hours.

Upon first hearing Ed's story, I didn't believe it. I didn't want to believe it. Extraordinary claims require extraordinary evidence. He didn't appear to have gone through the same lengths David Maher and I did when we broke the record in 2006. He had no video. Media? Witnesses? I wasn't convinced. But Bolian did have something extraordinary. His story rang true. He *had* called me under false pretenses seeking to know how I had planned our run. He *had* prepared a car correctly. He knew all of the details of the drive off the top of his head. His story was consistent. His GPS records matched.

Of all the people who've ever called to say they'd beaten our time, Bolian's was the only one that made any sense. As soon as I met him, I knew he was telling the truth. I'll never stop insulting him to his face for not shooting video, however, for I think he lowered the evidentiary bar, enabling frauds with times tattooed to their arms to claim they are part of the history.

But history isn't for me to decide.

No one person can ever own the Cannonball

history again, except for Brock Yates, who is now gone. All that is left is respect for the history. Go across in a car and you're part of it. Under 38 is good. Under 35 is better. For every hour under 34, your voice will be louder among those who know. Loyalty? Brotherhood? These things can't be bought. The entry fee? The cheapest car that will get you across safely will suffice. Cannonballing in the purist sense isn't for rich people. It's for smart ones…if you call risking your life for nothing smart.

I have absolutely nothing in common with Ed Bolian. We disagree on religion, politics, you name it. He's wrong, and I despise his traitorous and absurd opinions. Hypocrisy? Thy name is Bolian. What else can you say about a Sunday School teaching, Lamborghini-driving criminal with a lovely wife and baby at home? You can say that he has a friend in me, for I too have struggled to rationalize the art and science of getting in a car and attacking a problem that doesn't need solving. Actually, we have everything in common. What am I thinking? Who am I to judge anyone? I practiced going cross country by dressing like a German cop. And a Spanish one. And a Canadian one. And a storm chaser, going cross country in one of the worst storm seasons in recent memory.

No one who does this sort of thing can claim a moral high ground, and yet—

For all the differences between us, we share something that goes to the heart of car culture, and what it means to be American. As a wise man named Mr. Regular once said, "California is the finish line of the world." Why do people keep doing this? Why do people dream of doing this? Why are people afraid to try? Why do people keep lying about doing this? Why are people ripping off the name, and trading on the goodwill of the Cannonball mythology?

There are only three books on the topic. Brock Yates' *Cannonball*, my book *The Driver*, and now, thankfully, Ed Bolian's. All amazing — mine being the best one, of course — and yet even these don't tell the full story.

Like jazz, if you have to ask...you'll never know until you've gotten in a car and tried. Don't bother until you've read all three cover to cover. Twice. And even then, if you're serious.

People often ask me if — now that the record Dave Maher and I set in 2006 has been broken — we're interested in going again. As if something has been taken from us. As if we have something to prove. As if the team of Bolian and co-driver David Black are our enemies.

Nonsense.

Everyone who has ever tried shares as much respect for each other as contempt for those who would claim unearned valor. Everyone who has ever gone for the record — alone or against other cars — did so on the backs of those who came before.

Anyone who has gotten across safely knows that one's time ultimately doesn't matter.

It's that you tried.

I'm proud to have done it, proud to have had the help of countless Cannonball and U.S. Express veterans, and proud that our experiences (however unwittingly) helped Ed and Dave raise the bar even further. Their achievement is monumental. Their margin of improvement? Insane.

Bolian, Black, and Huang are now part of Cannonball history. Something tells me they won't be the last to join it, as it should be. Anything is possible, even if not everything is necessary. Someone is going to do the research, likely one of you reading this now, and surprise Ed as much as he surprised me. Given the tradition of the old guy calling the new guy a liar, I can't wait for Ed to know that feeling.

FYI, if I was going to go again, I certainly wouldn't tell Ed (or anyone) in advance.

Now enjoy this terrible book about terrible people doing terrible things.

For my son, Graham

The most important thing in your life is your relationship with God. The recognition of the grace that saves me from sin, rather than the works or good deeds that I may do, is what delivers me from eternal separation from God through the sacrifice that Jesus made to bear our sins. If I teach you only one thing in your life, I want you to understand God loves you even more than I can. He sacrificed His own son so that you, me, and anyone else who asks can spend forever in paradise with Him. I would, however, like to teach you one more important thing about our lives here on earth.

This awesome God that we get to serve set a stage for humanity to exist upon. It involves a constant struggle between pride and benevolence, comfort and fear, and winning and losing. One of the coolest things that God ever did was build the world so that we could have great experiences, make a mark, and truly achieve something great. I want to tell you about a goal that came to define a significant portion of my life and where the journey to explore and eventually conquer that idea took me.
I am writing these first words sitting just a few feet away from you. You are three days old.

Chapter 1 - All Roads Lead to Cannonball

The tires squealed for mercy as the Lamborghini Murcielago's differentials traded grip for lateral inertia. My seventeen-year-old hands feigned confidence beyond their skillset and the bloodless face of the inexperienced salesman next to me failed to exude his desired cool as we slid between a bicyclist and a road-going tractor. I was grinning ear-to-ear as the V12 howl reverberated off the Carolina trees. There is nothing like controlled power, except of course the sensation of power just beyond complete control - that is when you trade precision for general direction. Dangerous. That is how it felt; dangerous and seductive. In the most basic sense - I was alive.

Today's man is not invited to do ballsy things. Producers seem to travel to England or Australia to find a "real man" actor to play opposite a casted hero who is either a sexy nerd or "just gay enough" to be palatable and called "metrosexual." It seems like being up on the latest internet memes and reality show drama constitutes culture. We downplay the significance of education and actual explorative achievement behind internet anonymity and social media status. Where are the real heroes?

Men are supposed to be powerful, dangerous, nearly unapproachable. They need to be in search of opportunities to either find or demonstrate courage, toughness, and strength - both mental and physical. Perhaps to win the admiration of womankind or just to exhibit their dominance over other men. There is a communism of masculinity happening where we want to have all betas rather than the occasional regal alpha.

Regardless of how much these animalistic urges are repressed, they still loom quiet and persistent beneath the surface just waiting for an opportunity to act.

But where are we to do that these days?

Cars. Beautiful, powerful, beastly, outrageous, exotic cars. Challenges in cars. Beating records so impossible that they were relegated to myth. Being smart and tough and calculating and devious. Hitting the road on a mission with a couple of other guys with enough testosterone and reckless abandon to kiss the wife, job, and maybe freedom from incarceration goodbye.

You just have to wake up one morning and say, "Today I'm going to start planning. It is something I simply have to do." Then for the next ten years it nags at you, it pulls you toward it with a simultaneously terrorizing and exciting magnetism. It drips in the background like a toilet that won't stop running until that one day when it is all that matters.

It must have been around 8:00 PM. The car felt under control and all systems were functional. I did not know precisely where I was, how fast I was going, or how long I had been driving. My eyesight was blurring with intense halos around every light ahead and in my mirrors. My depth perception was gone. I could not comprehend what Dave and Dan were saying. I remember telling them to find the next gas station. I had driven for what felt like hours directly into the Western Arizona setting sun near Kingman, wedging my head against the roof of the car to use it as a makeshift sun visor since the actual visor completely obstructed my view of the road. My senses were disoriented and struggling to focus. When I got into the mountains headed towards the eastern California border, the winding roads felt completely alien to me.

Somehow, I made it to the last gas station we would need to finish the trip. I looked down at the trip data displayed on the Mercedes computer. I had driven for just over two and half hours at an average speed of 95 miles per hour. It was our slowest leg of the trip thus far. Our overall average was right around 100 mph and we were just over 500 miles from the Portofino, our destination. On one hand the Portofino felt unbelievably close, in fact we did not need to completely fill the gas tanks to get there. On the other hand, 500 miles was nearly the distance that I used to devote a day to in a drive from Atlanta to Palm Beach, Florida visiting family on holidays and summer vacations. Considering the distance in that light remained as demoralizing and draining as that leg of driving had felt.

It was no surprise that no scenes from the *Cannonball Run* film were filmed in this setting. Even Captain Chaos would have stumbled. It was at that point when it hurt the worst and exactly that point when it all made sense. Any combination of goals, desires, and motivations which could get me twenty-four hours into a drive, barely coherent, and on track to do something this momentous had to be truly special.

I love cars. I haven't always loved cars. I don't love working on cars, drawing cars, cleaning cars, or building cars. I love driving cars. It is the way that I make my living, the lens through which I view the world, and my favorite recreational activity.

It kicked in at the point when I was able to drive. Being a grossly overconfident teenager, I saw nothing wrong or disrespectful in walking into every exotic car showroom in the metro Atlanta area and asking the hard working sales people to test drive one of their fine automobiles.

Most people who are successful by any accepted metric could be deemed obsessive. My personality has been characterized by a series of obsessions lumped together in sequence - dinosaurs, basketball, athletic shoes, reptiles, Ivy League schools, cars. It could have been rattling off every Mesozoic era dinosaur at age eight, playing in AAU basketball tournaments with Dwight Howard and Lebron James at thirteen, collecting Jordans at fifteen, attending the National Reptile Breeders' Expo at sixteen, trying to get into an Ivy League school at seventeen, at age twenty trying to drive 200 mph in my first Lamborghini without enough cash in my bank account to make the next payment, falling in love with a girl that was way out of my league around that same time, selling supercars at twenty-four, and barreling through Arizona inebriated only by exhaustion at twenty-eight. Life was generally one obsession after another with everything else either falling into place or falling by the wayside.

I started my first business when I was in middle school. The idea first came to me through my pet green iguana named George. Impressing them with my keen interest in genetics, I convinced my strangely indulgent parents to invest in an Albino Iguana breeding project. Before long we had a basement filled with thirty-three six foot long gentle giant lizards. Given their appetite, we were on our way to becoming the largest consumer of collard greens in the state of Georgia.

Mine was not a lemonade stand, pet sitting service, roadside carwash or any of the cliche first entrepreneurial projects you might expect of a kid. I wanted my work, even as a young teen to signify a uniqueness to my character and be something worth talking about. Anyone could have a pet dog or cat. Not many people had a basement that looked, smelled, and sounded like Jurassic Park.

Great White Reptiles was a lot of fun. My father and I built elaborate cages together, learned the intricacies of incubation, and took the lizards to trade shows to sell. Peculiar is a good word to describe the demographic of people who buy breeding quality reptiles as a blended hobby and investment. Imagine simultaneous enthusiasm for leather clothing, body art, and living home decor in a fascinating emulsion. Add twenty foot reticulated pythons, eight foot Sumatran water monitors, and adolescent me to the mix and you have it.

I sold a breeding pair of iguanas that were heterozygous for albinism to a couple of interesting guys from Tampa. Their pony tails, self-customized denim wear, and general lack of hygiene were quite frightening to Megan, whom I had recently begun dating. We found out later how, soon after leaving the rest area where we had made the exchange, they had released both thirty-plus pound lizards to roam about in the cab of their truck. Intrigued by their genetic mutation Noah's Ark, they ran their truck out of gas en route home and were forced to play paper-rock-scissors to see who got to walk five miles to fill a gas can.

Success was limited. The iguanas seemed so healthy and comfortable that perhaps I convinced them they would live forever. Regardless of whether it was communal solace or some other herpetological libido diminisher, fertile eggs were rare. My short attention span soon had me searching for my next fixation.

I was sixteen when I became smitten with cars. The confidence games to solicit test drives, magazine racing, internet videos, and a burgeoning indoctrination into the local car culture led to the desire to become professionally engrossed in the car industry just as I had with iguanas. I thought I wanted to be an automotive journalist, but found out it was not a high paying industry. I would have had a lot of chances to drive uninteresting cars for a few days but only rare opportunities to drive an exotic car for five minutes, so it seemed worthwhile to explore other automotive careers. It occurred to me if a job was widely considered to be cool you'd probably not be paid much to do it. I needed to change that.

My parents are amazing people. It has been said they did not say "No" often enough to me but I think they are terrific parents. Both are engineers, intellectuals, and devoted Christians. They gave me every example and opportunity I could have asked for to live a well-adjusted, normal life. I missed that boat or at least routinely steered it off course. Fortunately they loved each other and loved me through the many ridiculous detours.

Most parents try to teach their kids to work hard. Mine wanted me to work smart and know what I was talking about. Soon enough I was good at one and proficient at faking the other. They raised me to be confident, set goals, and make decisions well. I am not sure they realized exactly how those traits might manifest. The process of developing an ability to solve problems in my own way led to some friction with most authority figures in my path and had some unique implications through my life.

I became an avid consumer of car culture. The criterion of car enthusiast movies was building quickly at the time. Historic greats like *Bullitt*, *The Italian Job*, *Gumball Rally*, *Vanishing Point*, and *Cannonball Run* were being joined by modern interpretations and remakes in *Gone in Sixty Seconds*, *The Fast and the Furious* franchise, a new *Batman* trilogy, and a remake of *The Italian Job*. There were also some phenomenal car cameos in *The Rock*, *Bad Boys*, and *The Transporter*.

From an entertainment consumption perspective it was a highpoint of exotic car film appearances. This was beautifully augmented by the dawn of amateur created film projects and internet publication of poorly shot and badly edited clips. Teckademics & the *Mischief* franchise were documenting events like the Gumball 3000 and grassroots street racing which added to the allure of long distance competitive driving. The juggernaut of *Top Gear* was also just gaining traction in both the US and UK markets.

When I was a freshman in high school I was given an invitation to learn what real pain felt like. I was diagnosed with a very rare knee disorder called Bilateral Osteochondritis Dissecans Disease. It is a deterioration of the outer chondyles of each of my femurs. Essentially, in the area where your femur comes down to meet your tibia in the knee joint it splits into two lobes. On the outer lobe, or chondyle, my bones started to crumble away. Sometimes the bit of cartilage that remained in place worked to maintain stability, sometimes it did not.

Regardless, it caused excruciating pain and would have had me in a wheelchair by age thirty if not surgically addressed. It would take me an hour to loosen my knees and stretch before a basketball game in order to be able to run due to the inflammation. The only solution was a cadaver bone and cartilage tissue transplant from a dead, but otherwise healthy, donor close to my age and height. I could not have imagined it then, but ten years later I would sell the guy who harvested the cadaver tissue in my knees a brand new Lamborghini Gallardo LP550-2 Spyder.

The knee surgeries were a lot for a kid to go through but it gave me an opportunity to bury myself deeper into automotive lifestyle and folklore. I had six surgeries and learned a valuable lesson about what I was capable of enduring. I love the stories of people going through boot camp or their first tour of military service. What I went through was not like that at all, with the exception of one psychological aspect. Being thrust into something difficult or painful without much understanding of what you should anticipate tends to reveal some interesting things about what you are capable of surviving.

Sports had been a big part of my life. The knee issues ended my AAU Basketball career and, from a medical standpoint, swimming was the only athletic pursuit that was an option. I hated swimming. To me it is a boring, pointless activity unless you add sharks or alligators to the mix. Unfortunately, I was pretty good at it. My six and a half foot body and high capacity lungs were even more useful stroking through a pool than dunking a basketball. I endured four years of varsity high school and club swimming. The potential was there to swim in college but it sounded as appetizing as another round of knee surgery. I retired happily to the hot tub.

I must admit daily swimming was a great time for deep thinking. There is nothing more mindless than paddling back and forth in a shallow pool looking at a line on the bottom of it. You have a lot of time for meditative introspection lap after lap. I remember just how lonely life at that stage could feel and how I wanted to achieve something in my existence that would be interesting. When the name Ed Bolian came up in conversations among my friends, I wanted the next sentence to be, "Oh yeah, the guy who _____." That blank needed to be something incredible. The adolescent urge to be distinctive was in full force.

Of course swimming was not immune from my efforts to push boundaries. Partially out of the controlled deviance of it, partially out of still trying to win, and partially out of the ridiculously alien sensation of it - I would convince a few of my teammates to cover our bodies in petroleum jelly before our swim meets. We would leave our shins and the undersides of our arms clear of it to maintain traction with the water. Elsewhere the water would bead off us like the hand waxed finish of an unreliable British Sports Car whose non-running ownership value lay redemptively in weekend polishing sessions.

If you have never taken a dive into a cold pool covered in Vaseline I highly recommend it. You won't be able to bathe normally for a week and the subsequent skin breakouts are a con but the feeling has got to be similar to being shot out of a cannon. It is ten times more effective than shaving your body.

It is worth spending a moment here to discuss something that materialized in my adolescence - an absolute inability to respect anyone or anything. I am not really sure where this started. I remember rebuking teachers into tears, breaking rules if only for the sake of doing so, and pushing against any line or limit that I could find. It was an elitist attitude that I didn't understand but it made me a very unlikeable person for a few years while in high school. It may have stemmed from the repeated pain of knee surgeries, the daunting challenges of academic future, or some flaw within me I had yet to admit existed.

I find it very difficult to maintain a peaceful relationship with my superiors in a work environment. I do not accept criticism well and my gut response to a rule or imposition is always to think of how far it can be pushed. There is some dark passenger inside of me that simply reacts badly to anything aiming to restrict me. I can say now this flaw is still a part of me but I have found better ways to keep it in check. I never knew what purpose my flaw served but I always hoped it might contribute to me doing something interesting down the road.

The path of youthful self discovery and soul searching led to the formulation of a life recipe. I wanted my life's goals to be a mixture 2 parts eccentricity, 1 part creativity, 1 part deviance, a splash of significance with a nod to historical precedent, garnished with some exotic flair of exhibitionism, filtered through some obstacle I felt like most others would not have the balls to pass through. It would be served, of course, in a glass of some sort of competitive victory. Evidence could indicate I was just a degree or two removed from either being a serial killer or confidence man. Or a lion tamer.

School came easy but motivation did not. I took a litany of Advanced Placement and high level courses in high school hoping to gain admittance into an Ivy League school. After applying to most of them I found out coming from an unheard of public Georgia High School; even an experienced entrepreneur and swim team captain with a high SAT & GPA who had overcome a debilitating physical condition was not going to get much attention from the admittance teams. In the end I was admitted to Georgia Tech where I eventually figured I would study public policy. The thinking was that if I didn't end up working for myself in some capacity, I would just go work for the CIA.

I did not pay a lot of attention in school. I blatantly read car magazines most of the time rather than listening to the lectures. I did well enough in the classes to get away with it but most of my thoughts went constantly to cars, businesses with cars, and driving cars. Every assignment I could bend towards cars and driving went straight there. The backs of each notebook page were filled with ideas for car clubs, driving experiences, and illegal road races.

One of the preposterous schemes was to get my grandmother to parlay the funds from a real estate investment into the newly announced Bugatti Veyron around 2003. The world beating McLaren F1 had appreciated strongly and buying what was guaranteed to be the new fastest car in the world seemed like a great idea. I set up a phone call with the CEO of Bugatti to discuss my interest in the car and my concerns about its approach to market. My barely post-pubescent deep voice came in quite handy. They sent me a letter guaranteeing my allocation of the car and set up an appointment for me to fly to Molsheim, France for seat and pedal fitting. When my grandmother decided hypercar speculation was not for her I set up a deal with a German exotic car dealer to sell my guaranteed spot for $100,000. The deal with their retail buyer fell apart but it was a great lesson in the art of faking it until you make it.

Eleven years later, as he sipped a cappuccino I had made him that he called "the best I have tasted in America," I shared that story with the very Italian but newly named President of Bugatti. He seemed amused but it was probably the coffee talking. My Lamborghini salesman barista skills were probably more impressive than the childhood schemes.

The first thought I had to start an exotic car rental company was in a conversation with my best friend, Kevin Messer. We both loved cars and we had heard about companies in Miami and Los Angeles that would rent them. The idea was born. The first fleet we thought about was a Diablo 6.0, Bentley Arnage, Ferrari 360, and Dodge Viper. Only one of these ended up making the final cut.

At the time, the automotive landscape was changing fast. In 2000, there were only a few impressive performance cars sold in the US. The E39 BMW M5 had a naturally aspirated 400 hp V8, the Porsche 996 Twin Turbo had 415 gargantuan hp and would go 0-60 in 3.9 seconds, and the Ferrari 360 Modena was emerging as the first truly usable supercar boasting 400 hp. The Corvette Z06 was on the horizon with 405 hp but the standard C5 Corvette was still an underwhelming performance car despite being great looking.

2003 and 2004 changed all of that - we got the Bentley Continental GT, Lamborghini Gallardo, Porsche Carrera GT, Ferrari Enzo, Mercedes McLaren SLR, Maserati came back to the US, Cadillac brought out the CTS-V, and Mercedes got into the true performance car game with 469 and 493 horsepower variants of a 5.4 liter supercharged V8 and a twin turbo V12 that they packed into several models. You could get a mid sized E Class, a convertible SL, a full-sized S Class, or a 2+2 CL coupe with a forced induction engine that would outperform just about anything else on the road, all while offering massaging seats and understated looks. It was a strange proposition to most wealthy prospects but a lightning fast Q-car could surely fit some niche.

I took it upon myself to figure out which of these cars were the best. While still a kid in high school, I would call up a car dealership that had one of these cars for sale, explain the nature of my business, being the breeding of exotic and interesting reptiles, and express my interest in purchasing a car. Of course their expectation of an immediate timetable for purchase might have been implied but I never had to lie to get to test drive the cars. I drove virtually every model of Ferrari, Lamborghini, Porsche, Bentley, Audi, BMW, Mercedes, Maserati, and others and began to grasp what the selection of luxury and exotic cars and the people who surrounded them looked like.

I remember learning the ins and outs of the modern day sequential manual gearboxes in a Cambiocorsa Maserati Spyder. I decided to see if it could be forced into first gear going fairly quickly around a ninety degree turn. It could. The car immediately kicked into a powerslide with a trajectory soon to intersect with an oncoming Ford F350. Somehow, through no learned skill of my own, I was able to right the car and point it where we wanted it to go. The utterly terrified salesman expressed his intense appreciation for my interest but asked that I return to the dealership in a slightly more conservative manner. As always, I found some convenient reason the car just wasn't for me at the time.

I had eBay alerts set up for anytime someone would list an interesting car for sale in the Atlanta area. I would call them during free time at school and go test drive the cars before swim practice, always offering some excuse not to consummate the purchase that day. One day a Ferrari 360 Spider popped up for sale as the personal car of the owner of a Toyota Dealership in my hometown. They were still selling at prices $100,000 over MSRP with eternal waits to get a new one. Our local Ferrari dealer was never very friendly to tourists so I had not been able to talk them into letting me drive one. I rang the Toyota dealer and took it for a spin. Hundreds of hours watching *Top Gear*, reading technical specifications in car magazines, and playing video games meant I was more versed on the car than the salesman. You can imagine his excitement at the possibility of selling the boss's $300,000 supercar as a departure from the mundane routine of Priuses sprinkled with the occasional Scion Xb. I showed him how the car worked and we drove and drove. We ran out of gas on the way back to the dealership and had to push/coast our way in.

When it rained I would test drive lightweight rear wheel drive sports cars like Honda S2000s, BMW M3s, and big engine Mercedes to hone my drifting abilities and to scare unsuspecting salespeople. I never would guess that a decade or so later I would be deflecting the same propositions from unqualified leads as a salesman of supercars.

The cars were great and the journalistic writing of the day was fantastic. For all of the multi-car shootout tests, fastest lap driving, drag times, and other metrics - the point that you couldn't test the capabilities of these cars out on a real road was present in every single article.

"Why not?" my 17 year old self kept asking. "I am glad that they can lap the Nurburgring quickly and it is great that they go from 0-60 so impressively, but which one could I drive the 590 mile trip to North Palm Beach the fastest in?" That was practical. That was interesting. It could be any road trip for that matter. How do I enjoy the drives that we do every single day? I thought of a cross country race. What cities would be interesting? Detroit, New York, Chicago, Los Angeles, Miami, Seattle, Atlanta? It had to be coast to coast. That sounded right. New York to Los Angeles then. That is America in a nutshell with cars. What could be better?

Offering gearheads admittance into a no holds barred cross country race sounded like selling picnic baskets to bears. The competitive proposition was simple but the problem solving strategies would be fascinatingly diverse. It seemed like the best game ever. I went home and told my father about the idea. He said, "Oh, you mean Cannonball? Yeah, that sounds like you. They did that thirty years ago. There are movies about it."

Mind blown, straight to Best Buy I went to get all of the DVD's I could find on the mysterious Cannonball.

My research led me to Brock Yates, a contributor to *Car & Driver Magazine* and the founder of this outlaw brand of cross country balls-to-the-wall street racing. Thirty-five or so years prior he had been sitting somewhere thinking the same thoughts I mulled over while in my high school chemistry class, and he decided an outlaw cross country race was a worthwhile endeavor. He was the Godfather of the dream which had just been ignited in my teenage brain.

I learned about the spirit of the idea, how Yates and his friends wanted to thumb their noses at the establishment and protest the imposition of a national speed limit. He had an idea for the creation of a Masters Level driving license and believed that well trained drivers in capable cars should be able to drive faster than an average Joe in an average car.

I was astonished to find out how many legitimate racecar drivers and teams had competed in the Cannonball. The cars were amazing, the people were interesting, the idea was endlessly compelling - I was hooked. People living ordinary lives had procured the most powerful high performance cars of the day, outfitted them with cutting edge gadgetry, and conducted an endurance test of both steed and operator through the unknowable frontier of the American highway system. I dove into dissecting the idea and thinking about what it would look like in the context of modern cars on today's roads. Many sleepless nights followed.

In my last semester of high school I took a class where I could define my own course requirements and content, pointed toward a large scale research project on a subject of interest. We were supposed to define a curriculum and an evaluation scale for ourselves. There was to be some field research and an interview with someone who was influential in the area of study.

I was continuing my habit of test driving as often as I could and felt like I was becoming quite the amateur authority on the latest crop of sports cars. I chose to investigate the profession of automotive journalism for the project. The expert in the field that I chose to interview was Brock Yates.

Chapter 2 - The Interview

The sales manager at the car dealership where I work from 2009-15 is named Bill Smith. Bill is one of my favorite people. He is as American as an apple pie shaped country music guitar being used as a baseball bat at Yankee stadium on the 4th of July by Miss America wearing daisy dukes atop the shoulders of Abraham Lincoln in an Elvis impersonator getup. He hates technology, loves the bumpy road of a past that has made him who he is, and is full of some of the best one liners and wisdom that you could ever find in a person. One of my favorite things to hear him regularly say is, "Why can't I just wake up and it be 1979 again?"

The 1970s in America was a crazy time. The idea of freedom was in the air and the national psyche was one of collectively testing limits, experimenting, and trying to build an identity in a collective fashion. I was born in 1985 and it sounds like I missed out on an era custom tailored for my mindset by just a few decades.

This was on the tail end of a glorious time for the American car culture and something that we will likely never see again. NASCAR racing had come out of the 1930's North Carolina bootlegging culture and had made its way into showrooms. This was the ideal racecar/road car selling relationship that every car manufacturer still wants. "Win on Sunday, sell on Monday" meant that showrooms of the 1960's were filled with cars that actually resembled the ones that were screaming around the super speedways, just without all of the stickers.

The muscle car era was a Great Awakening of car culture in America. You could walk into any showroom in America and buy a practical car with the biggest engine they offered at a reasonable price. No one cared about fuel economy, emissions, Al Gore, Ralph Nader, global warming, carbon footprints, safety, foreign oil, or motor vehicle regulations. Concerns about oil dependence and embargos were still a few years away. What a glorious time it was.

The early 70's ushered in a fuel crisis and a massive criticism of high performance motoring. Laws were passed that imposed safety, restricted engine capacity, mandated lower fuel consumption, and shackled down horsepower. It was the death blow to the muscle car. Worse than that, it also was the genesis of the 55 mile per hour national speed limit. This was like finding a world full of drug addicts who had enjoyed full legalization and an unlimited supply of anything they could ask for and then turning off the faucet and watching everyone squirm. Someone should have played the entrapment angle.

Brock Yates was a long-term staff writer for *Car & Driver Magazine*. He had an idea - what if we tried to see how fast we could drive from coast to coast? How would the world react if a group banded together to demonstrate just how preposterous a 55 mph national speed limit was? Eisenhower had built these roads to land military aircraft on. With cars that could go triple the legal speed, shouldn't we be allowed to use them? The idea was born and immediately gathered steam in the small underground world of cross country outlaw road racing, which at the time was his personal rolodex of racing contacts and connections.

The name Cannonball came from the legendary Erwin George "Cannon Ball" Baker who was known for doing hundreds of point to point motorcycle and car drives totalling more than half a million miles in his lifetime. His best known trek was from New York City to Los Angeles in 1933 in a Graham-Paige Model 57 Blue Streak 8 in fifty three and half hours. That record stood for almost forty years.

The route was born - balls out NY 2 LA. The name evolved into The Cannonball Baker Sea to Shining Sea Memorial Trophy Dash. The irony dripped from the erudite journalistic bravado of Yates who was both proud of and terrified by his new passion project. He knew it was an idea that tugged at the heartstrings of any car enthusiast and served as a rare continuation of the great American frontiersman spirit. The "Go West" idea had pervaded the United States psyche for two hundred years. Now it had a new context.

Yates chronicled the history of each running of the Cannonball in 1971, 1972, 1975, and finally in 1979 in his book - *"Cannonball! The World's Greatest Outlaw Road Race,"* published in 2001. The antics of the race were also amplified and depicted in the 1980's films by Hal Needham starring Burt Reynolds, Dom Deluise, and the Rat Pack.

The best Cannonball story/ruse has to be the 1979 strategy of Yates and Needham. It was in the actual race but also later used in the 1981 film. They outfitted an ambulance and carried along a woman who was purported to be a senator's wife. When they were pulled over for running lights ablaze at 130 mph past several hospitals the law enforcement officers asked what they were up to. Somehow without rehearsal, the man in the back explained how the woman had a unique condition which had to be treated by the staff of the UCLA medical center. She had to be transported there by ambulance because the pressurization of an airplane cabin would have caused her body to erupt into cysts. The cops asked them to slow it down a bit but let them continue without arrest or citation. Absolute gold.

Of course when discussing Cannonball it is impossible to overlook the opening of each film featuring two gorgeous women piloting a Lamborghini Countach toying with the police and spraypainting X's over the shiny new double nickel speed limit signs. Supreme Court Justice Potter Stewart said once that despite struggling to use words to define pornography, "I know it when I see it." I assume this was the mental image he was struggling to describe.

The epitome of Cannonball cool also belongs to Yates' own participation in 1971 when he solicited Dan Gurney as a co-driver and was able to negotiate a loan of a Sunoco Blue Ferrari 365 GTB/4 Daytona for the trip. They did the drive in 35 hours 54 minutes, winning the inaugural competitive event and setting the stage for the years to come. Gurney commented to the dismay of readers everywhere that "At no time did we exceed 175 mph." The Yates/Gurney time would be bested by a single minute in the 1975 winning run by Jack May and Rick Cline in a white Ferrari Dino 246 GTS. It is a painfully beautiful car still owned and routinely shown by "Cannonball Jack" to this day.

The best time from coast-to-coast to come out of the Cannonball runnings was held by Dave Heinz and Dave Yarbrough of 32 hours 51 mins. Heinz was a Jaguar Dealer and they drove a Jaguar XJS. The Cannonball cool factor permeated the dealership business for years after the race. Yarborough still runs a Lexus store in Charleston. The XJS they used recently resurfaced for sale, being bought for restoration by a character to come later in this story.

The Australian Jaguar Importer actually outfitted eleven XJS's with unique wheels, Cibie Driving Lights, a "Prince" trip computer, blacked out chrome trim, and other interesting modifications. They were sold as "Cannonball Editions." This was not the only "Cannonball" special edition car. In 1985 (the year I was born) Brock Yates partnered with Bob Snodgrass and Brumos Audi in Florida to make a run of twelve customized Quattro 4000 sport sedans. They had a similar suite of modifications plus euro spec lights, a larger fuel tank, and improved suspension. Cannonball was becoming a cultural phenomenon.

When Yates was pressured into stopping the organization of Cannonball both by the movie producers and by his employer, there were clearly still people wanting to continue doing it. An event called the US Express was born and run in 1981, 1982, and 1983. The best time out of this event was held by David Diem and Doug Turner of 32 hours 7 minutes. They drove a Ferrari 308 GTS, still owned to this day by David.

Over the years, various small scale copycat events continued to pop up, but the American appetite for such things was quickly waning. Cars were less capable, police patrolling was much greater, and the roads were becoming more crowded with more people owning and driving cars. Urban sprawl was quickly eating up the vast open areas of undeveloped regions of the country and the population was increasing fast. Bear in mind there were 50% more people living in the United States in the year 2013 than there were in 1971 when the first Cannonball was run.

In the epilogue to his book, Yates said very directly how he did not believe that the records from that era could be challenged today. The records had not advanced since 1979 in his mind, not acknowledging the spinoff style events. Even those had remained untouched since 1983. He cited all of the obvious reasons - more people, more cops, more cars, better anti-speeding technology, harsher penalties for speeding, and a completely different social mindset which he thought would prove much more hostile to the idea.

That was what I wanted to talk to him about as an eighteen year old high school student. I wanted to understand what the lifestyle of an automotive journalist was like but more importantly I wanted to know about Cannonball. Less than a year prior I had been dreaming of the exact same idea he had pioneered without any prior knowledge of its existence.

Why couldn't someone [I] do it? What would stop me? How much harder is it now? What would be involved with a modern attempt?

Yates was surprisingly forthcoming to a kid who had just gotten his home phone number by bluffing the receptionist at the magazine. He still loved the idea of Cannonball. It sounded like your grandfather recounting a night he spent with Marilyn Monroe. It was the pinnacle of his life, his proudest achievement, the tallest feather in his well adorned cap. He had all of the stories fresh in his mind since writing the book just a few years prior. They were like his fraternity stories from college. Those "you wouldn't believe what we got away with" type tales. He was the most confident sounding man I had ever heard speak. It was Tarantino wrapping production on the final scene of Pulp Fiction. It was Michelangelo cleaning his brushes while the last strokes of the Sistine Chapel dried. It was Jordan pushing off of Byron Russell for the winning shot in game six of the '98 finals. These were the glory days projects that can turn your resume into a single line item, perhaps just a single word.

Everything was cordial. He was extremely kind. He wished me the best in school and I told him one day I was going to break the Cannonball records. Brock Yates laughed politely and signed off saying, "Good luck kid."

Chapter 3 - Finding My Flaw

My childhood best friend was named Kevin Messer. His dad was a long-time muscle car guy and Kevin was ballsy enough to carry on a conversation with me about the things I was interested in. He was my partner in crime for the illegitimate test driving, car business dreaming, and repeatedly getting my first car stuck in the mud. It was a 1995 Land Rover Discovery with 150k miles. Appropriately green, it was an awesome truck with a crankshaft knock that would make an old farm tractor blush. We would sneak out and do donuts in his father's 1960's Corvettes and Camaros and dream about the days when we would have exotic cars of our own. Before we realized how weird the visual would be, we had a bet to see who the first person would be to be able to buy a Ferrari. The loser had to ride shotgun for a day wearing a dress. Fortunately I never made him pay up on that. Two dudes rolling around shoulder to shoulder in a Ferrari wearing proper attire is sexually questionable enough.

We dreamt of the record. We talked about how we might do it, we watched the movies over and over again, and we idolized the folklore of it all. Neither of us had any idea what we would end up doing with our lives but the conversations with him were actually where the exotic car rental concept came from as well.

Kevin was not one to behave himself. He never did great in school, got a lot of tickets, dated the wrong kinds of girls, and was the kind of guy your parents questioned you hanging around with. I, on the other hand, was the kind of kid your parents didn't realize was probably the wrong kind of person to associate with until it was too late. Kevin and I would download street racing clips on early file sharing sites like Kazaa and Limewire of Ferraris doing burnouts and Europeans getting arrested for bringing their cars to the US for driving events and getting pulled over at preposterous speeds.

An event called the Gumball 3000 was founded by a mysterious man named Maximillion Cooper in 1999. It continues today as an annual ~3,000 mile road rally for exotic car enthusiasts. It is not a race but anytime you get a bunch of supercars and their owners' super-egos together, adhering to the speed limit seem to fall just below humility at the bottom of their hierarchy of existential concerns.

It was widely assumed that this was some continuation of Cannonball. Participants would claim to "win" stages or the event altogether but the organizers seemed to make it clear that it was not a race and that the only competition was to embody the Spirit of Gumball using decorated cars and generally adding to the endless party atmosphere. It was tough to reconcile the folklore of Cannonball with entitled international celebrities testing the limits of sleep deprivation and blood alcohol levels but it was the closest thing that seemed to exist.

Similar events popped up - the Bullrun, Player's Run, Cannonball Run Europe Events, and others. As a senior trip after finishing high school I entered an event called the AKA Rally. It was the same idea, driving generally 3,000 miles across the country from New York to Los Angeles, stopping each night for a party. While I aspired to do Gumball, the finances never made it possible. This event had a lower entry fee which meant there would be more modified Japanese cars and fewer Ferraris and Lamborghinis. I registered and drove a modified 2000 Audi S4 I had been able to acquire due to the number of scholarships I had gotten exceeding the necessary in-state budget at Georgia Tech. The car was great - 350 upgraded hp with twin turbos for great torque, upgraded suspension, nice six speed gearbox, all wheel drive, and very comfortable to boot. It was a great car to eat up the highway on a long road trip. I bought my first Valentine 1 Radar Detector, the Zach Morris cell phone version of a Garmin GPS that weighed more than the laptop I am typing this on now, and a Radio Shack CB Radio.

I had seen the videos and heard the stories from Gumball. It looked like a blast but there was a clear demarcation between those who were treating it as a millionaire's holiday and those who were trying to compete, either with each other or just against the clock. I found the later hugely compelling. There were three names that stood out of the participants who seemed to take the point-to-point speed aspect seriously. They were Rob Kenworthy, Alex Roy, and Richard Rawlings.

Rob Kenworthy participated in several Gumball events and other rallies. He was British and took great advantage of not having US tickets impact his driving privileges back home. There were clips of him weaving through traffic in a modified Porsche 996 GT2 at nearly 200 mph. It was fantastic but he was seeming to just drive fast for the thrill of it, not bothered by where he actually finished.

Alex Roy was a different story. His objective was clear - he wanted to finish first on every single leg of the event, going to great lengths to do so. Where the other participants were clearly taking advantage of their selections from the cornucopia of exotic car offerings in the marketplace by driving Murcielagos, 360s, 911 Turbos, and even ultra-rare cars like Koenigseggs; he drove an understated Avus Blue E39 BMW M5. In fact, he outfitted it as an international police vehicle each year with a different country's law enforcement livery all over it.

Every time I would see a video or gallery of photos online documenting Gumball I was quick to pour through them. Just like the car statistic magazine racer that I was, I wanted to be an expert on this event I lacked the means to engage in. I was flipping through some photos from a European Gumball and saw a picture of Alex Roy sitting at a desk. He was decked out in some foreign nation's police uniform with the stickers on the M5 set to match. He was updating his navigation systems from a silver Apple computer similarly covered in vinyl decals. Upside down in the frame was a phone number in stickers on the outside of the computer. It had to be his cell phone number. What else would you put on a computer when you travel out of the country? I put it into my phone and saved it. I would not use it for years but I knew it would come in handy one day.

He also took an interesting approach to vehicle preparation. Most of the cars were hitting ridiculously high speeds without much in the way of police countermeasures. Alex did it differently. He had various radar detectors, police scanners, lights, radios, navigation systems, etc. It was clearly giving him an advantage in a race within a rally that not many people cared about.

Richard Rawlings was a third outspoken and thereby prolific participant in the event. He drove a variety of cars including a modified Chevrolet Avalanche and a Ferrari 550 Maranello owned by his friend, Dennis Collins. Like Alex, he had radar detectors, fuel range extending upgrades, and a CB radio antenna swinging off of the car. He clearly wanted to come in first and frequently did.

This was not true Cannonball but it was the closest thing to it I could find. I wanted to be as close as I could to whatever modern interpretation existed. As I was preparing my car for the AKA Rally in 2004, I purchased my suite of electronics to emulate their preparation. Some representatives from the *MTV True Life* production team contacted me and told me they wanted to follow three different teams in their participation in this event. They asked if they could film me, some backstory about me graduating from high school, and us driving. It was a lot of fun and the episode aired as *"MTV True Life: I'm Rallying to LA"* in October of 2004.

The trip was a blast. My co-driver was a good friend from high school and AAU basketball teammate - Lee Burrell. He learned to drive a stick in order to join me on the trip. He was the perfect co-driver. I knew him well enough to enjoy his company but the relationship was casual enough that we could still get upset with each other and be honest. Like the Gumball, this was not a race but a rally. That being said, there were four teams that treated it as a competition. Lee and I were constantly trying to get to every destination first, as were a two girl team out of New Jersey and a guy named Tom Greulich from St Louis. Another great competitor and co-participant was Nick Reid. He drove a Subaru WRX STi very well and was the life of every party.

The girls were an interesting pair. Alicia was a marine biologist from the Smithsonian and Kelly was covered in Tattoos and the owner of the brand new BMW E46 M3 that they drove proficiently. They had the advantage of actually having been to most of the cities where we were going as opposed to Lee and I who had traveled very little.

Tom drove a Honda S2000. His choice of vehicle for the rally didn't matter because Tom's parents had a Jaguar XJ220 which was one of the most insane hypercars to ever exist by 2004. I suppose that didn't matter either because they never drove it and I have come to adopt the position that if you don't have the testicular fortitude to actually drive an exotic car you own, you might as well not bother to purchase it in the first place, particularly if the car is of dubious investment potential like an XJ220 had been since its release ten or so years prior.

Tom and I developed a pleasant friendship through the trip. He drove fast but responsibly. He enjoyed himself but invested in making friendships along the way. We kept in touch for several years after the drive, talking cars and life. Great guy.

In the subsequent publicity of the rally and the MTV show I met a guy named Chris Staschiak. He had done Gumball a couple of times with Roy and

Rawlings, and was a real car guy. He drove a 1973 Corvette, dressed as an L88 with bass boat glitter green paint. He aspired to one day own a Ferrari or a Porsche 911 Turbo. Chris and I would talk regularly but actually didn't meet in person for three years. Chris was the only person other than Kevin who I knew that had ever cared about the Cannonball Record. He loved talking about the strategy of it, the best car for the job, and how we might do it one day. You could never really tell how serious he was about going through with the idea though.

Around that same time there was a new re-release of a 1976 short film by Claude Lelouch called *C'était un rendez-vous*. It featured an anonymous driver, in fact Lelouch himself, driving through the city of Paris at breakneck speed early one morning. The legend was that Lelouche's personal Ferrari 275 was the steed for this film but it was in fact a Mercedes Benz 450SEL 6.9 - the original German super sedan with the sonorous Italian V12 dubbed over in editing. During the drive you see the car fly past the iconic landmarks of Paris such as the Arc de Triomphe and Champs-Élysées. It had the fantastic reckless abandon to tug at the gearhead heartstrings in all of us. Pigeons being scattered, no hesitation in the running of red lights, smoky sideways slides around turns, the checklist completed with only a *Dukes of Hazzard* bridge jump left out.

The film ends as the car pulls up to an overlook and a beautiful woman walks up to meet the driver, blissfully ignorant of the drama of the drive bringing him to her. This would obviously be the exact manner in which I would meet my own wife someday. Who

42

could resist such a proposal?

The film, and more saliently its recent push to market where I found out about it, demonstrated the new spectrum of cross country driving events and the idea of point to point speed records were front of mind in American car culture. Even the production strategy - taking something that would be sexy to do in a Ferrari but actually using a more functional and capable German super sedan, mirrored the intellectual's approach to a modern Cannonball.

After we returned home from the rally I found my first job in the car business. I was a generic employee of a racing school at Road Atlanta called the Panoz Racing School and Audi Driving Experience. They did race licensing and general driving skills training at the track. I learned a lot, had a great time, and was not invited to apply there to work the next summer. Apparently they were not interested in seeing how high the Audi A4's could jump, how well their pit carts could do donuts in the unpaved areas around the storage facilities, or what an amazing off road rally circuit could be made connecting a few parts of the service roads through the infield of the track.

The New York to Los Angeles Rally and the subsequent car business job did quite a bit to quell my immediate interest in breaking the record. At this point, no one had made a recent attempt to my knowledge. The 1979 Cannonball and the 1983 US Express records still stood and the whole idea had not received a lot of press. The desire was still alive but there was no mental image of what a modern attempt would look or feel like. I knew it was well beyond my budget and I knew enough to know I was incapable of fully understanding the risks and long term liabilities of being associated with the record at that point.

In the fall of 2004 I entered Georgia Tech as a freshman, majoring in Mechanical Engineering. I hated pretty much everything about Georgia Tech other than Intramural Sports. It was challenging, my classmates were difficult to relate to, and it blurred any vision I had of what path my life was going to take. I was accustomed to exerting a mediocre effort and getting good grades. The expectation became to put forth an intense effort to get mediocre grades. I got by but found my own self worth in Intramural Slam Dunk Contest Championships and short film competitions rather than a Dean's list streak.

Growing up I was never one to shy away from an opportunity to try something that others were afraid of. Each year my roommates and I would enter a five minute film contest with something that we called Lecture Crashers. It was a montage of pranks and disruptions we would carry out in the large lecture halls and classrooms of Georgia Tech. In a school of reclusive introverts laser focused on their 9-5 futures, this was an above-the-knee skirt in Amish town.

I found the school to be full of the kind of people I knew I didn't want to be like. I do not pretend to think that most people approach life, rules, goals, and obsessions the way that I do, nor will I contend that my approach is better. I also know my worldview is typically diametrically opposed to the direction of happiness and contentment. At the time there was a staunch incongruence between where my world was pushing me and where I was hoping to steer. I needed to find new ways to interrupt that inertial pull of the institution.

I got pretty depressed. I couldn't sleep. I didn't eat well. I stayed in decent shape but was very emotionally conflicted. The ratio of guys to girls at Georgia Tech was 4 to 1 which didn't help. I honestly had never had a great deal of success in that department. I never found it difficult to find a date for prom or a homecoming dance in High School but the idea of a meaningful girlfriend relationship was still very foreign.

Georgia Tech is a very diverse place. You could usually count seven or eight languages being spoken in the student center or library. I became proficient at visually discerning between Chinese, Japanese, Korean, Vietnamese, Thai, and Malaysian people. One way I enjoyed relieving stress was playing what I called Godzilla basketball. Early on the weekend mornings the Asian students who never slept in would be up playing in the recreation center. Yao Ming was an anomaly and generally it was a fairly low skill game where you had almost no contact. I remember one game to 11 where I had 1 assist and 10 points with 7 slam dunks. Lots of fun and a self esteem boost I needed desperately at the time.

At night I would leave my soon to be condemned dorm, walk out to the nearest handicapped spot. My Audi S4 was parked there, still utilizing the ten year expiration from the high school knee surgeries. I would go out at two or three in the morning and drive laps around I-285 which is the ring road around the perimeter of Atlanta. It is about sixty-two miles and I would generally drive it in about forty-five minutes, an average almost thirty miles per hour over the limit.

I went fast but it was never about that. I always planned on trying to do it in thirty minutes but never got around to it. I was exorcising demons, not exercising myself or the car. It was brilliant. Just me, the truckers, and the street lights streaming by. Nothing was accomplished, nothing was learned, I just came home ready to sleep for two hours and to endure the doldrums of another few days.

The major selection of a mechanical engineering path was due to the business program having a terrible reputation and the assumption it was a better route to automotive journalism than the existing alternatives. I quickly decided that was a stupid idea. They don't pay you enough and the classes were harder than seemed necessary. I had already resolved myself into the idea that my profession was unlikely to be closely tied to my major and that the main service this institution was going to provide me was a name on a resume line rather than vast subject matter knowledge.

I looked around for alternatives and found the relatively new Public Policy Department. I was most attracted to the major by one of the professors who was an ex director of the CIA. Now that sounded like fun. In the introspection of my depression I had come to understand some things about myself. One was how I lacked an emotional sensitivity most people seemed to have. The awareness was too new to really grasp it. I wanted to find some goal or career where it might serve as an advantage. Working for the

CIA seemed to check a lot of boxes. I doubted they would issue me a license to kill but it sounded like fun anyway, particularly without any immediate entrepreneurial alternatives. I changed my major to Public Policy.

The second reason that I chose Public Policy was the scheduling. The major was so small that there was no need to offer multiples of the same classes each semester. This meant they were usually all on Tuesdays and Thursdays. I could maintain a full time schedule with 18-21 hours and still have four day weekends. I went to school from 8-6 two days a week and then sat around without much to do. It was perfect. Fortunately the classes were not very hard. Most if it was papers and presentations.

It was in those presentations that I learned something else about myself - I love talking. I love it even more when I don't know what I am talking about. I love it much more when I don't know what I am talking about and the stakes are high. I needed an adrenal high and this was the main line of it. Speaking into a sea of judgmental eyes having to sell a bluff and build a logic based on two or three handholds of factual information was a euphoric rush. When I could pull that off it tickled every nerve that I needed caressed.

It was an interesting time in political and psychological research. The accessibility to computers capable of running advanced regression models on particularly farcical notions was ushering in a generation of *Freakonomics* styled economists and researchers. Some people were looking at the world in a way that I related to. It seemed like an interesting, albeit functionally useless field of study. I loved the idea of removing emotion and typical assumption from an idea and getting to the bottom of what it might actually take to solve the problems.

The general curriculum and major requirements were new in the Georgia Tech School of Public Policy. The course load walked you through the political science process introducing a new element each semester and asking you to write a paper using that angle as a vantage point. What no one else seemed to get was you could use the same paper over and over again. Also, no one in the classes had any idea what was going on at all.

In my intro class I wrote a paper on alternatively fueled vehicles. This was, predictably, a topic I lacked any positive enthusiasm for and generally flew in the face of everything I believed in or held dear about the world. I did not know much about them but I just started talking. The faster I talked, the more people listened and the fewer questions they asked. I started with two or three things I knew for sure and then built from crazy assumptions into an actual presentation. I continued through each semester examining the same topic from the perspectives of balance of power, legislative process, partisanship, tiered government, bureaucracy, implementation, and blindly forced my way into the gamut of peer and teacher reviews.

By my senior thesis I had built the paper into a formula that actually quantified, in dollars, the incremental cost of every human vehicle mile driven on American society. It blindsided the professorial staff because it was a sixteen week assignment built over four years, half in fact and the other 99% completely fabricated with such an intense hubris behind it they actually believed I hadn't made up all of the statistical work. My professor asked if I would present it to a larger audience or explore publication of the work but I knew well enough to stop while I was ahead and in front of an audience that did not know enough to call me out on its shortcomings. Never sell past a yes.

Between the late night highway runs, trips to the hot tub, and recycling papers, I was searching. Trust me, I get that this has sounded a bit self-praising and while in hindsight I am proud of some of my independent thinking, this is all coming from a guy who found life very isolating through adolescence. Perhaps it was staging me for something interesting, perhaps it was molding me into the husband my wife would need, perhaps it was just making sure a struggling Italian car dealership would not go out of business one day. I had no idea where my life was headed and how I was going to get there. I had no shortage of aspiration and ideas ran fleetingly through my head with pop star wardrobe change velocity but I couldn't get any traction. I got into the habit of building a document each year I simply dubbed "The Plan."

The Plan was a state of Ed's union. It discussed my psychological state, social successes and failures, business ideas, life vision, friendships, and goals. I figured if I ever got arrested or accomplished something great there would be something entertaining about them. They also served as my personal Last Will and Testament to distribute the iguanas and my car.

A recurring theme of the psychological portion of these writings was actually psychopathy. I didn't understand it at the time but clinically I have been told that I am a psychopath, which is essentially defined as lacking proper empathy, fear, and sensitivity to certain risks and other social cues. Like most psychiatric conditions, everyone falls somewhere along a spectrum of psychopathy. Depending on test administration, I fall somewhere between 65% and 95% of the way toward the opposite end of the spectrum from the person who would be my future wife, Mother Theresa, and Elmo. All I knew was that I did not feel the way I assumed people normally did about daily situations. It doesn't make me a bad person, it just makes it a lot easier for me to make bad or dangerous decisions. I also really liked *Dexter*.

I struggled with a grasp of this as a college student. It was an emotionally insurmountable hurdle as a developing teenager. I grew up in a great family with awesome, well-adjusted parents. They worked hard and instilled some great ideas - the greatest of which was Christianity and an unwavering faith in God. Salvation is marked by a life change, turning from a life of sin and recognizing that grace saves us and reconciles us to God. This was a bit tough for me because I never knew a life where I didn't feel like I was a Christian. I was born the day after our pastor's daughter. All of the books I remember from my nursery were Bible stories. It was not dogmatically hammered in but it was always part of my life I gladly accepted and I developed a rational comfort towards it all. To this day, I find faith in God to be one of the simplest concepts for me to remain steadfast to.

The psychopathy manifested itself in what felt like not being afraid. I never felt embarrassed and I deflected insults without credence because my valuation scales for myself and the rest of the world felt so radically misaligned. It was a good thing that I was a Christian because it appeared I might make a very good criminal.

The problem I faced as a kid was that I just hated everyone. I couldn't stand my teachers or any person of authority. I was egotistical, overconfident, and did not care much for the feelings of others. It made me into a real jerk and cost me a lot of friendships as I navigated a glass case of emotions. I vividly remember the struggle of reconciling the Christian idea that we have to love people in order to truly love God. Feeling as though I could never learn to love or even like people, I had no idea how this made sense.

The disconnect between my sincere feelings and what I knew I was called to do both as a Christian and as a member of society was difficult. What truly matters? It is how you react and treat people? Is it how you feel on the inside? Initially they were very close. I could not suffer or indulge the shallow foolishness I perceived from the average Joe and I let him know that. Over time, though, I was able to separate my guttural proclivity from how I might act. It begged some moral questions regarding sincerity but that is a discussion for another day. Fortunately I found some balance that allowed me to earn some friends, some allies, and avoid some enemies that I deserved.

I knew God was real, I knew how He had

helped me through trials and tribulations, healed me physically and emotionally, and blessed me in ways I needed no other explanation for beyond grace. I believed the Bible and I believed I needed to care more about the opinions and well being of others but I just couldn't. Who else has full faith and understanding of the power and presence of God but felt the way that I did? Satan. The Devil. How many thirteen year old kids have to get their parents to talk them out of the idea that they are an incarnate form of Satan? Well I did. Fortunately they did a good job.

Chapter 4 - $1 Million in Debt at 20

Another frequent element of The Plan each year was a status report on my progress in starting my passion project business - an exotic car rental company. In 2006, the summer after my sophomore year at Tech, I finally made some progress toward the idea. My business plan as a fifteen year old five years prior actually materialized into something real. This was the peak of the US lending economy and also the climate that precipitated the downturn. You could get a mortgage without income and you could get a car loan pretty much just by asking for it.

I was twenty and I bought my first Lamborghini. I sold my Audi S4 to use as a down payment and started the business without enough money leftover to make the first payment on it. It was a Giallo Midas (pearl yellow in lay-carperson) 2004 Lamborghini Gallardo. I built a website that was just beyond the look of a well developed Angelfire page but it started to work. I got calls, got the car rented out quite a bit, made the business look like something beyond a shoestring project run out of a dorm room, and actually learned a lot.

What I learned most was how unprepared I was to run a real company with real risks. There was a lot of breath holding through the gambles of a startup environment hoping the odds never played out as they should have. Of course my accounting method was a box of receipts much like Vince Vaughan's "keepers" from *Dodgeball*, my marketing was me posting on message boards and driving to car shows, and my contracts had more holes than a butterfly net but I was in business.

It was the talk of campus. "The guy on that terrible MTV show has a Lamborghini and somehow rents it out." I got a random message via this new website called The Facebook that us college students used to figure out who had the same class schedule. Georgia Tech was one of the first schools to get it and it still had the "Mark Zuckerberg production" tagline at the bottom of each page. The message was from an exotic car enthusiast freshmen who wanted to know how a kid my age had a Lamborghini. His name was Dan Huang. The conversation was brief. Dan was one of those conspiracy theory freaks convinced you needed to guard your internet identity by using anonymous profile pictures so I had no idea what he looked like.

The rental company grew steadily. I bought a Ferrari 360 Modena a few months later and a 360 Spider (convertible) right when the company turned a year old. Gumballer Chris Staschiak actually flew down to Palm Beach with me to pick it up and drive it back to Atlanta. It was another one of those great life road trips. Six hundred glorious miles in a Rosso Corsa, six-speed gated manual, mid-engined V8 Ferrari with a Tubi exhaust. That car was so loud it would shake the entire building when I would start it inside my warehouse unit. Ferrari designed the catalytic converters on those cars to disintegrate internally over time so by the time the car had 50k miles it shrieked like a proper Formula 1 car.

The company was becoming established, gaining some notoriety within the Atlanta area car scene, and my customer base was increasingly loyal.

Most of my business in year two was from repeat clients. I found a transaction with a repeat renter was almost three times as valuable to me than finding a new customer. They did not have a learning curve in the car, they began to think of the car as theirs, and they frequently told their friends they owned them. These factors made them rent more to continue to keep the charade up and they treated the cars better. It behooved me to discount their rentals and offer return incentives. I did that and my rental volume increased in a much needed fashion.

Literally the same week I incorporated Supercar Rentals I went on my first date with Megan. She was the girl I would end up marrying thirty-seven months and twelve days later. I grew up with Megan. We went to elementary, middle, and high school together. She is a year older than I am so while we knew of each other, we never spent a great deal of time together in school. Her mother and my mother graduated from high school together and our grandmothers were actually in a high school graduating class of twelve together. Fortunately, they did the backtracking to confirm that we were not related before we thought to do it.

I knew she had a great reputation and that she was well out of my league but like every other area of my life - I was aspirational. I remember a conversation I had with Kevin Messer four or five years before I asked Megan out of our first date. I truly cannot remember how she came up in conversation but I remember expressing some interest. His response was, "Forget about it. She has a Master-Lock between those legs." His relationship goals and mine were very different at the time. The conversation did not continue but I remember vividly thinking that was precisely the kind of thing I would want someone to say about whatever girl would eventually become my wife.

Megan was the perfect girl both to date and to marry. Typically I had found most girls to be either one or the other. She had been in enough bad relationships to appreciate someone who was not a complete moron but she did so early enough to avoid serious issues or long term emotional scarring. She had spent some time being single and was very independent, had a career path in mind to become an elementary school teacher, and she cared enough about her family to love them and also learn from their mistakes. She was primed to be wooed.

Dating was like spontaneously giving presentations in college. Start with a couple of things you know and then just keep talking. I loved it. I loved the deep, engaging conversations where you learn more about yourself than the other person. We found our strengths and shortcomings were sufficiently opposite that we filled in each others' gaps in an eerily providential way. Megan is a phenomenal Christian girl. She helped me to understand how to live out the ideas that I cared about and made me a much more sensitive person to what it actually took to maintain healthy relationships with people. The love God/love people dichotomy was starting to make sense, even in my stunted psychopathic emotional growth curve.

She had more friends than anyone ever. We never went anywhere that Megan didn't see at least three or four people that she knew. I had to hone my skills of using vague pronouns to feign familiarity because I could not keep track of which ones I had met before. It is a skill that has translated well into the car business. I am truly horrible with names. There were lots of, "Hey man," "How are you buddy?" and "Great to see you! How are things?"

I would like to think that through our relationship I have made Megan a 10% better, more effective person. Not that such a service would be fair because she has improved all aspects of me, punctuality excluded, by 1000%. I was batting out of my league but I was continuing to enjoy every minute of it.

Megan is not great at math but she knew enough to understand the rental business was nuts. I had nearly a million dollars in debt by the time I was twenty-two and while I had good answers for all of it she was purely in the relationship through faith in me rather than in the visible outcomes of what I was doing. It would have been sensational to be a fly on the wall listening to her explain to her friends and family how everything was going to be alright even though most of the time it all felt held together by the thinnest of recycled tape.

Running the exotic car rental company by myself definitely detracted and distracted me from my school work. It was a line item of priority already hanging on by a thread. I still made progress through the curriculum and was on track to graduate on time. Despite these successes I was constantly challenged by the fact that I could not make strides towards readiness to attempt a New York to Los Angeles drive and one day do so faster than anyone ever had. No matter how exciting the foreground of my life got, the background presence of the Cannonball never stopped prodding me.

The best way to describe the mental occupation the New York to Los Angeles record held in my consciousness is this. You have a toilet that is always running. It is far enough away from your bed that you can still sleep. The leak is small enough that it doesn't impact the water bill. You have never fixed a toilet or even taken the cover off of one but you believe you can do it. You believe all you need to do is spend some time, free of everything else that so easily takes priority, and look at it. Once you do, it might take a trip to the hardware store but you will find the flapper you need to replace and you will pop it right in there. Before you get around to that, though, you use the bathroom a hundred times, go on a few vacations, have some guests over who wonder why you don't take care of the place, you do some math on how much the procrastination might have cost you. You gripe to some unsympathetic friends about how annoying it is and they don't care. Your parents come to visit and they think you are not handy enough to know which end of a nail to start hitting. You even avoid that washroom altogether for a little while before you finally break down and shut the world off long enough to fix your toilet.

Chapter 5 - Two Lightning Bolts in the Darkness

Even as it remained on the horizon I could not put my finger on why it was so compelling to me. The goal of breaking the record for driving from New York to Los Angeles is not a common one. It carries lots of risk and little reward. Based on my conversation with Yates and the history that I could research it was not clear if it was even possible. I continued to tell myself it could be done but was my hesitation actually due to a lack of means to accomplish it or the concern it was actually impossible? I had not generally allowed my life decisions to be controlled by fear, emotional risk, or limitations so I chose to believe I just was not ready. The daydreaming continued.

The cars were faster, roads were better, and the route was now shorter but there were fifty percent more people in the country and the number of cars using those roads had increased by a similar magnitude. There was no open competition so verification and validity were up to the driver. There was a real chance I would get arrested. There was probably a real chance I would die. It would certainly be extremely expensive. I knew I was unlikely to break it on the first try which would make it even more expensive. The process of attempting it could destroy a car or it could wind up requiring even more maintenance than I could anticipate adding to the expense. It was a terribly hard thing I would probably pour a lot of time and money into and end up getting nothing from. It was sounding a lot like golf. I hate golf.

The "Why?" question is one of the hardest and

most enjoyable to grapple with. The itch came from all of the cultural references and to the intrinsic joy of getting out on an open road in a fast car. It was an appealing challenge to the car enthusiast, competitor, and problem solver in me. I felt the skills and talents I had lent themselves to overcoming the obstacles to success in a fairly unique combination such that being me, in spite of all of the quirks, could actually be an advantage.

It also seemed like something that might appeal to the client base that I would cater to on a daily basis in the exotic car business. If just as a publicity stunt, surely it would be salubrious to my other efforts in some way. Of course that justification sounded a bit like buying season tickets to a baseball season just because you need a new hat.

The reality of it is both shallow and deep at the same time. Like Everest, a four minute mile, or a chicken across the road - you do it because it is out there. But was that enough? It is an idea that can permeate everything about you and potentially help to define who you are. I aim for Christianity and my relationship with God to be the first thing people see when they are around me but as we live in this world and pursue different things, this was one of those personal mountains and a resume item that truly mattered to me. Would anyone else care? I had no idea and I was not sure how much the public appeal mattered to me but I wanted to find out.

There was no way to know how the world might react. I had no real idea if owning Supercar Rentals would be the last job I would need. What would an employer say if they Googled me and found

I was notorious for breaking laws? Would they even find out? It seemed conceivable that the whole feat could actually go unnoticed. The media climate was much less favorable to acts of public disobedience than it was in the 1970s. Would I even be able to get insurance?

I worked at the racing school a few years earlier with a great guy. He tried to teach me how to properly clean a car. That was a failure and the water spots and caked dust on my Murcielago can still attest to it. His name was Tony. Tony's wife had sort of fallen into a gospel singing career but his greatest skill, beyond detailing a dozen racecars a day, was in storytelling.

In the early 90's he was the caretaker of a wealthy man's car collection. He had a nice variety of cars but he was getting ready to take delivery of his brand new Corvette ZR-1. It was an American car that, for the first time in over a decade, an Italian car guy could love. He told Tony to grab his Countach and that they would see which was faster on the way home. Tony got on the highway headed back right next to his boss in the new Corvette but it was no match for the mighty bull. Tony pulled away quickly in the Lamborghini and put some serious distance between them.

Tony crested a hill at around 180 mph and saw a cop coming in the other direction. Knowing what would happen next, he went ahead and pulled over to the side of the road. It took the cop a few minutes to get past Tony coming from the opposite direction, get turned around through the median, and pull to a stop behind Tony. The exchange went something like this:

"Do you know how fast you were going?" The officer asked Tony.

"I have a pretty good idea."

"I was surprised that you stopped."

"Yeah, didn't feel like running today," Tony defended, hoping that he might have found the good graces of the cop and get off with a warning.

"Well you can't outrun the radio."

"Sir I was doing about 3 miles a minute, I probably had a shot."

"Is this your car?"

"Do you know what? It isn't. It belongs to my boss." Sarcasm in a time of risk and adversity. No wonder I loved this guy.

"Well what does he think of you driving it like that?"

"You can ask him in a just a minute." Like the poetic clockwork it had the potential to be, Tony's boss blew right past them in the Corvette at just that precise beautiful moment.

His boss came and bailed Tony of out jail. He paid a $5,000 fine to avoid forfeiting his license but it didn't do him a lot of good because Tony could not get insurance for the next few years. Would this type of outlaw reputation bring an end or at least a temporary hiatus to my own driving career?

In May of 2007 I got a lot of those answers. At the start of the annual Bullrun cross country rally, someone bet Richard Rawlings $50,000 that he couldn't break the Cannonball record. Like Brock Yates, Richard did not acknowledge the US Express records so he viewed the 32:51 Heinz/Yarborough time from the 1979 Cannonball as the existing mark to beat. He was already prepared to do a more than casual cross country drive in a Nero Daytona 1999 Ferrari 550 Maranello with its owner, Dennis Collins. It was outfitted with radar detectors, a dated Scorpion radar jammer, CB, traffic light changer, scanner, fuel cell, and the general checklist of ambitious road trip items.

Rawlings accepted the challenge and diverted to Manhattan to start at the Red Ball parking garage. He rolled into the Portofino in Redondo Beach 31 hours 59 minutes later, beating the 32:07 US Express record as well. He wasted no time in proclaiming the victory, having already been in negotiations for a television deal. He and Dennis did several interviews and the story got some great internet publicity. It was generally positive and persisted on message boards for quite some time. There were questions about validity but they seemed to pass. There were questions about subsequent prosecution but nothing ever seemed to materialize.

For me, sitting in my dorm room reading the internet, this was a Mars Rover landing. This was the first modern publicized attempt at the record. It was in a great car by someone who was known to be of the ability to drive fast. It got a reasonable amount of positive attention and seemed to generally lack negative consequence. This was brilliant. It seemed slow, though, a two hour eternity away from the thirty hour time I had been considering my own benchmark. Was Brock Yates correct about such a time being impossible?

There was one strangely outspoken internet

voice in opposition to Rawlings's record. The naysaying, legitimacy challenging, and belittling came from his historic Gumball rival Alex Roy. He was critical of the lack of proof, the small margin of victory over the 32:07 US Express record time, and the general attitude that Richard had about the whole thing. Alex argued that the calculation and precision he felt would be necessary to accomplish such a Herculean automotive task was not demonstrated here. Alex kind of came out of nowhere on this and his authoritative stance was somewhat strange. He was sure quick to comment though. The assumption of the audience was that the new record would challenge the salience of the US Express documentary that Alex Roy had invested in and was working on alongside Cory Welles.

Roy's indignance made a lot more sense just a few short months later in October of 2007. He released his new book, "*The Driver.*" He revealed how on Columbus Day weekend of 2006 he and co-driver Dave Maher had driven his 2000 BMW M5 from the New York Classic Car Club to the Santa Monica Pier in 31 hours 4 minutes. Cory Welles rode in the back seat and captured video. Alex had waited a year to complete his book and to allow the statute of limitations to expire on some of the speeding laws. He had bested the Rawlings/Collins time and done it before their drive actually took place. To this day, neither believes the other actually did it. At least that is what each claims to me. Neither have published any wholistically conclusive proof they did it but the documentation that was publicly available and the perceived media fact checking made it much harder to doubt anything about the Roy/Maher claim.

Alex claims to have a cornucopia of video, photos, toll receipts, gas receipts, witness accounts, etc. Richard claims to have some video and a phone log with his wife. I hate the idea that anyone would lie about this type of thing and I find it emotionally useless to question either. Both had been repeatedly claimed online and there was nothing to be gained by claiming a "record" that was slower than either.

The game had clearly changed. I was no longer tip toeing towards this record in the dark. There were two formidable competitors who had staked their claims. One could more easily dismiss Rawlings's success as good fortune based on the spontaneity of it but Roy had made this his life's mission. He was scientific, calculated, and prepared. Was I capable of that level of preparation? Would I ever be able to afford it? Could I chase a goal as intently if I truly doubted I had what it took to compete on that level? I wanted to find out but I didn't know how. I also had the black hole of the rental business consuming any excess money I had in the name of fleet expansion.

Kevin, Chris, and I had frequent conversations about it. Megan knew that it loomed in my head and that one day I would probably do it but she never seemed to give the talks much credence. We set out to define the key variables in the equation.

The Car - We needed something very fast. It should could carry three people, lots of gas, have a suspension to handle the weight and performance, and get reasonable fuel economy. It also needed to be comfortable. It needed to be capable but also stealthy and able to fly under the proverbial and literal radar. If it became newsworthy it would be nice to use something interesting. Obviously an M5 was out.

The Route - I needed to find a balance between the shortest route and the fastest route based on a highway preference. I would also need the equipment necessary to maintain the course. It was more than generally New York to Los Angeles. Alex had driven from the New York Classic Car Club to the Santa Monica Pier. Richard adhered to the most common Cannonball end points - the Red Ball Parking Garage and the Portofino Inn. I loved the idea of this starting with Yates and the later was an easy decision. The question of obstacles also presented - traffic, weather, accidents, construction. Avoidance of these possible hindrances would also be critical.

The Prep - We would need a lot of anti-cop gadgets to avoid detection. I had some of these from the 04 AKA Rally but this trip was on a whole new level. Alex's M5 looked like a space station inside. The installation would need to be clean and purposeful. Ergonomics and access to the necessary data were top priorities.

The Team - This did not seem like something that I could fully plan and execute myself. I needed a real partner who could share the driving, the emotional load, and the finances of it. While Kevin and Chris both loved the discussion it remained questionable as to whether or not they would end up being willing to come along or contribute financially to the endeavor.

The Obstacles - Construction, weather, traffic, accidents, and every other roadway risk needed to be dealt with. Any shortcoming here could easily render the aspirational times impossible. These challenges would require an immense time investment in planning.

The Verification - I needed conclusive proof. This would be easy from the tracking devices I used for the rental company but I would need redundancy. Alex's crusade against the validity of the Rawlings/Collins time elevated the need for conclusive proof. Without an official governing body or organized event, providing layered proof was a challenge.

The Reveal - The release needed to be controlled. More press would be better and it needed to read right. It felt like a story which could so easily get crucifyingly negative. I needed to make sure we painted it in a light that was paying tribute to this compelling chapter of car history rather than in the same protesting-the-system spirit that had originally spawned the formation of the event.

The mental challenge of formulating a strategy to break the record was a hugely interesting. We had seen how Richard and Alex did it, an invaluable resource unimaginable just a few short months prior. We had a few ideas of our own to throw in as well.

While I was a student at Georgia Tech, I was told there was someone I needed to meet. Forrest Sibley was an electrical engineering major with a passion for police countermeasures. Everything about Forrest fit the eccentricity of this project. He loved distance cycling, had a sweet blonde ponytail, wore Hawaiian shirts and spandex at the same time, and had a fantastic laugh. An eccentric social awkwardness exists within all of us in this realm but his was a brand of its own. He fit in great.

His passion project was not breaking a New York to Los Angeles driving record but it was very complimentary to it. He wanted to build a fully effective civilian radar jammer. He called it the Bacon Blocker and at that point it was pretty much just a well formed theory in his own head. In my limited understanding of electronics it sounded like it might actually work.

He owned several laser guns for testing and had pretty much every existing anti-police gadget installed in his battle scarred Acura RSX. He had some other seriously interesting ideas that applied to my pursuit such as anti-laser paint, strategic police scanner programming, and a MiRT which is an LED traffic light changer as used in ambulances around the country. He offered some great [expensive] additions to my eventual shopping list.

Of course, life was not done getting in the way.

Megan and I got engaged in 2007. She was in her first year of teaching and I was nearing graduation. We intended to get married after I got out of Tech, at which point she hoped to move closer to the Atlanta area but at the time she was still teaching near the University of Georgia, from which she had recently graduated. I would frequently go up to read to her class, dress up as Johnny Appleseed, or borrow a friend's pet Alligator and go play Crocodile Hunter (due to some very effective crisis management on the part of the Discovery Channel, none of the kids knew he was dead).

Engagement was the most miserable time of my life. You have all of the stresses and anxieties of being permanently together without the benefits - operatively in our case were the convenience of living together and the satisfaction of sex. We had both chosen to remain sexually abstinent until marriage and while it certainly strengthened our relationship both then and now, it was a profound challenge at the time.

In 2008 a few things happened to bring the Cannonball goal closer to reality. One of my good friends and customers crashed my Ferrari 612. He was actually using the car for a cross country car rally and the accident happened in Texas. In Georgia and most other states after an insurance provider pays to repair your vehicle, they are still required to compensate you for the diminished value of the car. I was the recipient of the highest diminished value settlement ever in the state of Georgia at nearly $50,000. It was a great cash infusion into Supercar Rentals, allowed me to pay off Megan's engagement ring, and left a little bit for something discretionary.

Megan's parents were definitely not wild about the idea of her marrying an entrepreneur with a mountain of debt collateralized on depreciating assets and a cash poor business that was barely stable on a month to month basis. Despite the pressure - she held steadfast and kept believing in me. Even then though, life was not without its occasional pokes by Megan to explore something new and safer.

Graduating from college was one of those rare sensations that completely lived up to my expectations of it. The balancing act between Megan, business, and school had been so intense it felt like finally finding an exit from an intense night club. The ears were still ringing and it took time for the nervous sensitivity to subside but the cool, dark air just washes over your body and cleanses the anxiety from every fiber of your sensational being. It felt exactly as good as I had ever dreamt it would.

I moved out of the six bedroom/six bathroom/dual kitchen house I had lived in with my roommates and intramural teammates for the past two years. I found a quiet warehouse a bit north of the city, previously an ambulance depot. It had all of the appropriate fire suppression walls to legally store cars inside. It was off the beaten path enough to keep the cars safe. My business model primarily involved delivering the cars to customers so it was simply a great place to store the cars and as it turned out - me.

The warehouse was built out with a bunch of offices. It was only a utility sink converted into a shower away from the perfect bachelor pad. I dealt with this issue employing my caveman level of carpentry proficiency. Of course, subsequently I found out the warehouse only had a five gallon water heater so I could take a warm shower at about a thirty percent flow for 45-60 seconds at a time. Megan did not visit often.

I made one of the offices into a bedroom, another into a kitchen (room with a microwave, hot plate and a fridge), and another into a closet. That left a lovely space for an office, client seating area, and then an open space to store the cars. It was perfection. You have never slept until you did so in the only room of a warehouse where the heat is fully functional that happens to be forty feet from any room with an exterior window.

Ferris Bueler advised us all to purchase a Ferrari 250 GT LWB California if we had the means. Great advice. If you happen to not have the means to afford traditional housing, I strongly recommended warehouse living. It was everything I wanted it to be. I lived there for thirteen months between graduating college and getting married. I regularly ask Megan if we can move back. It is vacant.

It had always seemed to me that such an interesting automotive feat could serve as a great marketing ploy or publicity stunt for a manufacturer. It certainly existed on the fringe of social acceptability but I wanted to bank on the idea that there is no such thing as bad publicity. A company like Mercedes or BMW was likely too big to take this kind of risk but some of the fringe exotic or luxury brands seemed like good candidates for a proposal.

After the Bentley/Rolls Royce split, BMW bought Rolls in 1998. The reputation of Bentleys as cars that you drive and Rolls Royces being the cars that you should be driven in was starting to blur. Volkswagen took Bentley into a much more mainstream market position with the introduction of the Continental GT. It was very similar to Audi's influence on Lamborghini with their part in the conception of the Gallardo. Rolls Royce was a bit slower to the corporate growth strategy.

They phased out the Silver Seraph and created the new Phantom for 2004 much to the delight of every hip-hop artist ever. In 2008 they brought out the two door Phantom Drophead and then in 2009 they were going to release a fixed roof version. Rolls Royce billed the car as the best way to travel long distances. They said it was a true alternative to private jet travel. This was an interesting claim. Surely they needed someone to test that.

I sent a letter in 2008 to the North American marketing representatives of Rolls Royce with a proposal. Send me one of your cars and I will use it to break the Cannonball New York to Los Angeles record. Surely there could be no better testament to the distance capability of the car than the most legendary point to point record ever.

I received no response. Good - now I had someone else to prove myself to.

The rental company was floating along with the occasional bob but I was periodically able to add something new to the fleet. Of course, such additions usually detracted from cross country car buying resources. One day I got a call from the local Ferrari dealer's service department. Given the dubious reliability of Italian cars and the stresses of rental driving I was quite the consumer of their wares. It was the end of the month and they needed to close out a $9,000 ticket on an Argento Nurburgring (silver) 360 Modena. It had around 21,000 miles and although they already had it torn apart the customer had said he could not afford to pay to finish the job.

It turned out that he had been given the car as a gift when he signed to a hip hop label. He had never driven the car much and it had sat in his parents' garage until one day they decided to see if it would still run. Trying to jump start the car, they put the cables on backwards and fried the entire electrical system. The car needed engine computers along with brake pads/rotors/calipers (due to the fluid solidifying), a big service, and some minor cosmetics. It was certainly not the caliber of car they wanted for their used car inventory so they went flipping through their rolodex looking for someone that would put a hard number on a non-driving Ferrari with a laundry list of needs. Fortunately, they had just the right non-discerning customer with an appetite for a cheater car - me!

Mark, their service advisor, called me and asked if I wanted it. "Sure," I said assuming it would be cheap but still having no idea how I might pay for it. They just wanted their service bill paid and they had the owner's permission to share his contact info with me if I was interested. I got the owner's phone number and gave him a call.

The car was worth about $75k at the time if it were perfect. It was not a particularly interesting example of a 360 and the owner was out of options. There were also no competing bidders because the dealership was not wild about being stuck with an unpaid service bill. After they found me they stopped looking.

I offered him $30,000 for it. He was a shrewd negotiator so he ended up making me pay $31,000. I settled up the bill at Ferrari and ended up owning the car for $40k. Well, I should say Megan owned the car for $40k. While the income earning and money retaining tides have shifted since we got married, Megan came into our relationship with about $50k in an investment account from living inexpensively, getting lots of scholarships, and working hard in the summers. I don't think the rainy day fund was intended to be either a dowry or the means to be a cash purchaser of a Ferrari as a 23 year old schoolteacher but she was now precisely that.

We bought it, rented it a couple times, drove it a bit, and sold it for $60k. That was a big help in engendering her belief in the great things that can come from owning exotic cars. It was a quick, easy, handsome profit.

Life was moving fast. When I had gone off to Georgia Tech and started the rental business and then met Megan, Kevin Messer and I were not nearly as close as we had been growing up. He was involved in a muscle car restoration and brokerage business and doing well. We spoke once or twice a year and our paths intersected occasionally. The conversations always involved a status report revealing my lack of progress toward the record.

Early in 2009 I got a call from my father. Kevin had been out drinking one night and accepted a ride home from a friend who had also had a few too many. On their way home, a police officer saw them and attempted to pull them over. The driver decided to try to evade the cop and in doing so ran off of the road and into a field. Kevin was impaled by a fence post and killed instantly as a passenger. The driver was fine.

The death of my childhood best friend hit me really hard. He was the person that had been there at the genesis of the idea of Cannonball and I had always assumed that no matter how distant things had become it would eventually be something that we finished together. It always seemed like the the odds had been if either of us were ever to die in a car, the other would be riding shotgun. It reignited the fire in me to pursue the Cannonball even more aggressively. With some money left from the 612 diminished value settlement and some of the proceeds from the ex-rapper 360 sale, it was time to go car shopping.

I found a white 2003 Mercedes Benz S55 AMG on Craigslist for $25k. It had 90,000 miles, a lot of cosmetic needs, a minor accident on CARFAX, and was the cheapest one in the world...ever. In my discussions with Chris and Kevin of what car would be best for breaking the record, the AMG Mercedes cars kept rising to the top of the list. It turned out Carmax had offered him $16,000 for the car. We settled on $16,001. It was utter perfection.

I drove it for about 90 days until someone made an illegal left turn into my lane, hitting me head on when I was on the way to a couples' wedding shower. I remember the accident vividly. I saw his decision making process and the inescapable trajectory toward my front right bumper. There was a clear feeling I was about to find out what it felt like to be hit by an airbag. Fortunately, they did not deploy but the rest of the safety systems did. The seat repositioned, the belt tensioners fired, radio went off, and the hazards turned on. It decimated that silver Honda Accord but fortunately both of us were fine.

It was a borderline total loss but I called in a favor at my local body shop, another local business where I had frequent flyer privileges. I told the owner I would rather not see the car again. They wound up totaling the car and that gave me a renewed invitation to go car shopping, my favorite pastime.

The best person to ever sell a car to you is someone else's insurance provider. With the ink of my signature barely dry on the title, they got me a check from the insurance company for $27,500 for a quick 72% profit. I used that to buy a much nicer gray 2003 S55. The dream remained alive.

The week before our wedding, in June of 2009, I rented two of my cars to a repeat client. He was previously an Atlanta Police Officer. He rented the Bordeaux Pontiveccio Ferrari 612 Scaglietti and the Giallo Midas Lamborghini Gallardo. That Wednesday night I was at my bachelor party racing go-karts and I got a call from an unknown number. The woman on the other end of the line had some interesting things to say.

"My husband is the guy that bought your Ferrari today and gave you our BMW and the $15,000 in cash as a down payment. He made a mistake and we want to undo the transaction." I am Jack's unexpected gut punch.

There were so many things wrong with that statement. I could see the next few days of what was already the busiest week of my life starting to crumble into chaos. The rental customer had decided that he was going to sell the car, which I came to find out was called Auto Theft by Conversion. He took a BMW 750 and some cash as a down payment and agreed to let the buyer pay over time. Of course my customer was now failing to answer his cell phone.

The tracking device on the Gallardo said it was in midtown Atlanta. I found it in a body shop with the front smashed off of it. That granted me a half sigh of relief. I got it towed to my preferred body shop and filed a claim with the renter's insurance company. Fortunately his participation was not required. The Ferrari was another story.

Without a way to get the BMW and their money back the "buyer's" self proclaimed lawyer wife was not willing to give my Ferrari back. Obviously I told them I was reporting the car stolen but their response was to hide it rather than give it back. Clearly the caliber of person who buys a Ferrari without any paperwork or documentation is on a slightly different level of reality. They made many questionable decisions in other areas of their lives as well.

I finally got in touch with the rental customer on Friday. He did not have the guy's name, address, phone number, or anything other than the fact that he went by Lucky. He had no good reason for selling the car but seemed to have convinced himself I might be happy about it. There was a general derangement about him not entirely inconsistent with the rest of my customer base at the time.

When you know who stole your car, the police don't try very hard to find it. Since the theft officially occurred in one county and the car was in another county, the normal BOLO/All Points Bulletin reclamation strategy did not happen. I would get reports of the car showing up in restaurant valets, mall parking lots, etc. but it kept moving. Beyond the whack a mole location effort, my satellite tracking device was malfunctioning within the typically unreliable electronic system of the Ferrari so that was no help. Fortunately, GPS/Cellular technology, particularly in capacitance, has been quickly improving since then.

I was on the phone with friends who were out looking for the car, police, my lawyer, the rental customer, valets around town, and everyone else I could think of throughout the evening of our rehearsal dinner and the day of our wedding. We couldn't make any progress. Predictably this was not a great way to impress my new wife and her family. Fortunately, we were able to get a few wedding photos without a Blackberry sticking out of my ear.

It is worth noting here that exotic car rental insurance is one of the hardest to find products in the insurance marketplace and it is laughably difficult to keep. Not only is there a clear understanding that if you ever file a claim against the policy you will not be able to renew, but also if they find out you experienced a loss that you end up paying out of pocket they still may drop you. Reporting the car stolen through the company insurance policy would have gotten me paid but put me out of business just a few months later.

We left the next morning on our honeymoon to Jade Mountain Resort in St Lucia. The car was still missing and progress was at a stalemate. I left it in my lawyer's hands and told him that I would be back in a week. It is difficult to enunciate in written form the level of anxiety I had to suppress to enjoy my honeymoon with my new wife but I managed to. We had a great time and despite the odds my blood pressure stayed where it needed to be.

When I got back there was still no progress. I was finally able to get in touch with Lucky. He agreed to return the car for $5,000. I had been in communication with the police officers running the case so I told them about the request. Their answer was to ask Lucky if he would take a check. Then they said to stop payment on the check after I gave it to him and got the car back. I reminded them that bouncing a check for that amount of money is a felony but they told me not to worry about it. Law enforcement at work.

Lucky was happy to take a check. We met at the sketchy downtown parking lot where he had stashed the car. The battery was completely dead so I called a tow truck to take it back to my warehouse. He was cordial and helpful. He even brought out a Maserati that he had purchased more legitimately that was some seafoam green metallic color repaint. The paint has falling off in square foot chunks so I gave him a body shop recommendation.

I am not one for gun ownership and personal protection. I don't value my life enough to invest a lot of money, time, and energy into assembling a personal arsenal. I did marry into a one family militia though. I had called my father-in-law of one week and asked him to follow me to the meeting just in case things went a bit pear shaped. I later found out that this was not the best foot forward in my burgeoning marriage to his daughter. Resentment has to start somewhere I suppose.

Everything was fairly uneventful. After we parted ways I got a call from my bank. "There is a guy here trying to cash a check very suspiciously," the very polite representative of the bank asked calmly.

"Oh yeah, that is an extortion payment for the return of stolen property. Please do not honor that request and destroy the check. There should be a stop payment in your system as well." She was happy to oblige. Lucky was not. He showed up at my warehouse a few hours later, made some empty threats, and we parted ways. I never heard from him or the customer that had rented the car again. I did get his insurance to pay the $30k to fix the Gallardo though. On to the next one.

Chapter 6: Lawyers, Politicians, and Used Car Salesmen

I met Alex Roy for the first time in early 2008. He was in Atlanta for a BMW event organized by a mutual friend. We shared a three minute conversation I am sure was easily dismissed. He was in town to take part in the setting of another record. It was one of his stops around the country promoting his recently released book.

The mutual friend was named Mitch DeFrancis and he was organizing an attempt to break the record for the longest convoy of cars from a single make - in this case BMW. I had actually helped Mitch locate and finance a very similar 2000 E39 chassis BMW M5 to the one Alex Roy used to set his transcontinental record just two years prior. Alex was in attendance to serve as a lead pace car for the event. He was cordial even after Mitch and I had relayed my interest in breaking his record one day.

Later that year Alex and I spoke at greater length. I dug into my phone book, found the number stored from the Gumball photo gallery, and placed a call to him where I reminded him that one day I was going to make my own attempt. At the moment I had a different request.

One of my frequent rental customers loved my Rosso Corsa Ferrari 360 Spider. He would rent it once every month or so, generally often enough to keep up the appearance to his friends that he owned it. One of his car guy friends was arguing with him that the obsession that he had for the 360 was foolish because of the new bargain performance option of the

505 hp Chevrolet Corvette C6 Z06. It was the amorous affinity of every car magazine at the time and it was winning most comparisons.

The customer called me and said he wanted to rent my car and his friend wanted to rent a Z06. They wanted to "race cross country." He had been to my warehouse and seen the S55 that I intended to use for the record myself and he actually wanted to make it a three way race with me in play as well, betting the rental charges. I told him I was not quite ready to make my own attempt yet but I would look into what it would take to put something like that together.

Of course this type of rental usage was not something I was excited to hear but I was truly not in a financial position to impulsively turn down any big business propositions. I decided to figure out how much it would take for a booking like this to make sense and give them an offer. I also told them that I was [loosely] friends with the guy that currently held the record for doing this and that I would contact him to work on the best preparation for the cars. Of course this was a self serving proposition because I fully expected the astronomical rental rate I would propose to cause their interest in this idea to subside rather quickly.

The quote came to about $25k per car to which they gracefully and thankfully bowed away. The conversation with Alex was great though. He was as against the idea of this as a race as I was but he was still extremely helpful. Every conversation I had with Alex prior to my own attempt was totally forthcoming, friendly, and positive with the ever-present demand not to hurt myself or anyone else. He, like everyone else who had ever been associated with the Cannonball pursuit, was very proud of the safety record of the pursuance of the idea.

The only known injury in 45 years is a broken arm from an all girl team in the 70s that ran off the road in an undramatic one car incident. I do not think seat belts were in play. I believe this was the team where the racy nylon driving suits worn by the Countach movie girls came from, pink in the real life example. If my head fit inside and I could touch a single pedal at a time, I don't think I could resist the allure of a Countach.

Alex and I talked at length about car prep and countermeasures. I had read his book and knew generally how he had done it. We discussed which systems worked well, which ones did not, and what further improvements might be possible. The main topic we discussed was actually verification. He was very critical of the lack of verification offered by Richard Rawlings and was proud to have full video of the entire drive. No one has ever had the interest or patience to watch it all but if a tree falls in the woods and there is no one around to hear it I suppose a lumberjack can still claim the kill.

In this rental race scenario I would need to officiate who won. I told him about the satellite tracking devices I kept in the cars and asked him if he would have any issue with that. He agreed it would be the most conclusive and easily shared form of proof available. It had not been available on a consumer level when he tried it or he said he would have used it.

As the rental race proposition fizzled out, the

steam of business for Supercar Rentals was starting to quiet as well. From the time when I started the company in 2006 to that point in 2008, the US Economy had experienced a surge and then a massive decline. Depreciation in luxury assets was at an all time high, dealerships were closing, new car sales were down, financing was difficult, and as other businesses struggled it became less and less socially acceptable to be seen driving around in an outrageously colored expensive automobile.

That decline had actually helped the rental business. I was selling my usage product as an ownership alternative. Renting a car for $1,500 per day was a lot cheaper than the real cost of owning one. People were paying me to rent my cars because it was a more intelligent decision than paying a quarter of a million dollars to own one. These were higher quality people than the normal impress-someone-for-the-night crowd so I enjoyed that fortuitous circumstance. It did well until it didn't anymore.

Early in 2009 prices had bottomed out. Even five years later as I begin writing this, the prices for Gallardos, Murcielagos, Ferrari 360s, 550 Maranellos, and others were still higher than they could have been bought for back then. The market recognized this and people started buying again. That meant my rental customer base shifted from people who were cleverly beating the depreciation game into those whose credit was so bad they could not take advantage of the inexpensive cars that were widely available in the marketplace. That lower caliber of person meant the cars were no longer being treated well, collection of payment was more difficult, and bookings were much more last minute.

People look at the daily rental rates of exotic cars and the normal finance payments for a 60 or 72 month term and assume the profit must be insane. They estimate that the cars must go out 10-20 days per month so I must have been rolling in the dough. Of course, the real numbers of days out per month for most exotic car rental companies is 3-8 so the margins remain fairly slim.

The Georgia Tech Alumni Magazine named me one of the "30 Alumni under 30 Making a Name for Themselves." My vocation was a far cry from anything requiring a Public Policy degree but I appreciated that they found my current life situation interesting enough to tout. I framed a copy and put it in our office at the house. They had a great picture of me in front of a couple of the Ferraris and the yellow Lamborghini Gallardo. It was fast becoming an ironic image.

Megan and I were struggling financially and the quality of our marriage reflected that. She could see the stress the business was putting on me and had the wisdom to say it was time to find a way out.

I was more stubborn. I took some time away to do some writing, consider some alternatives, and to try to figure out the right direction to go. The Cannonball record could not have been further from my mind since making the monthly payments on all of the cars already felt like a herculean task. It was common for us to end months with less than ten dollars in our bank account. I remember having some friends over to watch a basketball game and literally not having enough cash in my wallet or bank account to buy some food and beer. Something was going to have to change soon.

My reputation within the local car scene was still elevating based on my persistence within the marketplace. I was a board member of the local chapter of the Ferrari Owners Club of America. I was a frequent judge and attender of local car shows. I was always searching for owners of these interesting cars that actually wanted to drive them in lieu of simply parking them in heated garages and occasionally charging the batteries back up to make it to a show.

In the exotic car world you find plenty of people with the money to buy cool cars but the lack of talent or interest to actually drive them. I always found this type of person to be terribly uninteresting. I met a guy named Tom Park who had graduated from Georgia Tech just a few years before me. He had created quite a system for flipping cars and had purchased his first Ferrari in his 20's. I met him while selling a used Ferrari part on a message board we both frequented. He loved driving on the road and track and was quite competent at doing so. Tom turned into a great friend and business confidant over the coming years. He remains one of my favorite and most admired friends.

I had long been courted by both the Ferrari and Lamborghini dealerships in Atlanta to join forces in some capacity. I never thought that selling exotic cars or selling any kind of cars sounded like much fun. I remembered the general morale of the people who I would harass requesting test drives in these types of cars and it was far from enviable. As I looked at the Venn Diagram where circle one was good people and circle two was exotic car owners I always saw very little intersection. It seemed like I might just be trading one unpleasant customer base for another.

As time drew on, the finances of Supercar Rentals got tougher rather than easier. I knew I had to do something. The cash flow required was too high and my cash reserves were too low. A very bad month could be beyond crippling. Additionally, as the credit markets had dried up, the loans I had come by so easily just a few years prior were no longer available. Losing the ability to leverage my investment in the company by using a small down payment and financing most of the cars shifted the risk into the unacceptable range of even my chronically miscalibrated risk-o-meter. Megan thought selling exotic cars was a great idea and I eventually conceded to try it out for at least a short time. It seemed like I could supplement the cash flow into Supercar Rentals and potentially find a few customers to convert.

I was planning on coming and going as I pleased to continue the daily operating requirements of Supercar Rentals. That proved impossible. The car sales business generally entails a 100% commission based compensation plan and there is an expectation that you are there whenever the doors are open. As my career progressed I came to the realization that it doesn't matter how much time you take off, it just costs you a ton of money in lost or split deals.

It turned out car sales was a lot like my experiences swimming competitively. I hated it but I was actually pretty good at it. My ability to speak and progress a conversation through a deliberate logic that made it easy for a customer to agree with me and commit to a purchase served me well in the industry from day one. I actually sold a BMW 650i Convertible the first day I worked there.

The dealership was an authorized retailer for Lamborghini, Aston Martin, and Lotus and I fairly quickly assumed the seat as Sales Director for the Lamborghini brand. It sounds sexier than it is, ultimately just a glorified salesperson. Eventually we got McLaren as well and I handled that brand too.

Sales had struggled badly in the previous couple of years with only 5 new Lamborghini cars sold in 2009. In 2010 we passed 15. 2011 was over 20. 2012 was over 30. In 2015 we were over 50. I was finding a stride and relating well to the customers. My experience in owning and dealing with these cars on a daily basis was creating quite a reputation of expertise. By 2012 over 75% of my business was from repeat customers. In fact, I was cultivating a crop of customers that wanted to purchase cars in the same way I always had personally - financing as much as possible, a few years old, with some miles, shielded from depreciation, and aimed at driving rather than parking.

It was an unexpectedly glorious respite from being a full time entrepreneur. I had none of the risk, some great upside from a reasonable commission structure, and free run of the existing customer base since no one else working there seemed to care to cultivate it. It did not take long for it to take my attention away from pushing the rental operation.

The income was nice and as consistent as is possible in the industry but there was no time for Supercar Rentals. It was clear that the landscape for the business model was not going to improve anytime soon. Seeing the writing on the wall, I made the decision to close the business. It was a challenging concession but one I was able to come to peace with faster than I had anticipated. The car business in any form is not one that can be tip-toed into. It always had to have a big business feel, even when it was just me. The 2010-12 fiscal reality in America was not entrepreneur friendly and everything was a bang-your-head-against-the-wall challenge.

I sold the customer base to a guy that I had helped start a similar business in Palm Beach, Florida just a few years prior. He was looking to expand operations into the Atlanta market. It was not a lot of money but it neatly closed that chapter of my life. I sold the cars individually throughout the next year into 2011.

I enjoyed spending time getting to know the customers and leading them on drives to help them enjoy their cars. That was even more fun than the transactional aspect of the business. I learned that increasing the denominator being used when calculating their own costs of ownership was the best way to keep them coming back for more. I had limited control on the top line of the equation, that being how many dollars it cost them to own the car. When I invited them to divide that number by more miles, friends, pictures, shows, drives, and events - the cars became more valuable and it was easier to make the decision to upgrade to the next one.

I really liked selling the types of cars that would appeal to me. I call them "cheater cars." They look like a million bucks but they are cheap relative to the average market for one reason or another. It could be high mileage, accident history, bad colors or options, service or maintenance needs, etc. They are the kind of cars you can generally buy, drive around for a year or two, and then sell for nearly what you paid for them. Most of the time, they are not nice enough for dealers looking for inventory. That means the check writing value is usually less than true wholesale. I was never in a position to own these cars when they were primed for depreciation but if the values were stable then I could make it work.

One way we got these cars as a dealership was by buying the press cars that the manufacturers use for magazine tests and customer events. One of the press cars we bought as a dealership was a black 2011 Lamborghini Gallardo LP570-4 Superleggera. It was a nicely optioned car that Lamborghini had used for some driving schools, car shows, and display events. It was an admittedly tough life but the price reflected it. It was an Ed Bolian car. No one else would have gotten a chance to buy it if I could tolerate black cars. I drive them too much and despise cleaning up after myself enough that black cars are out. Bright metallic colors do not show dirt badly. This was the perfect car for someone looking to stretch into a Lamborghini that they normally might not be able to afford.

Dave Black was a previous employee of Apple who had moved to Atlanta and worked for the Intercontinental Hotel Group. He had purchased a barely used Maserati GranTurismo Convertible a couple of years prior and thought it was the end all be all of automotive perfection. I was organizing drives to the North Georgia mountains every two or three months. I met Dave at our local cars and coffee get together and invited him to join. He came along and began to notice how vast the gap in aggressive street driving performance is between a Maserati grand touring convertible and a new Lamborghini.

Dave was actually wrapped up in the dissolution of his department at IHG and was about to go into free lance consulting. The problem was that he now had the Lamborghini bug. We looked at older Gallardos that would be closer to an even trade to his depreciated Maserati but those just didn't work. When we got the Superleggera press car in, it was perfect. It was a great cheater car that had a bit of paint work but was under warranty. The downside was somewhere between low and non existent. Dave bought the car and joined our group of regular drivers. He had a top of the line 2011 model for the price of an 08-09 and it was everything that he wanted it to be. I am not sure the seat ever got cold.

I was no psych major but I loved the mental aspect of sales. The process was truly exhilarating to me. You ask leading questions, make it easy to say yes, and carefully sculpt a logic that leads to a decision. It is a style of hypnosis. I was very green when I started but the general manager and sales manager of the dealership seemed to notice some promise. They invested a lot of time into teaching me what they had learned in long careers in the car business. Before long the word tracks flowed like honey and whether I liked it or not, I was a salesman. I assumed that before too long I would develop that twinkle in my incisors every time I smiled. They say that psychopaths exist most effectively as lawyers, politicians, or salesman. Seems there is some truth to that notion.

I still loved driving the cars but giving up ownership was challenging. It had been one of my favorite things about myself and while the successes at the dealership were nice, it did not compare to the pride I felt in owning the rental business. When a guy is asked what he does for a living, the answer matters. "I sell Lamborghinis" sounds cool but, "I own and operate an exotic car rental company that I started in college" sounded a lot better to me.

That was by no means the beginning or the end of my issues with pride. Humility and sports cars have a bit of an oil and water relationship. Making the best of it was still sort of scraping the bottom of the barrel. That led to a lot of soul searching. I have always found myself to be good at things that you probably should not be good at. If you tell someone that you are highly adept at getting away with things, bending a questionable truth into an appealing reality, and rationalizing breaking the law; it does not always paint an attractive image. It is not the way I want the world to see me but it remains difficult to escape.

Megan and I had purchased our first house in a northern suburb of Atlanta late in 2010. It was not geographically close to anything that I liked going to but she fell in love with the house and it was an aggressive short sale so I agreed that we could buy it. It was a long way from where we both worked which created some tension in the relationship. For all her amazing qualities, understanding of maps is not Megan's strong suit. It also only had a two car garage which accommodated the S55 and her Cayenne but did not invite a new exotic addition to the family.

I tried to get her to understand that a small garage was like only having one bedroom. No room for kids. I guess that means we won't have any. She did not seem to get it and, of course, the house had four bedrooms.

I hate home ownership. I think the polarity of my interests has always made it easy to become irrationally obsessed with certain things very few people even care about while having an apathy towards conventional goals. The grass is always greener but I look back on renting and truly question why people are so obsessed with owning houses. Of course those people who spend all of their spare time and money taking care of their treasured house probably think, "Why does that idiot spend more on his car than we spend on this beautiful and satisfying home we have here?" Touché theoretical opponent.

Despite some financial success and stability I was extremely unhappy. I never intended to consider divorce as an option in my marriage but we had completely different goals and views of what we wanted our life to become. I had grown to vehemently oppose the idea of having children. I missed my cars. I still had the gray S55 but Cannonball was a distant priority. We were struggling to find a church that we could enjoy being a part of. Her parents were not wild

93

about me and I was growing to care less and less about their opinions. It was a fairly dark place below the surface of some finally calm seas.

Over time I took steps to give up the priorities in my life that were keeping me from a happy marriage and it did begin to improve. Megan and I began to tithe diligently to a church we had joined in Alpharetta and helped start a new Sunday School class for newly married couples. She and I were getting along better but the rest of my life still felt pretty empty. I had lived my life up until marriage in a very selfish but effective way - bouncing from goal to accomplished goal. That felt over.

The struggles in marriage had taken a lot out of me. I remember the day that I made the decision that the only thing that mattered to me was honoring my covenant of marriage. That was a much more open ended answer than I was looking for. My wedding vows to Megan were these:

I am not here because I love you
I am not here because you are the most amazing
person I have met
I am not here because I want to spend the rest of my
life with you.
*I **am** here because I know, beyond the shadow of a*
doubt,
that God made you for me.
All of those things are also true but it is the
recognition of God's plan for our lives
that gives me confidence and joy to marry you.
So I do promise to love you

From this day forward
Just as Christ loves His Church
For better or worse
In sickness or health
For richer or poorer
Until death do us part.

I knew that the "Just as Christ loves His Church" part would come into play. Ephesians 5:25 commands us to do just that but it is both an impossible standard and something we do not see play out very often. The idea of loving someone truly regardless of what they do for you is hard but I learned a lot through trying. I would stay with Megan and trust that God could make me happy through that act of faithfulness. I knew it meant continuing to sacrifice anything standing in the way of our union. I truly let myself buy into the idea that if I proceeded through life with that priority first, I would find greater peace and happiness than if I were to pursue the selfish goals that had pulled us apart early on in our marriage. I had reached this conclusion after a lot of soul searching, prayer, secular counseling, and Christian counseling with the pastor of the church that we grew up in and who had married us just a few short years prior.

My God is one of endless grace and faithfulness. I was in for a wild ride.

Chapter 7 - A Prostitute and a Lamborghini

People ask me a lot about what I want out of my life, how I want to be perceived, what I might want my legacy to be. I want to be known as a devout evangelical Christian, a good family man, and a loyal friend. I believe their questions are different though. To answer the true essence of the questions - I really want to be the most interesting man in the world. At least I want to be the most interesting person that people who know me know.

I don't care how wealthy I get, how educated, how admired, or how popular I am. All of those metrics are awesome but when I look in hindsight upon how I have made the decisions that made me the happiest, they were generally chasing after ideas that I thought would be interesting to talk about later.

The steps I had taken to stabilize my marriage had confounded some of my efforts to do interesting things but as the top level priority improved it began to feel more acceptable to add back in some things I was missing.

Early in 2011 I met one of the most interesting people whom I have ever known. A flatbed tow truck arrived at the dealership with a non-running Blue Caelum (metallic royal blue) 2004 Gallardo. Every wheel was curbed, the tires were bald, the clutch was fried, and it was pouring oil from everywhere it could find. The door handles were broken off and the interior smelled particularly exotic. The two East Asian guys dropping it off didn't speak much English. Best we could understand it, we were being asked to put together an estimate of what it would take to get the car back up and running. With quite the laundry list, the rehabilitation came to right at $20,000.

We called the number they left and did not get an answer. We had the car all apart and did not have anyone to pay for it. A man showed up a couple of days later and told us it belonged to his girlfriend's daughter and that she was very attractive. It was a strange unsolicited comment but he did not present himself as being the most socially conforming type of person. She was in jail at the moment but would be out soon and probably wanted to sell the car. My ears perked up.

The car was too rough to even wholesale. It needed a lot more work than we anticipated she would be able to afford so we parked it out back and waited.

A few days later I met Kimmi.

Kimmi is a prostitute. Political correctness might ask that I say Kimmi is an alleged prostitute but that wouldn't be fair to the criminal justice system that had already convicted her of the charges three times in various metro Atlanta jurisdictions. While her mother's boyfriend had insinuated that she was in jail for speeding it was, in fact, a professional appearance. Kimmi had paid $100,000 in cash for the car in Miami about nine months prior to her most recent incarceration. While she was away some of her friends went joyriding fairly destructively in the Gallardo and thus our paths began to cross.

We were correct in assuming Kimmi was not in a position to write us a check for the service so she asked if we would buy the car. There are never many bidders on a car like this. You could not know what else it needed until the first $20,000 was spent fixing the obvious items. The risk made me the one and only suitor. I offered her $30,000. She wanted $60,000 as it sat. We settled on $30,000. I expected more out of a career negotiator.

I paid the service bill and stuck my detailers on it for a week. It had some occasional electrical and mechanical quirks but it was a great car. It also said Lamborghini on it and had cost me less than a new Hyundai.

Kimmi was half black and half Vietnamese as best I could gather. She had blue and blonde hair and usually wore very tight, nylon, animal print, short dresses. She had a lot of tattoos and they were conveniently displayed, even the ones in more private areas. She wore some weird zombie-like light blue contacts with catseye pupils. Kimmi's most compelling and presumably marketable feature was her backside. She had a reasonably proportioned, albeit augmented, torso but then she had 50" hips. I mean that she could take breaks while hula hooping. It was the kind of thing that you could never stop looking at, with or without it being arousing to you. She was taller sitting in a chair.

The demographic market for her specialty was a far cry from myself but I found her to be a phenomenally interesting person. She wanted a pink Bentley like the one Paris Hilton had on the TV. You can't buy a Bentley and paint it pink for the $30,000 I owed her for the Gallardo so we decided to see if we could get her financed for the balance.

That meant Kimmi and I got to talk about her credit. I asked her if she had ever gotten a loan for anything and she said, "No." That would normally be a death blow to a big car loan but if she was financing half of a $60-70k Bentley we thought we had a shot. Beyond that, the conversation was too much fun to stop. She pulled out her social security card which she apparently carried all of the time and she gave me her driver's license to copy. The address that was on it matched the title for the Gallardo that she had but it was a strange location for a residence. It was off a big road in the center of town so I Googled it. It was an establishment called the Gold Spa. She unashamedly confirmed that was correct.

I asked Kimmi who to list as her employer and she gave me a name of a pornography production company. She seemed to have her hand in a variety of businesses. I asked her how much she made and she said that it was between $10-50k per month, "So why don't we just say $500,000?" That was on the unbelievable side of the scale for a bank.

"How about this, what did you put on your most recent tax return?"

She shook her head.

"Does that mean it was not very much or you just haven't gotten around to filing."

"That." She said.

We estimated.

When we pulled her credit it was strange. There were no records at all. She had never used her social security number for anything. Not a cell phone, library card, credit card, not even a bank account. That became clear in the next step.

We had no banks that would step up to be the first credit offering to Kimmi. Without a Bentley to apply it to, I told her we would give her a check for the Lambo. We printed it out, signed it, and handed it to her.

"What do I do with this?" She asked.

"You can deposit it or cash it. Do you have a bank account?" Head shakes. "Then just take it to our bank and they will give you cash." The dots were not connecting.

"Really? Can you guys just give me cash?" She was perplexed.

"No, we don't keep that much cash around. It is super easy, they are right down the road." I said. "Have you ever used a check?"

She had never seen one.

Kimmi went on her way and I owned a prostitute's Gallardo. I had a bear of a time getting the second key from her though. I called, texted, emailed, and tried everything to get in touch with her to get it. I wanted the second key and wasn't wild about someone in her profession maintaining access to the car - not judging.

One day she sends me a text message.

"It's my birthday tomorrow. Do you still want that key?" she asked. Interesting combination of ideas.

"Yes, please. Would you bring it up here?" I asked.

"Can I get $100 for it?" I shouldn't have been surprised given her normal income earning strategies.

"Sure. Get it here by 5 PM and I will give you $100." No response. No show by 5.

The next day just as we were about to close, Kimmi walks in. The best way to describe the dress that she was wearing is that it was a basketball net. More holes than stretchy white fabric. It left even less up to the imagination than her normal wardrobe. There was a woman with a small child at our service counter. She saw Kimmi's dress, grabbed the child, and literally ran screaming out of the building.

"What are you all dressed up for Kimmi?" I asked. She came over and hugged me. Kimmi was a hugger.

"Itsma birfday!"

"Well you are halfway to that outfit, aren't you?" I am not sure she got it.

She handed me the key. I paid her the $100. Given her attire I felt like the obvious question was sufficiently appropriate. My curiosity persisted on a zoological level. Utterly fascinating. No pun intended although our local Atlanta, low budget implant installers need to brush up.

"Kimmi, do you have butt implants?" I was at the edge of my seat.

She was proud to answer, "No. I got a fat redistribution. You see, they made me gain thirty pounds, and then they suck it out, and they injected it right here." She pointed to the injection site. They clearly used a turkey baster.

"Does it feel strange?"

"No. Feels normal." She seemed quite pleased with it. I was proud to have lived long enough to encounter the recipient of such a pioneering medical procedure.

I haven't seen Kimmi since then but she does occasionally like and comment on some social media posts of mine. Now that is interesting.

I was very pleased to once again be an exotic car owner and I drove the wheels off of it. As I said, the house that we had purchased only had a two car garage. That meant that there was no place to put the Mercedes. I ended up enjoying the blue Gallardo as the first exotic that I had owned that finally had no strings attached. One consequence of the rental business was a hyper-consciousness about the cost of driving them.

It was $5.71 per mile on average to drive a Ferrari 360 or Gallardo including the cost of consumable items, servicing, depreciation, insurance, cost of money, etc. With the financial risk removed from ownership of the Kimmi car, It quickly graduated into daily driver duty. The carefree feeling of a car that looks cool, is fun to drive, and was fresh out of a monster service was excellent.

Working 60-70 hours per week, trying to build up some savings, volunteering a lot at church, and continuing to work on my marriage meant that the Cannonball still occupied a space somewhere between a backburner and the lowest cabinet shelf in the kitchen. As much as I wanted it and while the toilet was still running in the background, there was just no time or money to allocate to it. I also had no idea how much it was going to cost to do. It is challenging to budget for an unknowable expenditure.

I wasn't driving the S55 very much and it was coming up on needing a ton of maintenance. It needed a major service, brakes, tires, a suspension/power steering pump, and a bunch of other stuff I knew meant I was further from the record than I wanted to be. Reluctantly, I listed it for sale on

Craigslist and it sold quickly. Very quickly in fact. I got a call on the way to the airport from a seriously interested party. I was headed to Las Vegas for a Lamborghini event so I told him I would be back in a few days. He wanted it now. "Well you can meet me at the airport parking lot if you want." I told him, expecting that to end it.

"That works. See you in 15. Text me the lot and section."

He got there, agreed to pay me what I wanted, gave me half in cash, and we agreed on the other half when I brought him the title. I had Megan grab the title and pick me up after my return flight into Hartsfield and we went to the buyer's house to wrap it up.

The Gallardo was my only car and I was quite fine with that, despite the fact I didn't fit in the car comfortably. My knees frequently hit the wiper stalk and my head was usually against the headliner. Jeremy Clarkson, who is only an inch shorter than I am, said it best. "I can fit in any car that I want to." I drove it as much as I could, putting over ten thousand miles on it in the next year. We ended up driving Megan's Cayenne whenever we required more space or comfort.

Chapter 8 - Finalizing the Playbook

Time flew by but life still felt mercilessly boring. I lacked energy, had no goals, and had made a lot of materialistic sacrifices for the sake of our marriage. Megan was happy but she was itching hard to have kids. I was not.

I was talking to Chris Staschiak. With increasing entrance fees, Gumball was now out of reach for him as well. It was time to start planning the drive. If we were going to make an attempt at the Cannonball record we needed to stop making excuses and start taking strides toward making something happen. You can always tell what is right outside the fringes of my deliberate consciousness by what I jot down on the backs of and in the margins of paper left lying around on my desk. Within the prior few weeks those spaces were full of shopping lists and budgets for radar detectors, laser jammers, CB radios, police scanners, and everything else we needed based on the last nine years of planning.

Chris was broke. He was very interested and ready to drive when asked to but he was not able to contribute financially. I knew we had about ten grand worth of equipment to buy and I still needed a car to do it in. I had sold the Gallardo a couple of months prior and was actually driving a 2005 Porsche Cayenne S that had spent some serious time under water. It had a Florida Certificate of Destruction rather than a normal vehicle title so we were unable to sell it as a dealership and just kept it around to run errands in. It had been a trade on a Lotus Evora. You get weird trades on Lotuses.

Cory Welles spontaneously released the movie that she had been working on for nearly a decade. It was called *32 Hours 7 Minutes* and it chronicled the US Express events of the 1980s. It intersected early on with Alex Roy. Alex had found Cory mid-project and offered interest, investment, and continuation. Cory was a friend of Doug Turner, half of the team that set the long standing record in 1983. Their phenomenal time was met with doubt and criticism by other US Express participants. Her film set out to prove the time was possible. Alex became her vessel of proof.

The movie was brilliant. It told the story in an exciting, historically relevant way. It continued to reveal more and more about how Alex had broken the record as well. This was an idea I found particularly intriguing. It filled in some of the gaps left by his book. Seeing parts of the drive on video was also great to help address the massive foreign elephant in the room of what the in-car psychology of attempting this might be like.

I made a list of cars to consider. The Mercedes AMG cars were still mathematically about as good as it gets but they were getting old. The high mileage ones were nearly cheap enough to be disposable but they would require an unforeseeable amount of maintenance to get truly ready to go. The newer 6.2L AMG cars got bad gas mileage and were 200-300% the price of the earlier cars without any clear benefit.

The 2010 Porsche Panamera Turbo was getting closer to affordability now that the Gallardo was out of the picture but based on the $16k I had paid for Megan's five-year-old Cayenne S just a couple of years prior I had a pretty good ghost-of-Christmas-future idea of what that $70k investment would turn into before too long. Also, when I put the fuel cells in the rear hatch I would need new heat shielding to protect the passenger areas due to the open design.

The 2004-2006 Bentley Continental GT had always seemed interesting. They were the same $70k they had been for the prior three years but it almost seemed worth it. The twin turbo 552 hp W12 was beastly. It had a slightly more confined rear seat than a CL and a very complicated vacuum system that could be perilously expensive to address if something went wrong. Parts and maintenance were sure to be a problem. I would rather be associated with breaking this record in a Bentley than a Mercedes if that counted for anything.

The Lotus Evora was the only car capable of exceeding 150 mph and getting 30 mpg on the highway. The North American headquarters was thirty minutes from the authorized dealership I worked for. The back seat is optional which is another word for useless. A third passenger was not possible and there was no great place for the extra fuel.

I toyed for a bit on using the 2005 Ferrari 612 from the rental fleet. It had some room for fuel and 532 hp out of a 5.75L V12. The car was extremely comfortable and difficult to identify by anyone but a die hard enthusiast. It did not have cruise control which seemed like a risk and I was not sure I could cut into the dash for all of the electronics. I also had about 11 years and $198,000 worth of payments left on it. I could not imagine having another decade of debt obligation required just to keep the car I came to prize. Those remaining payment coupons would add a lot of salt to the wound if the car were seized or destroyed in the process.

Clearly I had never been one to keep a car for a long time. I knew that it would be tough to part with the car that we broke the record in if everything went to plan so vanity weighed on the decision a bit. It would be the car that I would show my grandkids, the grandkids I was clearly not going to be able to avoid having based on the persistence of my wife.

Life threw another wrench in my Cannonball-car's way in the form of a kryptonite car. An Arancio Atlas 2008 Lamborghini Murcielago LP640 Roadster popped up on the market with 24k miles. It had $80k in recent service history and was the cheapest one there had ever been. It was my dream car, in my favorite color, in the roofless configuration that would allow me to sit up straight for once. I had to have it.

It exuded every positive impression that had been tattooed on my brain during that first Murcielago test drive as a seventeen year old, screeching around a slow moving tractor to the chagrin and terror of the unsuspecting salesperson. Getting a ghost-faced passenger praying to God while his fingernails dug into the leather of a $300,000 Italian sports car is not the evangelism that Matthew was talking about but it must count for something. It was nirvana seeing an orange LP640, believing that I could get financed for it, and having some trade credits sitting at the dealership from previous disposal of the rental fleet that I could use to avoid any taxes.

Being around exotic cars all day poses some problems in the personal preference front. I obviously want pretty much all of them but I am constrained by budget and my ability to finance these cars. That set some parameters but because of having the huge car loans open for so long with Supercar Rentals, I had better car-buying credit than all but a handful of my customers. The finance terms were amazing. I put down nothing, paid no sales taxes due to the use of the 612 and the prostitute Gallardo as trades, financed the car for 12 years/144 months, and had a payment of $1,799. It was perfection.

For me, though, the LP640 iteration of the Murcielago is the benchmark. It occupies that $175-250k price point where you also find the Ferrari 458, McLaren 12C, Aston Martin Vanquish, a nice 599, and some other options. The thing about it is, they are just not as cool as the big V12 doorstop-wedge-aerodynamics Murcielago. It is the most useless car ever built and it comes from a heritage of other completely useless cars. You can't see out of it, the transmission barely works in traffic or reverse, the engine is completely inaccessible and must be removed for most servicing, the all wheel drive system is tuned to work perfectly at 200 mph and only marginally at daily speeds, it gets eight miles per gallon most of the time and five when you are having fun, women can't get in or out without revealing the color of their underpants, and it can barely go over a speed bump. Add in the Roadster factor and you can't drive in the rain, even with the roof on. It leaks and the only windshield wiper hits the leading edge of it every swoop even after you've spent twenty minutes installing it under an overpass. Imagine a car still worth it even after all that! It is the male version of a five-inch stiletto. Worth every ounce of the pain for that look and performance.

Because I had purchased the Murci, the more expensive record car options were out the window. Five days later I bought a 2004 Mercedes CL55 AMG with 100k miles. It was a nice car with a little paint work, good options, needed some tires, and some general cleaning. I bought it for $17,000.

The feeling of getting back on the horse with these two goals of having a cool exotic car and pursuing the Cannonball record was phenomenal. My life was at a point of stability with Megan and with our finances that these decisions could be justified. I also went to our local reptile trade show and purchased a baby Sunglow Albino Red Tail Boa Constrictor and named her Sunny the LamBoa. I suppose while the thought had been to dip a toe or two in the proverbial swimming pool of the vices I had been neglecting for a few years, this was probably more of a cannonball.

It felt real this time. It was as close as it had ever been. The conversations began to get more intentional with the compatriots I needed to make the drive a reality.

Through local car events I had become good friends with a guy named Adam Kochanski. At the time he had a great vertical collection of BMW M3's. He had a 1995 Daytona Violet E36 M3 coupe, a Phoenix Yellow 2001 E46 M3 track car, and an Alpine White 2008 E90 M3 Sedan. I get more impressed than I probably should by these types of vertically generational car collections. It carries a true connoisseur status. I had long aspired to amassing a similarly generational collection of the V12 Lamborghini lineage.

I told him about the plan to try to break the record and he was immediately fascinated by the idea. Like Chris, he was not in a position to contribute financially but he was available to drive or help as needed. I needed a co-driver, support passenger, someone to stay home and monitor weather, people to help with installation, and some help with verification. There would be lots of roles to fill and he seemed capable of bringing some strong skillsets to the table. Adam had read Alex's book and was enthusiastic about the outlaw craft of cross country road racing.

Work continued to pick up and I stayed very busy. I was thoroughly enjoying the Murcielago and daily driving the CL. Megan had driven the CL on one occasion and managed to run over something the size of a mobile home park. It broke the undertray and one of the front wheels. I needed a set of spares anyway so I found some on eBay and wound up with 1.75 sets of AMG wheels for the car. Fall was fast approaching and it was clear that there would be no chance for a 2012 attempt before the weather got too risky.

I called Alex Roy to catch up. He was still engaged in a bitter legal battle with Cory Welles where he claimed he had not authorized the release of the film or the final cut. Rather than pursuing a theatrical or festival release she had done an internet straight to DVD release. I told him again that I was serious about an attempt and we talked for a bit about

110

the landscape of challengers he had faced since going public with his record five years prior.

He believed that five to seven people per year attempted the drive. He said in the time that he had held the record, he only believed that three had a shot, me being one of them. That felt like quite an honor. We talked through my strategy, the car that we were using, route preferences, legitimacy, and verification. It was an extremely positive and helpful conversation. He was a bit cagey about his approval of my decisions, but I could tell that he just loved talking about it. It was like asking Kimmi about her favorite swimsuit bottoms - right in the wheelhouse.

I started building the war room in our home office. I met various times over the winter with the team of people that were interested in some level of involvement in the project. I still had no one who was interested in or capable of helping me financially with the undertaking but I had resolved myself to the idea of footing the bill myself. The target date at this point was May of 2013.

The car was right. It had 493 hp, a great advantage to the 400 that the M5 that Alex had used. The forced induction would also help with altitude variation and fuel economy. Fuel range was a huge issue. You have to go extremely fast to make up for each stop. Alex had used an auxiliary sixteen gallon fuel cell to extend his range but he still required six fuel stops. I wanted to cut that to three. The easy math was 3000 miles = 4 tanks of gas = 750 mile range @ 15 mpg = 50 gallons required. The stock tank on the CL was 23 gallons so I needed at least another 27. Full emptying was not likely so building a cushion was necessary. Also, even though the actual route was 2813 miles, fuel economy would be less than 15. I enlisted our resident Lamborghini technician to help me with sourcing and installation. He was friends with Vincent Luongo, the Lamborghini technician who had installed the fuel cell in Dennis Collins's Ferrari.

That fuel was going to be heavy. I needed an adjustable suspension to compensate for the weight reduction over time as we burned through the fuel and to keep the car level. Gasoline weighs about six pounds per gallon so we would have just over four hundred pounds of fuel on board when full. The achilles heel of reliability for that generation of Mercedes was the Active Body Control hydraulic suspension. It was perfect but getting it fully operational at this age was going to be quite an expensive undertaking. There was no better option out there. Also, the CL was already a heavy car so the weight change was less likely to alter the handling characteristic than a smaller sports car. I would have been fine with a CL or a third S Class but after spending 10k miles driving this CL it was clear that the big 2+2 coupe was a much better handling car than the S sedan.

Although 2003 was the first year of availability for this car, it was poetic that it was a 2004 - the year of inception of my idea of personally challenging the record. If I had unlimited funding for the project back then, I would have certainly wandered into a Mercedes showroom and purchased one brand new. In fact, in 2004 I had pretended I was going to do just that and driven a $137,000 white version of this car that was now being prepared for electrical dissection. I think the excuse I had used to avoid a commitment to purchase at the time was a need to check out the newly released Bentley Continental GT before making a decision on which would make a better cross country race car.

The list of countermeasures was growing. I had long used a Valentine 1 radar and laser detector. The positive reviews you find about the V1 on the internet are all correct. Forrest, the countermeasure enthusiast friend I had from Georgia Tech, and I went through the shopping list and we decided since the frontal reception in the units were stronger we needed to use another one mounted backwards on the rear glass. His Bacon Blocker Radar Jammer remained in the "nearing completion" phase it had enjoyed for three years.

For the sake of redundancy we also wanted to use the Passport/Escort detector system for radar. That included a frontal laser Jammer that had fairly poor reviews so I bought a full Laser Interceptor system to install for redundancy as well. Navigation and documentation were key and the ten year old system in the Mercedes was useless so I bought two of the biggest and best rated Garmin Nuvi systems with XM Traffic Data to use. I ordered a Cobra 29, a fully adjustable and programmable citizens band radio with a K40 whip antenna. I also got a Uniden Bearcat Digital Trunking Police Scanner and its associated GPS and radio antennas. I called up GeoForce, the tracking company I had used for the rental cars, and asked them for another unit with a monitoring plan. We started looking into methods of enhancing the lighting of the car as well but struggled to be impressed by any available options beyond an HID kit.

I built a shopping list for other supplies we would need for the car - a jack, fire extinguisher, urine bottles, bed pans, duct tape, electrical tape, double stick tape, spare fuses, spare fluids, fasteners, flashlights, binoculars, chewable vitamins (C, B, Multi), nutrition bars, candy bars, energy drinks, pure sugar candy, sports beverages with electrolytes, and bottled water. Lots of time was spent staring at the car and the cockpit trying to imagine where everything might fit.

The biggest advantage that Alex and I had discussed in doing this type of thing in 2013 rather than 2006 was the prevalence and capability of smartphones. He had an early generation Blackberry on his runs but that was nothing compared to an iPhone and tethered iPad for apps like Waze, Trapster, and Google Maps. I made sure to stock up on cradles, chargers, and mounts for multiple phones and tablets. These were the only potential game changing factors that he saw between 2006 and 2012-13.

Forrest was continuing on the Bacon Blocker and the MiRT. A MiRT is a traffic light changer as employed by ambulances. Rawlings had used one of these as well. Both of them were coming along. He had the control board designed for the radar jammer and he claimed that the MiRT was a walk in the park. We talked for a short moment about the penalties of using each. It was illegal to use any active radar jammer without FCC permitting. I hear that speeding

114

is actually illegal too. Obviously our use did not merit such a permit. Violation of those rules can result in a one year minimum prison sentence and a $10,000 fine. The MiRT was legal to own but illegal to use or sell. We were good there since it would not be in use during any heavy speeding.

We needed a plan to control the uncontrollable variables. Weather, traffic, construction, and accidents could each throw massive wrenches into our time and progress along the route. Also new since Alex did the run was traffic information by satellite radio and by mobile internet. Weather was impossible to predict very far out but we knew that spring and fall were better than summer. I also ruled out summer due to the heat and the likelihood that we would not use the air conditioning during the ride to conserve power and fuel economy. Later contemplation and experimentation revealed that using the AC was an absolute necessity and that other comfort options such as windows/sunroof created much more parasitic drag.

Construction data was available by phone for each state but not compiled in a very digestible way. Waze kept good data but there was no way to know how many users would be available in a given area as we passed through. My plan became to deploy some spotters up ahead. This would effectively create our own custom Waze style network for people up ahead to alert us to pertinent issues.

The route was also a challenge. For me, the starting and ending points were easy. This had always been the bone of contention between Alex Roy and Richard Rawlings. Richard claimed a

Cannonball Record, Alex claimed a transcontinental record. Technically the route that Alex took was only a few miles shorter but those miles were at the extremes - the slowest portions of the trip. His exit point from Manhattan could save up to twenty minutes depending on traffic and the exit point at the end of Route 66/the Santa Monica pier was navigationally much more simple. I simply could not stomach the idea of using a non-Cannonball tribute route based on how the idea had developed for me.

I sought to unify the two records by breaking both while adhering to the Cannonball route of starting at the Red Ball Parking Garage on E 31st Street, originally chosen because it was used to house the *Car & Driver Magazine* test fleet and to finish at the Portofino Inn in Redondo Beach which was now called the Portofino Hotel and Marina.

The traditional route is to take the Jersey Turnpike to 70 and then drop down through St. Louis onto I-40. 20 and 80 were the theoretical alternatives although the southern route using I-20 was far too long and unfeasible. Some of the Cannonballers had tried it but it had never been terribly successful. I found I-80 to be compelling, particularly due to the Iowa, Nebraska, Colorado, Utah component. It felt like a great opportunity to put in some high average times. Some of the others voiced concerns about traversing the Rocky Mountains that far north but it seemed worthy of consideration. It would be a much more weather dependent, gametime decision.

Timing was tough. The last two weekends of each month are very hard times to take off in the car business due to the accounting procedure of closing the books each month. Also, let's not kid ourselves that being a cop is unlike any performance based job. They have ticket quotas to fulfill and the patrolling was going to intensify toward the end of each month.

I went into this embracing the sobering reality that it would likely take three or four attempts. You can really only try once per month when coping with the logistics of getting the car home, re-serviced, and back to Manhattan. It seemed to make sense to shoot for Spring for a first attempt so that you would at least have time to try once more that year, likely in the Fall. There would be more rain in the Spring but you could never know when snow would present in the Northeast or Midwest forcing you to write the rest of the year off. Each attempt is also expensive. Lots of gas, flights, shipping, oil changes, tire replacement, etc. I had driven the car hard but had barely given it a taste of the torture test to come. It was tough to guess how the CL was going to react.

Verification was a serious issue. There was no sense in doing this and not being able to convincingly prove it. I wanted there to be excessive redundancy in this area. The satellite tracking device was truly enough. It could not be cheated by flying the car but theoretically it could be counterfeited. The GPS trip data would be extremely valuable. The Garmin units had a screen that showed distance driven, average speed, top speed, time driven, time stopped, and total time. That would be the easiest way to show the result to someone in a set of pictures. The preponderance of circumstantial evidence would be compelling.

The Mercedes on board computer was also

great. It had a two screen system. One showed the statistics since the car was started. The other showed them since a reset. I knew they would be useful for the driver on each leg to evaluate how they were doing on a more immediate basis so we planned for those to be the resets. I planned on the data "since start" to serve as the trip data. This required that the engine not be shut off throughout the trip including during refueling. That would not pose any mechanical issues other than popping a check engine light for an evaporative system leak. While the extra fuel plumbing was not fully planned, there was a pretty decent chance those codes would already be present regardless.

Each screen would show total time, total distance, average speed, and fuel economy average. It was a beautiful and holistic depiction of this trip containing all of the operative variables. In addition to these, we would have toll records from the fast passes and credit card records for gas receipts. I felt like we had this area sufficiently covered.

The psychology and physiology of it was very tough to predict. I had done long distance drives, rallies, and high speed runs but there was no way to forecast what the adrenaline was going to do to us during the drive. I was glad to have comfortable, massaging seats in the Mercedes and it was a relatively roomy car up front but would we be able to sleep? Would our eyesight suffer? Would we dehydrate badly? Would the onboard bathroom facilities be necessary? How should we eat? What should we eat? When should we eat? How do you pre-game for something like this? The litany of unanswerable questions was a real concern.

I decided that some of those were simply unknowable and I just needed to accept that as something that went with this explored, but truly uncharted territory. The first attempt needed to be treated as a reconnaissance run anyway. Success was unlikely and it would be the only way to learn the answers to some of these questions. It sure was some expensive and risky research.

A broader question was of driving protocols. What was the goal? My personal goal, even before Alex and Richard established their records had been to break 30 hours. It felt like the benchmark of the idea within current technological parameters. It was also a comfortable margin ahead of Alex's 31:04 time where I would be able to fail at my own goal while still breaking the record. 31 hours was a 91 average. 30 hours required nearly 94. Estimating three fuel stops at ten minutes and four driver changes to evenly divide each tank of gas at two minutes, forty-five minutes stopped seemed like a good guess on the time that we would not spend making progress. That upped the required average speed to 93 mph for 31 hours and just over 96 for 30 hours. That was really moving and pretty daunting from my perspective.

I took the CL out on a few trips to try to see how long I could keep an average like that up. The answer was not very long. The style of driving that would be required and hopefully possible in this attempt would be in stark contrast to anything I did on a regular basis. Rally driving is the only form of auto racing where two people are actively engaged in the process of driving. This is necessary because the course cannot be memorized and success requires attacking the course as though it is memorized. This demands constant instruction. Maintaining the speeds to be competitive requires driving beyond what the driver can comprehend by themself. High speed road driving is the same way. This type of driving hinged on the co-driver/navigator so the selection was critical. I needed someone who was as invested in this working as I was. As the preparation went on, I began to question whether or not finding a useful car co-driver was actually possible.

It was clear how a few hours of extremely high averages (110-120) would massively relax the required pace for the rest of the trip. I had driven 111 miles in one hour during a leg of the AKA Rally back in 2004 and I had averaged 85 miles per hour on one 600 mile trip from Palm Beach, Florida to Atlanta including all required stops. Those were a long way from what I needed here. The wild card was the co-driver. The speed that you achieve and the rhythm you settled into depended on the comfort level and confidence instilled by the person calling the shots. The driving protocols needed to encourage clear instructions that would foster confidence and relax the driver.

Alex had used two things I felt were flashy but unnecessary. He used a private plane to fly ahead of him and watch out for cops. From what I could read and see in the documentary, it appeared to have had limited use and the air to ground communication was difficult. He also used a thermal night vision camera. I spoke with FLIR, Raytheon, and several distributors of night vision systems and none of them seemed to have enough range to show anything the headlights wouldn't. Both of those ideas also ended up being prohibitively expensive for my current position so they were scrapped. It was nice, though, to leave myself some outs in tactics to employ in future attempts as I would try to improve my time.

I had formulated a good playbook and the boxes of tools and goodies came in over the course of the next few weeks. As winter set in, life got extremely busy and my attention began to wander. We had gotten extremely involved with the church and were enjoying the connections being made there. It seemed like there was a wedding, a birthday party, a couples shower for something, or a car event every single weekend. It was easy for weeks to go by without me having much time at all to devote to the contemplation of and preparation for the record. None of the other guys were much help in making progress. Business was good at the dealership and I was actually growing more content in the areas of life where I had struggled in the past.

Chapter 9 - Becoming a Christian Outlaw

As an outspoken Christian, I am asked frequently how I reconcile extravagant spending and working in such a materialistic industry with living by faith in a relationship with God. Mine is usually the only Lamborghini in our church parking lot and I don't recruit a lot of customers there. I do not believe that there is anything inherently wrong with having or using the ability to buy something expensive but we will all be called to answer for those purchases sooner rather than later.

We do a lot of volunteer work through the church. One of my favorite things is leading a discipleship group of high school seniors every spring on a weekend retreat. The youth ministers love it because the kids get excited to go hang out with Mr. Ed and I just love getting to know them and figuring out what is going on in their lives.

The car, the jobs, the celebrity clients, the social media presence - it all helps me to get to them and makes them open up about what they struggle with. If maintaining a big car payment and chasing crazy dreams serves as a foot in the door to start a conversation with one of these kids about Jesus and how to balance life with what is truly important then it is worth every dime.

Showing people how much you don't care about your stuff is equally important to how much you do appreciate and take care of what you have. I am never shy about letting people take pictures, sit in, and even drive my cars when situations permit. I can't preach that my treasure is in Heaven if I jump on top of every kid that leans on my car to take a selfie. It is a big box of carbon fiber and paint. It can all be fixed and no one would be more excited to call the AllState people than I would!

I get a lot of customers whose wives and children all hate their cars. They resent the time and attention the cars get and they are critical of the requirement the car stay in such pristine condition. Guys walk into my showroom all the time to trade into their next car. They will tell me their current one never sees rain, they spend days in the garage detailing it after every drive and then they promise me that I won't find a blemish on it. It is the cleanest one ever! Woohoo.

Inevitably a comment comes up within the next few minutes about how upset their significant other will be that they just increased their investment in the recreational expenditure department. I always ask, "Does she drive it?" and the answer is always to the contrary. When I ask them if they would like their wives to drive, use, and enjoy their cars alongside them the answer is generally, "Yes."

The problem is, the wives are smart enough to know that it simply is not worth the risk. They know how devastated their husband would be if they came home with a scuffed bumper, scraped wheel, or scratch. Their distance from the car serves as a security measure to strengthen or maintain the wellbeing of their relationship.

I told them all the same thing. Megan is not going to grab the keys to the Lambo and go grab coffee with a friend. She knows that she is always welcome to but she also knows that you can't see out of it, the transmission is challenging, and the parts are expensive enough to bother her if we had to replace them. What she loves doing is driving the car in an easy situation. It is my job as someone who wants her to tolerate this obsession to create these opportunities for her.

I told my customers to take their wives on a road trip somewhere reasonably close. 200-300 miles away is perfect. Once you get out of metropolitan areas hop off an exit and switch seats. Anyone can drive one of these cars on the highway. They learn how the car feels, how the controls work, and they get really comfortable in it. It is a great opportunity to give some encouraging words about how well she did, how fun it is, and how much her enjoying it adds to your enjoyment of it. Exotic cars - strengthening marriages! I think there is a seminar series in there somewhere.

Once you get to the destination, get out and tell them how cool it is to see this beautiful car covered in bugs, brake dust, and filled with garbage from the trip. Be happy about using the car and make it clear that the next stop does not have to be the detail shop. Show her that you are not saving it for the next owner to enjoy. You want to have fun with the car and you are making her a part of it.

After that you get to buy whatever car you want!

I try to showcase that attitude with all of the cars that I own and drive. They are special things that do not require special treatment. Give kids rides. Let them take pictures. Answer their questions and show them you don't have to be Kanye West to have and enjoy something cool. In fact, our recent election has shown that you can be a multi-Lambo owner and go on to become President of the United States. For better or worse, driving around in an expensive car makes you a role model to an impressionable audience. Even though I sold a lot of cars to people who should not be imitated, ownership comes with responsibility.

Over the past ten years I have owned four Ferraris, six Lamborghinis, two Porsches, a Ruf, four AMG Mercedes, four Land Rovers, a BMW, and an Audi. The process of buying, driving them, and selling them has been a lot of fun but what I love most is sharing them with fellow car enthusiasts. I think that is what drew me to the rental business in the first place. Every day I was giving someone a supercar experience and creating memories they would have for a very long time.

The ethical question pertains to the record in a similar way. Was the record my idol? Was breaking the law sinful? Was I putting people at risk? Each of those questions merit some discussion.

We serve an amazing God that built a beautifully complex world for us to hang out in while we get to know Him. The idea of a record is a celebration of so many things about creation. It embodies the competitive spirit of humanity and the drive that allows us to attempt something extraordinary. It demonstrates how social groups can come together to collectively pursue and accomplish something truly special.

The grace of God allows us to actually enjoy our time here, to win things, to set goals, and the have a lot of fun along the way. I love my God for that.

What is even cooler is that because I set this record - you just got to read those words from me. Whatever we do can become a platform for a message that is much, much greater.

Is it sinful? When I was interviewed on the TODAY Show, the hosts asked how I could reconcile being a Sunday School teacher with breaking so many laws. I told them this was an example of goal setting, planning an idea to fruition and being who you want to be. The actual answer is somewhat deeper than that and it was something that I spent this entire journey trying to figure out for myself. The "Why?" question is piercingly hard to answer.

The safety question is similarly difficult and unwinnable. As I contemplated attempting this record it was clear that there was an element of danger and that I needed to understand what the true risks were. I would still need to sugar coat them for Megan and the rest of my friends and family, but I needed to be honest with myself about what was on the line.

As the Spring drew closer I steered more conversations toward the record. The idea of accountability was something I wanted. If a year passed and I was nowhere closer to having this done then I needed someone to call me out on it.

Throughout my life, I had never been shy about making my goals clear and then delivering on them. This felt different though. The longer my friends heard me talk about it the higher their perception on my personal investment in it went. Adding humiliation to the devastation of failure was a double-edged sword. It pushed me harder but it added some emotional tension and trepidation to the idea. I have always said I am not afraid of anything other than spiders. I do not really count the spiders because everyone should hate spiders. They are sneaky and they bite you. I suppose as I reflect on it I am afraid of the day that I find out I cannot do something that I truly wanted to do and what the people around me might think of that.

At that point the group helping me consisted of Chris Staschiak (co-driver option #1), Adam Kochanski (co-driver option #2), Taylor Clark (support passenger option #1), and Forrest Sibley (technician and support passenger option #2). Taylor Clark was a great friend, bookkeeper for my exotic car rental business [read "masochist"], and a true source of good advice. I thought he would be a very big asset to pose the questions as to how hard I was pushing in a way that I might not immediately reject outright.

Starting in 2012 I formed a group of ten friends that I occasionally met with to brainstorm entrepreneurial ideas and projects. The group included Tom Park, Taylor Clark, and several other people who knew about my interest in breaking the record. One of them brought Dan Huang to a meeting we had about an exotic car track driving experience concept. We actually entertained using the Cannonball World Record project as a business endeavor but the monetization aspect is so difficult/impossible it felt too risky as a profit seeking business.

I had not spoken to Dan more than a handful of times since college. We had talked about a couple of cars he was interested in and he had come along on a couple of our drives. He would soon become very important.

I told Forrest that we wanted to make an attempt in the spring so he needed to get the Radar Jammer operational. The Bacon Blocker had been a couple months from completion for about four years. Interestingly, his quest to build the device and my quest to break the record were very similar in duration and expense. Forrest was also building me the MIRT which was closer to completion.

From **Forrest Sibley**
Countermeasure Expert

Our testing of countermeasures goes back to 2009 when Ed was still at Supercar Rentals. We discussed several options for disguise. Ed had a white Mercedes at the time and had the idea to rebadge the front and rear of it with something like an Audi emblem in the front and a Lexus emblem on the back. I remember very clearly that Ed wanted to have BMW hubcaps or center caps on the wheels because it is an obvious logo when the wheels are turning and the blue color is still discernible at speed.

We were obviously very concerned about speed measuring devices. The two main devices used today are radar and lidar. There are a few other methods employed for measuring speed, namely the stopwatch method (VASCAR), but there isn't much that can be done for this other than slamming on the brakes. There were several options available for lidar. One was passive protection. This involves decreasing the optical reflection of a laser beam being pointed at the vehicle.

Ed and I discussed various methods of doing this such as painting the car black, putting a dull vinyl bra on the front, and wrapping the car. I found an infrared-absorbing polymer that could go on the most reflective parts of the car: the headlights and license plate. It is a green powder that costs more by weight than Heroin, several hundred dollars for a few grams.

I found a solvent for it that would dissolve in automotive clear coat and ended up with a lidar-absorbent green clear coat. I purchased an airbrush and sprayed down my license plate, headlights, and a piece of test plexiglass. The results were excellent. The reflectivity of whatever it was coated in was nil. I was having a hard time getting readings off my car at long distances with my lidar gun. However, everything was green, and within days, sunlight destroyed the polymer, the item turned clear, and the coated items became reflective again. This would not work in the long term, and so we abandoned the idea. For lidar, Ed purchased a set of Laser Interceptor jammers which I had had a lot of success with. That took care of that problem.

As for radar, I had something in the works and had been working on it for a few years at the time that I met Ed. It's my long-term hobby project, and I can't talk much about it, but let's just say that they would have a hard time getting a speed reading with their radar guns. At the time of the first run, the main circuit board was being produced in New Jersey. We were anticipating the first run to just be a test run and were going to do it without active radar protection. I had seven of these boards produced, front and rear each for six cars plus one spare. I have the spare hanging on the wall in my office. Since we were planning on using one of these devices on the run, I put a Mercedes logo on the bottom to make it match the car. We would have had points for style if we had used this. Instead, we went with a couple of Valentine One radar detectors. One pointed through the rear window and one pointed through the front windshield. Ed and I checked with one of my radar guns to be sure that the detectors could "see" through the metallic coating on the windshield after he pointed out the faint trapezoidal aperture at the bottom. The detectors worked well for the little that we tested them in this configuration. This was it for radar.

Ed and I discussed two methods for radio communication: a police scanner and a CB radio. Ed had me pick out the best scanner that money could buy, I found it, and he ordered it immediately. The same went with the CB. Not quite a week before Ed made the run, I went over to his place, and the two of us spent hours upon hours going through the road atlas of the route state by state, county by county, and city by city. I picked frequencies to upload to the scanner as Ed poured over the road atlas and named the geographic locations. Many of the frequencies had GPS metadata attached to them so that the scanner would automatically pick them up as we approached the particular municipalities. In practice, there were too many frequencies without GPS data that the scanner had to go through all the time for our sorting to be of any use, and the scanner was so bogged down that it did no good during the run. Hey, this is what test runs are for, right?

The CB radio was another important item that Ed and I worked on. We decided on the latest and greatest Cobra 29 radio, and he went with the K40 antenna since that was what I had used in the past. The antenna was a bit on the large size, and when I had one on my car, everyone referred to it as "the lightning rod." We had some problems with the radio being crammed back into the dash. When Ed got the car back from the installer, he noticed that he had no reception on the brand new radio. The installer had shoved the CB enough to break the connector from the coaxial cable. Reception was maybe good for a few hundred yards, and the VSWRs were through the roof. I ordered a 90-degree angle adapter to make more room behind the radio and installed it the following week. It seemed to do the trick, the VSWRs dropped below 2:1, and we didn't have time before the run to get a new crimp connector in case the connector was really bad. Several days later--and I don't know whether this was before the run or during it--the connection was bad again, and the CB was performing fairly badly.

A few months before the run, Ed asked me about controlling traffic lights. A few years prior, I had built a device that could do this on unencoded systems. It consisted of an infrared light source controlled by a microcontroller that pulsed it around 10 Hz. It worked on some lights and was a "nice to have," but I don't think that Ed ever used it. (By the way, Ed, if you ever take out all of the "good stuff" or sell the car, I want this thing back!)

Chapter 10 - The Criminal in the Mirror

Spring quickly became Summer and I was not ready. None of the other team members were available and I was insanely busy. The car still needed its laundry list of service items and I did not have the cash to pay for that. Megan and I were doing well in our marriage but she was annoyingly anxious to have a kid.

I agreed eventually I would hop on board the procreation train but I told her that I had to break the record first. Our office was full of enough devices that she knew that it was close enough for that condition to be acceptable. She was finally egging me on to complete it sooner rather than later. The clock was ticking in more ways than one.

That Summer I bit the bullet and bought the rest of the countermeasure items I needed. My optimism was waning but I wanted to make sure I at least had one attempt in by the end of the year. I knew the big construction projects in Oklahoma and New Mexico had finished and I was running out of excuses.

Every conversation I had with planned co-driver Chris, though, was less than encouraging. He was busy with work, his girlfriend at the time had some health issues, and he was making it sound like he was not going to come through. Each commitment came with some kind of way out.

Backup co-driver Adam's wife got pregnant. She had indulged the two of us in believing she was ok with him participating but when little man started baking she was out so he was relegated to the sidelines. It was quickly becoming clear I might not have a co-driver. It was also becoming clear that if someone had much time to think about the cornucopia of calamity that could come from attempting this run, it just might make it impossible for someone to remain engaged in the task.

In the same summer of 2013 I sold Dave Black a second Lamborghini. He was enjoying driving his Superleggera but he wanted a convertible. He had been driving the former press car very hard and it actually had transmission failure. I used that mechanical hardship as some leverage with the Lamborghini factory to help get him a great deal on a new car. Over the course of a few weeks I worked out the details for him to buy a new Lamborghini Gallardo LP570-4 Performante Edizione Tecnica at a handsome discount. I placed the 2011 Superleggera with a West Coast wholesaler who gave him $20k more than he had paid us for it nine months and 5,000 miles prior. This was one of the final special editions of the Gallardo and a truly unique car for him. Dave was excited; still unemployed, but excited.

He had a lot of free time on his hands. He would find minor imperfections in the car and bring it in for us to fix it. He lives about two miles from the dealership so I would see him scream by in the car every day on his way to QuikTrip to buy the largest cup of fountain soda that he could carry. He would drop the car off and then explain how flexible and accommodating he would be in yielding to our timing to repair it. Then he would stop in every day once or twice to check on progress. Dave proclaimed himself to be the most laid back customer ever. The irony stuck and he earned himself the nickname Laid Back Dave Black or LBDB for short.

During one of our conversations Dave mentioned that he had seen a movie recently called *32 Hours 7 Minutes*. This was the documentary by Cory Welles about the US Express and Alex Roy's record breaking attempts. He remembered reading the article in *Wired Magazine* about Alex and the preparation that he had done to the car back in 2007 when the news had broken about the record. He thought it was such a cool idea. He wanted to organize a screening and wanted to talk to me about the feasibility of organizing a race along the same route today. Of course I was familiar with the litigation between Alex and Cory and I was not looking to endorse Cory in that fight. I still wanted Alex's acknowledgement of my record when I set it.

I also explained that due to the way tortious litigation works there was truly no good way to organize a race on public roads. It had been tried, failed to launch, and was generally socially unacceptable. There could not be anyone on Earth more interested in starting or participating in a race of that kind than me but it simply could not be done. I told him that was why all of the recent attempts were single car, one-off efforts.

I quietly revealed to Dave I was in the process of breaking that record. That meant setting up a screening for a film that would be yesterday's news before too terribly long might not be the best use of his time.

It blew him away. He was very excited and

135

asked if there was any help he could offer. At the time I had a team together and was holding out optimistic hope that they might actually come through so I did not have a role for him to play. I told him the CL was already at CarTunes getting everything installed and Charles was getting ready to build the fuel system. He offered to lead me out of Manhattan if I wanted. I told him that would be great.

It was a difficult conversation to have because I could see how truly excited he was about the idea. By historic precedent and I am sure by his own admission, Dave was far from the ideal person to do this. In one of my conversations with Alex Roy he mentioned that he felt the ideal age to try this was 28-35. I was 28 when I did it. Alex was 35. Dave was 45. He had a 15 year old daughter. He still needed future employers not to brand him as an outlaw. He was well outside whatever narrow demographic of morons I exist within that allows me to stomach the risks of doing this.

Of course, I could never fault anyone for an interest in the idea but when I thought about the person sitting in the passenger seat next to me the mental image was different. There is an overconfidence bred by the planning of this type of thing. In order to believe I had what it would take to challenge this record, I needed to convince myself that there was some aspect of my skill set and abilities that makes me make better decisions than the competition. Without such a distinction, how would I feel capable of success?

That meant when someone offered well-intended advice or an alternative to the direction I was headed it was very difficult for me to accept it. My character flaws are plentiful. They make me who I am. Nestled among the defiance, hubris, and snake oil shilling charm is a part of me that equally weighs all obstacles between me and a goal. Arrest, my own risk of death, and financial ruin kept equal ground with the weather and traffic patterns.

This is as good a time as any to mention this - there was a moment just a few months before the attempt where I had an unsettling moment of clarity. It was probably while driving to work, brushing my teeth, or selling a $500,000 car - some mindless task. There was an instant where it hit me. I am a criminal.

Throughout my life I had seen many circumstances where I truly admired criminal enterprise. It could be the Guy Ritchie movies talking or the emotional psychopathy acting out but I had always seen a greater appeal there than it felt responsible to admit. It could have been the sleepless nights in college researching the intricacies of counterfeiting currency, getting a bit too caught up in thinking how interesting a modern life of piracy might be (eyepatch-aaaargh! piracy, not Napster piracy), or the adrenal need for occasional rationalized deviance but I always felt like I would be a good criminal. I do love pyramid schemes.

I had always seen Christianity as an opposing force to this and I had never identified myself as a candidate for a life of crime. Then it hit me. I was a criminal. I was, and had been for quite some time, planning an elaborate scheme to break the law. As a professional rationalization consultant I spend a lot of time telling people it is okay to scratch that itch and take the plunge into an extravagant purchase. I clearly do it to myself too.

One hangup that I always had with the idea of Christian salvation was my need for Jesus. I never felt that much like a sinner, at least I talked myself into thinking that my sins were ok relative to everyone else's. One day, though, it hit me. God sees all of our indiscretions with the same weight. The same way everything that could go wrong on this drive had the same amount of real estate in the "con" column, all failures were the same to him.

Saying you ate one Oreo when it was in fact all of them was the same as being an axe murderer of babies. We all clearly sin and from there, the insurmountable nature of reconciliation to God apart from a just sacrifice in Jesus made sense.

Of course, nine years of planning into an idea that was illegal, when a recognition like that hits you, it can cause some kind of a quandary. It didn't. Maybe it was the fact I was not doing it for any personal financial gain, to gain an unfair advantage over anyone, or to hurt anyone. I was not doing it for any particular reason. It had just become the latest notch on the obsession belt. That next glance into a mirror felt very strange.

From **Dave Black**
Co-Outlaw

June 19, 1981 was not just my 13th birthday, it was the release date of The Cannonball Run movie. My brother and his friends saw it before me. They came back talking about a car called a "Lamborghini." Up until this point, I had only known about Ferraris and Maseratis - especially the 308 GTS driven on Magnum PI. The next morning, I rode my bike to the theater and watched the matinee. The movie fades in with a black screen and an amazing exhaust note to reveal a black Lamborghini Countach driving across a stretch of desert highway. My jaw dropped - it was the most amazing thing I had ever seen. The other 308 GTS driven by Sammy Davis Jr. and Dean Martin was virtually invisible compared to the Lamborghini. After watching the movie, I wanted to see the car again. I snuck into the neighboring auditorium and waited for 15 minutes until the next one began, and snuck back in. I repeated this three times, and returned with a friend the next day to watch it two more times. When we eventually rented the movie on VHS, I probably watched it a dozen more times.

I was a crazed car enthusiast. I liked cars and loved driving. My first car was a canary yellow '79 Camaro (hand-me-down from my sister) that I totalled while racing a friend on an empty, rural Texas highway at 2 am. My second car was a charcoal grey '83 Firebird. I drove this to college for a couple years before trading in for a new, red VW 16-valve GLI Jetta that I totally abused. Within the life of this car, I had been pulled over by police over twenty times, and I developed a first-name relationship with my traffic ticket attorney. While I had always tried to achieve high average speeds during my commutes to college, spring breaks, etc.; I eventually got a job taking photos at gymnastics schools around the country. It was during this time that I checked off 30k miles of interstate and developed a "sense" for highway driving where I could avoid tickets while going fast.

When I turned 25, I traded in the GLI for a new, green '93 Jeep Grand Cherokee, followed ten years later with another one in 2003 that I kept until 2010 when I bought a diesel Jetta station wagon. I was enjoying being ticket and accident-free, and having economical cars that supported my mountain-biking hobby.

In 2005, my family moved to Beijing China where we lived for four years. I bought a Tian Qi Mei Ya TM6500 or Tian Qi Qi Bing which translates to "vehicle of the sky...great warrior" - a Chinese Mitsubishi 4 cyl. manual shitbucket of an SUV. Driving in China can be approached with two mindsets - 1: "OMG...look out...these people are crazy," or 2: "Hell ya!...this is how I've always wanted to drive."

I was #2 and had fun driving on curbs, service lanes, and oncoming traffic. The signature idiocy is at left turn lanes where people lock bumpers and never let oncoming cars through. If I were trying to pass through the intersection, I would go full speed at this cars as a game of chicken and would get them to open up a slot for the rest of the traffic to flow through. It didn't hurt that I had installed massive steel bull bars on the front of the car my family dubbed "the soldier."

I drove the diesel Jetta to San Francisco and maintained my highest record to Dallas from Atlanta - 83 mph including stops with a rolling average of 86, completely shocking my mother when I arrived 4 hours earlier than expected. While the car was a great car, the diesel Jetta began to push some wrong buttons - it was too small, too practical, and too...um...dorky - like a pair of orthotic shoes. Twenty plus years of suppressing my love of cars combined with a 100x increase in value of my company's stock options became the fuel and air that would soon ignite an intense emotional fire for something more "me."

Christmas 2010, I was walking through Phipps Plaza mall in Atlanta with my family when I came upon a Black Maserati GranTurismo on display. It stopped me cold in my tracks. My family went on to go shopping while I walked around the car mesmerized. It was funny...from my youth to young adulthood, I struggled with being materialistic and jealous of other people's things - the result of being the youngest of three siblings. But once I hit my 40s, I learned to live rather practically...just give me a good laptop, a good bicycle, and a humble roof over my head and I was content. This was different - it was the first time that a physical object possessed me. For the next nine months, I configured this car online over ten times, had screensavers of it, and kept looking online at it.

Then, one day, I saw that our local dealer had a used one in a color combo that I liked. I went to the dealership, test-drove it, and found myself in the midst of an existential crisis about the meaning of life. I couldn't resist - I went to the bank, got a cashier's check, came back and bought it. I thought I should win an award for the most awesome mid-life crisis ever.

As someone who has been a travelling consultant for an entire career, I didn't have any local Atlanta friends. My entire social network was in San Francisco, South East Asia, and Europe, and none of my friends were "car guys." I found myself looking for group car events and stumbled upon Caffeine and Octane. I awkwardly attended my first one, then a second one. During one of them, I remember seeing a Lambo, and couple of Aston Martins pull in. It was Ed, his wife Megan, and some others. They seemed like an intimidating bunch - young, attractive, and driving cars that cost twice as much as mine, but the C&O show was a comfortable place where I could chat with other car people and not feel like the only fool who parts with a good portion of his wealth on a car. The next C&O, I connected with a guy from Maseratilife (an online Maserati Forum) - Scott Shetler who brought his Verde Ithaca Gallardo. While talking with him, Ed approached and we were introduced. The intimidating aura was gone.

Ed invited me to go on a mountain drive and a few months later invited me to a supercar owners' dinner. These were a blast and over this time, I got to know Ed better. One of the first times I met with him at the dealership, he said "you know...a GT car like a Maserati is a 'gateway car.' You'll either go with more luxury like a Bentley, or more performance like a Lambo."

"I see what you're doing there...you're trying to plant a seed in my head," I said. "But I'm cool with this car...if I sell, it will be to the end of my foray into cars altogether." But over time, I appreciated that Ed had a deep understanding of the relationship between a person's psychology and the qualities of a car - it's brand / design language, sound, and other visceral qualities. Ed proved himself to be the only car dealer I've ever met who could sustain a conversation at this level.

A few months later, I was looking at used Maseratis online and saw that my car was catastrophically depreciating. A friend of mine suggested that I get a Lambo, and even had a line on one that would be a decent value. It was the first time I seriously thought about owning one - it would be another famous Italian marque...a checkbox. I didn't love the idea of such an impractical car, but as a means of staying in the car hobby a little longer, it made sense. I started getting into serious discussions with Ed about a buying a Lambo - looking for one that would cost about the same as my Maserati. That meant a Gallardo five years older with twice the miles. I still didn't think I would actually buy one...yes, it would be cool, but no, I shouldn't. Ultimately, I thought I had a "kill switch" to prevent me from actually buying one - my ridiculously steep driveway.

I told Ed this, who quickly replied, "Let's try it." So we did, and at the right angle, we were able to climb the driveway without scraping the front. To see a Lamborghini in my driveway sealed the deal - I was going to buy one. The next few days were exhausting, I couldn't sleep. I finally decided to go to the dealership and buy the car we had test driven - it was close to the price of the Maserati and would make sense financially.

When I arrived at the dealership, Ed did the "let me show you something else" trick (which I now appreciate). He took me to their back lot, showed me a different one - a black 2011 Superleggera that was still under warranty. It was a press car that had been slightly abused, but the price was such that I could own it without losing money - it just required a significantly higher payment.

Sure, why the hell not? Within the first few days of ownership, I was looking at some photos I had taken of this black beast. It hit me - the wing, the black, the big air intakes - it was the modern day equivalent of the black Countach in *Cannonball Run*. Realizing this ignited the thirteen year old in me. It's probably why I enjoyed showing it, and giving rides to teenage car enthusiasts - I was reliving my teenage years through their enthusiasm.

My company laid off my team the next month. Unemployed, I found myself attempting another startup. My daily ritual to clear my head, was to go to QuickTrip for a soda. The QuickTrip is across the street from the Lamborghini dealership. Frequently, I'd stop in to look at the new arrivals by driving around the parking lot, and frequently, I'd go inside and say hi to Ed and everyone. Without a job, they bore the brunt of my need to get a daily fix of human interaction.

Ed also organized a trip to Palm Beach, Florida for the Lamborghini Esperienza track training event. I drove my SUV while Ed and others followed along in Lambos and various supercars. I would have driven mine, but I was too tall and got frequent back pains while driving short distances. I averaged between 85 and 95 mph, and would drive ahead a few miles, spot for police, then call back to the group to proceed. Within a minute, they'd be blowing past me, slowing down, letting me pass to do it again. On one particularly empty stretch of the turnpike headed south I opened up a few miles of space and Ed started closing the gap quickly in his orange Murcielago LP640 Roadster. He blew past me so fast I was not sure his tires were still on the ground. I called on the two way radio to see how fast he had gotten and he said to me "194." I made him repeat that a few times.

The Lamborghini training event was a lot of fun and gave me a lot of confidence at higher speeds, even when the brakes were fading the tires were so soft that they felt like sponges.

April 27th, I received the DVD "*32 Hours 7 Minutes*" - a documentary about the transcontinental races and speed records. It ignited something in me - the desire to escape with an epic road trip...check, the desire to speed...check, the desire to thumb my nose at laws clearly designed for the lowest common denominator...check, and using technology and innovation to do it? CHECK! i.e., it resonated strongly with me. But seeing Alex Roy break the record, all his expense and preparation made me shy away from the idea of wanting to do the NY to LA Cannonball. This was clearly not something that could be casually approached. Instead, I started plotting out a longer route from Seattle to Key West - the corner-to-corner run - much longer than the Cannonball, and something that could be established as a new record.

During one of my visits to the dealership, I shared this rally idea with Ed. He mentioned that it's a terrible idea in this legal climate to promote a race. Untimed rallies are ok, but when a timer got involved, the organizer could find himself catastrophically broke or in jail. I was disappointed, but it also explained why Cannonball races don't happen anymore. Given the spirited drives I had joined Ed on in the prior months, I believed that if there were a way to organize a large scale Cannonball race today, he would have figured it out.

At this point, he motioned that we should walk into the other showroom away from the other employees. He put on his serious-face and lowered his voice. Having experienced this before, I knew this was going to be good. "Can you keep a secret?" He asked. Wow, it's going to be real good.

"Totally," I replied. "Working for Apple for twelve years requires it."

"Ok, you can't tell anyone what I'm about to tell you."

"Ok," I replied...this *is* serious. I was starting to think that he was going to tell me some juicy gossip about someone I knew, or offer a business proposition, or tell me he was going to start his own dealership - something big.

"I'm going to break the Cannonball Run record," he said solemnly. I nearly choked with laughter on the water I was drinking.

"Bullshit," I replied.

"Nope...I'm serious...I've got a car at CarTunes getting equipped with everything...I'm going to do this in the next couple months."

146

"Ok," I thought...I started to believe him and it started sinking in. Then, possessed with the ghost of the teenage version of myself, I rapidly replied "DO YOU HAVE A CO-DRIVER?!!!!!" It was a bullet-time moment where I imagined that the entire "hush-hush secrecy" was a prelude to him asking me to be his co-driver.

I was envisioning the next moment where he would say "that's what I'm talking to you about", but instead it was "Yeah, I have this guy in Ohio..."

I couldn't hear anything else after that point. I was so bummed...all these boner-inducing theatrics leading to a total letdown. Despite my disappointment, I replied "Hey, I totally want to be a part of this somehow...let me know if I can help." Ed explained that he might need some help getting out of New York. "I'd totally help you with that...just let me know and I'll fly up, rent a car and tear it up on the turnpike" - this probably came from watching *Smokey and the Bandit* dozens of times.

I went home and swore Lisa to secrecy before telling her the news. She had known me when we were teenagers so she understood the significance of this to me. Unlike my experience just a couple of hours prior, when she thought that the next element of the story might be me telling her that I was co-driving with Ed, she was relieved rather than devastated as I was.

Months passed. I saw the equipped car at the dealership one day and again, I was struggling with my jealousy over being part of the attempt. But I just kept quiet...waiting for the call to fly up to NY to help. The only problem was that I had been unemployed all these months, and the idea of flights, tickets, and increased insurance premiums were starting to look like real money. I wasn't so sure I would be in a position to help.

Chapter 11 - Assembling the Bomb

There are not many jobs where the pursuance of this record would not pose a serious problem and threaten the future of your employment. If I were an elementary school teacher like my wife, a politician, or a cop; this recreational activity would be frowned upon. Fortunately in the car business, it works. My boss and the owner of our dealership were unsure of whether or not they would still be able to have me on our insurance policy afterward but they did not bother to share that concern with me. They thought it was great idea and Brandon, our general manager, actually agreed to have the store contribute $5,000 to the project. It was an unbelievable help at a moment when I was not sure where the final cash infusions were going to come from.

I was pot committed at this point. I was beyond the point of counting receipts and maintaining a consciousness of what this effort was costing me. If I needed it and had the money it was on its way. In addition to the financial support, the dealership had given me permission to proposition our twenty-year tenured master Lambo tech into devising a fuel system for the car as a side job.

Charles gave me a shopping list for the Jegs catalog and I ordered two additional 22 gallon fuel cells with pumps and tubing. Charles devised a transfer pump strategy to take the fuel through the factory gas cap into the existing filler neck. The smaller cell in Alex's car was gravity fed because BMW puts their fuel tanks under the floor of the trunk on a 5 Series. Mercedes puts the tank upright, between the rear seats and the trunk. I liked this because it meant that the factory heat shielding was between me and the extra forty-four gallons of fuel.

Charles's strategy kept the check engine light on for an evaporative system leak but it was elegant in its simplicity. He spoke at length to Michael Luongo who was the Ferrari technician that Rawlings and Collins had used to install their fuel cell in the 550. It worked very similarly to ours but was smaller in capacity. In my experience techs love talking about working on cars more than actually working on cars. This was the type of project that you got some miles out of talking about.

From **Charles Carden**
20 Year Master Technician
Lamborghini Atlanta

There is only one Lamborghini technician still at a dealer in the US that has a longer tenure with the brand than I do. In the twenty years that I have been with Lamborghini Atlanta, the only person who has come along with as strong an affinity for the brand as I have is Ed Bolian.

Ed was hired as a sales guy a few years ago but we knew Ed well through servicing the cars for his rental company. We watched as his early Gallardo hit a deer at the beginning of rut one year, spun a connecting rod bearing and sent pistons through both sides of the block due to oil starvation, and required a few paint repairs ranging from a wheel scuff to colliding with a Ferrari.

When Ed came on, he really shook things up. Our new car sales exploded and our customers became a lot more active. That helps me because we started to see a lot more customers actually servicing their cars. When life gets in the way, neglecting the care of your supercar is quick to happen. Ed seemed like the kind of guy that could sell ice to an eskimo and then somehow get that eskimo to come back in six months and trade for some nicer ice. He was pushing cars out faster than we had since the heyday of the exotic car industry in 2007. Ed also built quite a brand for himself. People came from all over the country and internet to buy cars from him.

He was never shy about accumulating miles on the cars. He is the only sales guy I have ever seen care anything about owning the cars himself. Even after he was finished with the rental business, Ed would always wander back to my corner of the shop and ask for my advice on cars to buy, issues to look out for, and my thoughts on the significance of each model. We both grew concerned about the futures of some of the technologies that were being added to our favorite supercars. Those conversations would also occasionally drift something else entertaining - Cannonball.

I am old enough to be Ed's father so I remember the tales of outlaws racing across the country, no holds barred, sea to shining sea. I stay close to the racing community and live a couple of miles from Road Atlanta, a circuit used annually but many top racing organizations. My son, Casey, is the head instructor at Skip Barber Racing School. They are the tenant that replaced the Audi/Panoz Racing School Ed told me he had worked at years ago. My weekends are always spent re-building Vespas or race cars with my son. Watching him grown up from Karts to top level racing seats has been one of my proudest achievements. Early in 2013 Ed approached me to start making progress towards his own competitive driving goal.

Ed told me about his plans to break the Cannonball Run record around 2010. It was clearly something that he had been working on and thinking about for years. Having watched many racing efforts take years to develop, this was not new but the context was definitely peculiar. I had seen Richard Rawlings on *Fast & Loud* bragging about his forearm tattoo and talking about his 31:59 time but I asked Ed how many people were actually trying to do this. He told me about Alex Roy and some of the other history that existed in the gap since 1979. It was fascinating stuff, particularly when it came to outfitting the car.

In 2012 Ed showed me the blue-ish CL55 after he had bought it and he ran down the list of gadgets that he had ready to be installed. It was clear that he had put a lot of thought into this idea but there was something different about Ed. Normally the guy exudes confidence like 9 bar brewed espresso but I could sense the nervousness in his voice. The stakes were different than his normal half a million dollar car transactions. This mattered. He asked for my help in rigging up the auxiliary fuel system. We talked about the range that he was looking for and how the packaging needed to work.

Ed told me that he never cared if the car could be put back to stock but I could not help but think that even our super-human-salesman might be over his head with this one. it seemed like a shame to build something onto this Mercedes that could not eventually be taken out. That was also likely unnecessary because there was clearly not going to be any easy to way to gravity feed the cell into the main tank due to the elevation of the factory tank within the car. If there was ever anything Ed lacked, it was certainly not confidence but the parent in me never stops trying to be the responsible advisor.

One Saturday I took the Mercedes up to our shop, opened a case of beer and just stared at the open trunk, lining removed. I remembered reading about the guys who had engineered a system of 55 gallon drums within the hull of an airplane and used surgical tubing to feed the fuel into the wing tanks as they flew all the way around the globe. I called Mike Luongo who I knew from Lambo training in years past. He had moved over to Ferrari and then started an independent shop. My thought had been some low pressure transfer pumps coming out of each cell and T-ing into a line running through the gas cap. He confirmed that their approach was similar. I gave Ed a shopping list and a JEGS catalog.

I fashioned a bracket to bridge across the spare tire well under the factory trunk floor that would support the weight of the tank. I mounted the cells, plumbed in the lines, got power to the pumps, rigged up some gauges for the tanks and mounted them on the dash, and created a 180 degree turn that would keep the factory gas cap cover in place. It was removeable during the refueling process so that Ed could use two pumps at the same time to fill the three tanks. Ed bought a spare factory gas cap and I cut into the old one.

The guys from CarTunes, our local stereo and aftermarket electronics gurus, had wired a switch for the transfer pumps into a custom panel where the car's ashtray used to be. It had controls for some of the radar and laser systems, a kill switch to the relays sequenced into all of the wiring for the rear lights, and a traffic light changer that one of Ed's Georgia Tech friends had rigged up for them. The gauges were not very accurate but bench testing revealed that it was moving about a gallon every ninety seconds. When Ed and I tested the transfer, the latency of both the auxiliary gauges and the stock gauge was significant so I told him to transfer four times for fifteen minutes to drain the tanks. Each transfer session should have moved about ten gallons of the forty-four that he would have. It was a simple enough system.

At least that is what I thought until I got a call from Ed on his way to New York telling me that they had just sprayed gas all over a silver Impala that was following them on the highway...

Chapter 12 - The Nine Thousand Dollar Tune Up

It took CarTunes about three weeks to install everything in the CL. The build had more devices drawing more power from more locations than they had ever put in a car. It came with a discounted labor rate and a solemn disclaimer that if this skunkworks project went sideways it was still my inoperable dune buggy and they were indemnified. I was not exactly reassured by that caveat but I knew Monty was their best installer and he was on the job.

The victorious car becomes the trophy so I spent a lot of time thinking about what I wanted it to look like on the other end of this whole experience, maintaining at least some semblance of optimism. On one hand you want to have a clean install without wires running everywhere and all of the devices tucked into a nice, neat place. On the other you want something that can portray the grit of the road and the bootstrapping spirit of a decade long passion project. The car was the vessel to complete the task but also served to tell the story. I hoped it would be a time capsule of a true high point in my life.

If everything went well, fifty years from then when my grandkids were reading this, the garage where I kept the car would be the next stop. It needed to be something to behold. The dated navigation equipment, the antennas, the fuel tanks, it was all going to give them a glimpse into what those couple of days in October felt like.

Sales at the dealership were not letting up. I sold 50% more cars in 2013 than I had in 2012. It kept me so busy I questioned whether or not I would have time to do this. Taylor Clark, the Supercar Rentals accountant and voice of road trip reason, got a new job and was unable to take time off to serve as the support passenger and reality check in the car. Gumball Chris was out with work and girlfriend problems, Adam's growing baby still kept him out. Forrest had been called up to the A team upon mini-Adam's conception but he was working insane hours at a research lab and he was not sure if he would be able to take the time off. Without him, the Bacon Blocker was a no-go. Any functionality he could achieve would not be usable by anyone else who was unfamiliar with the inner-workings. I kept pushing forward but the outcome was even more of an unknown.

Money was still tight despite my successes in selling cars. I needed a few more devices and countermeasures. I was looking for something to sell. I found just the thing - my $50,000 Lamborghini engine block coffee table.

In January of 2007 I was eating dinner with a fellow student from Tech. I remember the seat I was sitting in at one of my favorite Mongolian restaurants. We were discussing whether or not these new smartphones were going to catch on. I got a call from a friend in south Florida saying, "I saw your Gallardo on a flatbed heading down I-95. It looked like it was in pretty rough shape." As the Atlanta rental market had quieted for the winter, I rented the car to a guy in Palm Beach that was promoting an exotic car show. I tried to call the rental customer. He did not answer.

My heart sank. The next morning I began

calling around to the exotic car shops in South Florida that were likely destinations for a broken Lamborghini. I found the car at Lamborghini Miami. The diagnosis was "catastrophic engine damage." The car had thrown one and a half connecting rods, most of a piston, and a rod bearing out both sides of the engine block. Their preliminary parts estimate was $56,000.

This was an unfathomable blow to a young student entrepreneur. The business had been doing well but this was going to be a huge hole to climb my way out of. The customer was someone whom I had known for years and who knew better than to mistreat a car like that. He had been paying me by the mile for his use of the car but in this most recent billing window had driven the car nearly 3,000 miles including some very abusive low speed maneuvers. This had run the car low on oil and the sustained high RPMs had popped the motor.

I ended up finding an engine in Europe that had been taken out of another early Gallardo which had been involved in a front end collision. It was $15,000 and I had it shipped to the dealer in Miami for install. A new clutch, seals, and labor was another $15k or so. A month or so later I got the car home and began the lawsuit against the customer. It never yielded anything beyond continued headache, heartache, and the legal bills.

I ended up with a very cool looking blown Gallardo engine. I bought a heavy duty dolly from the local hardware shop and a big piece of plate glass to put on top of it. It became the centerpiece in the customer waiting area where I stored the cars. It also served as a good warning to customers not to abuse the cars.

I had actually sold the engine a couple of years before that point to a company engineering turbo systems for Gallardos. They had stripped it down, used the heads for a project and they were left with a very clean aluminum engine block. That was only of scrap value for them so I asked if they would ship it back to me. They did. It was a great momento to the rental company that was now a few years in the rearview mirror but the Cannonball goal was close and I needed the cash. I sold the decorative engine block for $3,000 and placed the order for the few remaining supplies.

The list of items installed in the car ended up being:

- Valentine 1 Radar/Laser Detector x 2
- Passport/Escort Radar/Laser Detector & Diffuser
- Laser Interceptor Laser Diffuser/Jammer
- 2 x Garmin GPS Units with XM Traffic
- 3 x iPhone Cradles with Chargers
- iPad Cradle and Charger
- GeoForce Satellite Tracking Device
- Uniden Police Scanner with GPS & Radio Antenna
- Cobra 29 CB Radio with K40 Antenna
- Toll passes for the pertinent areas
- 2 x 22 Gallon Auxiliary Fuel Cells with Transfer Pumps
- Custom Switch Panel with kill switch for rear lights, fuel pump control, manage power to all devices, Passport & Laser Interceptor Controls
- Power Inverter with Outlets in Center Console
- MiRT - traffic light changer

- Full Size Spare
- Fire Extinguisher
- Full Size Hydraulic Jack
- 2 pairs of binoculars - 8x and 10x
- 3 digital timers
- Cooler

The fuel system was finished. Servicing the car was the final step remaining to be ready to press the GO button. The trip was going to impose more stress on the car than I could anticipate. I also knew that Alex Roy's most promising attempt got derailed by a clogged fuel filter and pump assembly in Oklahoma. His M5 was six years old at the time of his run. My CL55 was nine years old with nearly twice the miles. I wanted to make sure the car got an exhaustive tech inspection and a redundantly clean bill of health before departure.

One of the reasons for choosing the Mercedes was the abundance of independent service options. I assumed I would find a shop that thought the idea was interesting and they would bend over backwards to get the business. I was wrong. Many were scared. I was vague about the purpose of the car. It was pretty much just a request to replace every fluid, filter, consumable item, and to address the suspension issues. The best service offer and quote actually came from one of our local authorized dealers - RBM North in Alpharetta, GA.

We had just hired one of their best sales guys to come and work with us at Motorcars of Georgia. It is not uncommon for new hires at the dealership to do something extravagant to celebrate their new job. The broken record cliche is buying a motorcycle. The first week that Nick was at our store he took delivery of a new Victory Motorcycle. In Georgia, you have to take a class to get a motorcycle license. You must provide your own motorcycle to take the test to get your license. You have to have a motorcycle license to buy motorcycle insurance. You do not have to show proof of insurance to buy and take delivery of a bike. You may be noticing a sequencing issue here. He was planning on taking the responsible steps to ownership such as buying a helmet, taking the class, and getting insurance within the coming months.

One of our other employees was going to move the newly delivered bike into our shop for safe keeping. Nick, the new guy, asked to sit on his bike for a moment. He then grew bold and decided he would try to see if he could make it move. He did and managed to hold on for about thirty feet straight into the back of a Porsche Panamera. He shattered the rear hatch glass with his un-helmeted face.

I was on the phone trying to buy a Bugatti for a customer when I heard the crash. I went outside to find blood pouring out of Nick's face. It was a scene that would make an axe murderer queasy. The rest of our team at Motorcars of Georgia seemed fairly perplexed by the whole thing so I took charge of getting our new man some proper medical attention. They were scrambling to pick the bike up, ascertain the extent of the damage to both Porsche and Nick, and generally freaking out. I walked out, grabbed Nick by his shoulders, smiled, and said "We are in for a long night!"

I loaded Nick into Megan's Cayenne, which

was at the dealership for some reason. Fortunately, it had some large moving quilts inside that I used to cover the leather seats from the unspeakable amount of blood all over him. I took him to the emergency room and watched the A, B, and C teams participate in stitching his face up. It was at least eighty facial stitches. At one point, the doctor pulled back a loose flap of skin and an ant walked out of Nick's face. I told him that whatever stories we got from today, they would never hold a candle to what that ant got to tell the next grasshopper he ran into. "I was minding my own business, hanging out on this bulbous Porsche station wagon thing when all of a sudden..."

He had not been working at the dealership long enough to have health insurance so before we left the ER I did some negotiating with the financial counselor. We got his $8k bill down to $800 or so. I took him to a pharmacy to get his prescriptions filled and got him home. The experience made me look like a great friend and earned me some favors. I cashed a few in on help negotiating this service with his former employer. Strange way to earn a discounted labor rate but I do enjoy the story.

I dropped the car off at RBM North Mercedes-Benz in Alpharetta. My instructions were fairly simple. The service advisor Nick had referred me to was aware of what I was doing but the techs were not initially. Fix or replace everything that needs it or might need it and then look the car over so I can drive it without worrying. The latter was the issue. The 115k mile CL55 was not without needs in the service department.

They replaced the tires, brakes, fluids, and

filters like I asked but it also required spark plugs and wires, two shocks, some other suspension components, motor mounts, a new battery, something called a flex disk, we agreed to do all bulbs, etc. for a retail total of over $17k and a discounted price to me of $8,800. The technicians and the shop foreman were very intrigued by the project but they looked at me like I was crazy when I proposed it. The car was barely worth the price of the service bill and it was obviously not the type of request they expected to encounter in their careers of servicing daily use cars for businessmen and their overly entitled wives.

Even though I had been hoping for something closer to half that, it was a good deal. That being said, I was still short from being able to pay for it. A few months prior I had come across a young guy whose father owned a coffee growing operation in South America. He was using his entrepreneurial chops to expand the business into a bottled, ready to serve, iced coffee beverage. The company is called Blue Donkey Iced Coffee. He felt like the car guy market was great for his product and he asked me if I might be interested in some marketing assistance for one of my events. He came along on a mountain drive and we talked about a few other ideas.

When I mentioned that I was trying to break this record he thought it was terrific. Driving for a long time with caffeine needs equalled his product in his mind. It came pre-mixed with milk but I wasn't going to argue. He came through with the last $2,500 that I needed to finish paying off my AMEX bill after the Mercedes service.

There were a lot of other modifications I had

163

explored doing to the car prior to the drive. The goal was obviously to make the car faster but also to improve the fuel economy. A popular package of modifications for that type of supercharged AMG engine was a combination of a smaller pulley for the supercharger, headers, exhaust, higher flowing air filters, and an ECU tune.

The first few of those would have been helpful to me but the ECU tunes that were available were not designed for this type of drive. They were mapped out to change the air fuel ratios to make the car accelerate faster from zero to sixty and improve the quarter mile time. I spoke with the three major Mercedes Benz modification houses - RennTech, Kleeman, and Carlsson. I filled them in on my objectives and all agreed that it was theoretically possible but they were not sure when they would be able to deliver it. When I had felt I needed to get closer to 15 mpg this was necessary. Based on the amount of fuel I was planning to carry at that point, this seemed unnecessary. It was added to the pile of ideas to be used if we ended up making our first run in 32-35 hours and needed ways to improve upon the time significantly.

I also decided to keep the car as stock as possible for the purpose of reliability. While it is popular to modify and personalize a car to suit the needs or wants of each user, the mechanical aspects of the car were best left to the original engineers at Mercedes in my opinion. It was easy to make a car go faster for a short time but building an engine that was still capable of doing this drive seemed best left up to Marco Weissgerber when he signed the hand assembled AMG engine in the first place.

Throughout that summer the sheer enormity of the project had started to set in. It was finally happening and this was truly the most dangerous thing that I had ever done. That was a new and very strange realization. I could tell that my brain was telling my inescapable desire to do this that it was really a pretty bad idea. It felt sort of like smoking with a label that says it will kill you, or buying a pet tiger, or dating a woman who cheated on someone else with you. You know the odds say the situation will not end well but you see how cool, fun, and sexy it can be as rational calculation just flies out the window at 150 mph.

I bought a $2 million life insurance policy. It seemed like a good idea given the developments in planning and the imminence of the first attempt. It also may be the only thing I ever did that made my father-in-law proud. We did not have any unhealthy amount of debt at the time but it still felt like a good bet.

From **David "Klink" Kalinkiewicz**
Former Master Technician at
Mercedes Benz of Alpharetta

I really did not know what to make of this guy.

I first met Ed Bolian in late 2012. I was then serving as a general "go to guy" in the service department at a Mercedes Benz dealer in metro Atlanta. I was told that he had recently purchased a 2004 Mercedes-Benz CL55 AMG and that he had a question or two about it.

I was predisposed to dislike him. I was told that he was "some kind of sales guy at the Lamborghini dealer." Yes, I realize that my mental imagery was out of date, possibly by decades, but perhaps you'll forgive me if I admit that I was expecting to see verdant waves of chest hair circled by loops of gold chain, and a huge ring on one hand counterbalanced on the other by an oversized watch so encrusted in diamonds that the hands could not be viewed without polarized sunglasses. I was kind of hoping that his inevitably white shoes would be marred by our usually, and in that moment unfortunately, immaculate shop floor.

The Ed Bolian that I was introduced to was not that guy. The guy I met had probably never even seen a prostitute, much less aspirated the cocaine off the thigh of a very expensive one with a Giorgio Moroder soundtrack pounding in the background. Maybe this was only the gofer that the "Lambo person" sent to drop off an MB trade-in, that for some reason they weren't simply auctioning off? This fellow was

166

remarkably unremarkable; Mr. Rogers, not Mr. T. He could have been a Sunday school teacher.

He certainly did not seem like the kind of guy that could be making a living by fogging dodgy six-figure lease arrangements and balloon notes past gullible finance company agents before an inevitable appearance in the collateral confrontation scene on an episode of "Airplane Repo."

The man I met was calm, polite, thoughtful and articulate, with knowledge of automobiles that went to a much greater depth than my unfair biases had predicted, or that his obvious youth made likely. I was starting to like this guy, but then again, my pre-meeting prejudices had set such a low bar.

At least he had good taste in cars. The one he had chosen to spend his own money on was everything that high-line cars attempt to be but often aren't: responsive, fast, stable, comfortable, durable, even reliable if maintained, and with a restrained industrial design aesthetic that emphasized form over contrivance. Like many of the big Mercedes-Benz coupes from the '60s to the present, this car has a look that is now lost on a generation raised on Ritalin, particularly so in its rainy day blue/gray hue - Granite Gray.

Ed told me that he had experience with Mercedes-Benz cars, and the rest of our conversation bore this out. He expressed his desire to keep this car for some period of time.

I had no idea what mission this car was being prepared for. I also never would have guessed that this much younger gentleman would become a personal hero of mine in just a few months.

In March 2013, Ed brought his MB to our shop for a few repairs and a routine maintenance service. I was happy to see that his "new old car" appeared to be working out for him and that possibly through, or maybe only in spite of our conversations, we had earned a chance at some business his employer was more than capable of providing. We performed an "A" service and generally looked the car over.

Well, we must have done well enough on that visit, because in early October 2013, Ed again brought his CL55 to us, this time for a strangely comprehensive preventive maintenance…

Ed's instructions were to change every fluid, filter, and consumable maintenance item. He asked us to carefully inspect the suspension in particular, and to address anything else that we saw. This was a change of pace in this new age of all show/no dough customers. It is not uncommon to get carte blanche to make a newer S65 perfect again after some unfortunate accident, or to bring great-grandad's 1964 230SL back to road worthiness, but this was a somewhat alien request for a high mile CL55, a car that by this point was usually in the loose and uncaring grip of its insolvent third owner.

And this CL had definitely accumulated some life experience. The bones were alright but it had clearly received a bit of paint work. The mechanicals of the car were pretty sound, but as happens with complicated cars, the "what you really should do if you're serious about keeping and DRIVING this thing" list was growing.

We knew that Ed had negotiated some discounted pricing, but even considering that, this was going to get spendy. When we went over the list, Ed said, "I want to be able to drive this across the country without ANY trouble. Do whatever it takes to make that a certainty."

We all wondered what possible future this newly revived car would have. At this visit, the car was already full of radio gear, tablet computers, GPS screens, jacks, tools, spare wheels, and had 2 huge fuel cells in the trunk. Why the hell someone would muck up a perfectly serviceable CL like this, I had no idea.

Someone muttered, "Maybe we should call Homeland Security" and they were serious. Those of us that knew better could tell that this wasn't the way one would package fuel if he was actually planning on blowing it up. Then someone said, "I heard he's doing some kind of gumball thing…"

Now it finally made some sense to me. This guy was cobbling up some kind of servicing vehicle to chase after and care for his customers, some of whom were obviously about to commit some sort of exhibitionistic misallocation of wealth, youth, and hedonism while they still had some of each to spare.

The following is a compilation of the so called "nine-thousand-dollar tune-up" that at least one media account had mentioned. It should have been the "ten to eleven thousand dollar tune up" but of course the "Lamborghini guy" negotiated a substantial discount. I remember thinking that this was a lot of money to invest in a somewhat impractical douche-hoon ambulance on call for people "doing some kind of gumball thing." If nothing else, he was going a long extra mile trying to take care of and entertain his customers, and it was certainly interesting looking.

Ok, now there was work to do. The work was performed by one of our most respected technicians, the relentless perfectionist, Ralph Mandoeng. Don't look for Ralph there anymore. He has since defected to Tesla.

On this job, Ralph was managed and assisted by his shop foreman, Mr. Bill Peek. Bill is a legend well known to most of us that work on these things for a living and even to many who don't. There is no way to overstate the esteem and respect that this man has engendered in so many of us, and I wanted to take this opportunity to thank him for his outsized positive influence on me and so many others. The success of Ed, Dave, and Dan's excellent adventure owes so very much to Ralph and Bill's dedication and fastidiousness.

The pre "gumball thing" work performed at RBM of Alpharetta included:

- Automatic transmission fluid/filter change. No abnormal wear particles or debris were found in the transmission fluid pan or filter
- Brake fluid change
- Brake pads and rotors
- The inner elastic bushings of the front axle rear lower control arms ("spring links" in MB jargon) were worn and cracking through. They were replaced.
- 4-wheel alignment
- Install 4 Michelin Pilot Super Sport tires - Tires are arguably the most important part of any car. This

tire was then, and still is, an overall performance benchmark.

- The left front wheel had a slight bend that was repaired before the new tires were installed.
- A fuel filter replacement was done. It is also a specified maintenance item at every 60,000 miles or 5 years. At 114,106 miles, it was near the end of its service life.
- Coolant flush and pressure test
- Engine air filters
- Cabin air filters
- Replace all light bulbs
- Replace wiper blades
- Replace key batteries
- Oil change - Mobil 1 Formula M 5W-40. This is a version of Mobil 1 that is sold to M-B dealers in the USA. It is labeled to meet only one engine oil specification, that being MB 229.5, which was at the time, and currently still is the highest specification for MB and AMG specified gasoline engine oils. It is essentially the same as the readily available Mobil 1 0W-40 "European Formula" except with 5W base viscosity. While any oil meeting 229.5 is fully up to any possible road use conditions, including the German autobahns, if I had known that these guys were planning an actual full-on Cannonball, I may have suggested the similar MB and Porsche dealer sold Mobil 1 5W-50, or the readily available at parts stores 15W-50 for possible lower oil consumption at speed. Most engines develop an appetite for oil at extended high speeds and loads, and these are no exception. Needing to make oil stops between the

fuel stops could knock an average speed down considerably.

- The inoperative windshield washer fluid pump was replaced.
- Replaced the ABC (Active Body Control) high pressure hose/metal line assembly that carries the pressure from the hydraulic pump to the main pressure regulating valve of the system. A gas pressurized diaphragm type pulsation/noise damper was also replaced. This damper protects the system from those same pump pressure pulses.
- Both right side ABC suspension spring struts were replaced due to slight leakage. This was one of the only areas of the preparation where Ed showed any financial restraint. We suggested replacement of all four struts because replacing one of an axle pair on a car that has already developed a strut fault is a little like replacing one shoe. While there can always be more wear and tear on one side relative to the other, it is reasonable to assume that one could expire not long after the other. This small gamble proved to be well played. Other than the high pressure pump developing a nasty noise near the completion of the trip, no ABC related failures occurred.
- ABC hydraulic fluid system was flushed out and filled with new oil.
- The hydraulic ABC oil filter was also replaced.
- The seeping valve cover gaskets were replaced.
- The crankcase vapor separator chambers on the tops of the valve covers were resealed.
- The spark plugs and wires replaced.

- There is a wound/woven fiber reinforced flexible rubber joint disc at each end of the driveshaft. The rear disc was showing some wear and crack formation, so we replaced it. The front disc on these cars usually shows deterioration sooner than the rear disc, yet it was in perfect condition, so it was safe to assume that it was recently replaced.
- The expired original motor mounts were replaced.
- The original battery from the 46th week of 2003 was still fitted. We replaced it.
- The most favorable of the removed tires and Ed supplied an additional wheel that we used to create an non-speed-limited spare.
- And everyone can breathe easier, because, yes, the Georgia state emission inspection required for renewal of the license and registration was passed.

The completed vehicle left our shop, and neither I nor anyone else had another thought about it.

Not that you should care, but here's why I love this. Maybe some of it resonates for you, too. I hope so.

I grew up in a small town where all acceptable recreational activities ended in "-ball." For reasons that I still don't fully understand, and certainly didn't choose, I didn't fit in. I was the geeky kid that took my dad's power tools and my mom's appliances apart. Later I could put them back together, too.

I was fortunate enough to be raised in a time

when my rampant ADD wasn't simply medicated away and I became attracted to order as an antidote to the chaos in my head. Not social order, but mechanical order. As a young child I had two obsessions. I loved fans. The big window fans that were ubiquitous before even the poorest among us became wealthy enough to have air conditioning were the best. My grandparents had the best one, their belt driven type being more interesting and making better sounds than the direct drive one we had at home, which was still, quite literally to me, awesome. The love of fans beget the second obsession.

I was around three or four years old when this happened, and I remember this like it was an hour ago. My dad picked me up and held me over the open engine compartment of his 1959 Impala coupe to show me that the car's engine also had a fan. A nice big noisy fan! And with belts! Cars, places, motion, fans, fun!

From that day, I was obsessed with cars. To paraphrase another Cannonballer, "cars became the monocle through which I viewed the world." My mother would bribe me to go to school by offering to buy another quart of oil to add to my collection after I got back home. I was lucky enough to ride in the trifecta of the 260, 289, and 427 Shelby/AC Cobras. God bless America, and save the queen while you're at it. The guy with the 260 powered car actually gave the best rides. He thought nothing of driving it sideways in the rain while somehow never spilling the open bottle of Iron City that he kept wedged between his legs. If my mom had known, she would have beaten the both of us comprehensively senseless.

The car became my vision of a better future, and by extension, even my present got a little better. From the time I could read, I devoured everything automotive related that I could. This was the sixties, and the "muscle car" era was in full flower. I was also fortunate enough to have a service station at the corner entrance to our neighborhood, and this station was the "hangout" for many of the local hot-rodders, street racers, bikers and motorcyclists (yes, there's usually a difference). I got to sit in, ride in, and "help" wash, wax and fix just about every American muscle car, '62, through '69, and even a few of those odd ball fancy "furrin" cars.

And some of those were where it coalesced for me, this combination of order and precision along with visions of freedom and fun, the adult and the juvenile seemingly integrated without conflict. I became fascinated with the deliberateness of German cars, and the most deliberate of all German cars were those from Mercedes-Benz. I admired their fearless embrace of complexity, especially since it was usually tempered with just enough practicality to actually work most of the time. I loved how nearly everything had a purpose and could be explained. I liked that modern materials and manufacturing methods were not eschewed in the superficial service of tradition, yet this company had a pedigree without peer.

Still later I got to appreciate that unlike with some other engineering heavy makes, little of that heavy engineering was needed to mollify those characteristics that were the inevitable result of overall bad design. To have this precision, order,

175

practicality and excellence marshalled to serve the ideal of unlimited operation at top speed? Well, at least for me, it just didn't get any better.

What could have seemed better was the spirit of the times. The malaise that gave the era its name was really starting to take hold. Though short in reality, the years that I had left to stay in school felt like a death sentence. The political and intellectual war against private transportation had recently started anew, but in that dismal zeitgeist, it was fashionably fresh and unquestioned. The future of private motoring was going to be bleak, and an armada of technocrats and authoritarians was hell-bent on creating that reality. The same people that couldn't make a single show about animals without attempting to convince everyone watching that they were somehow personally responsible for killing them all were now going after the device of my obsession. This was personal now, dammit!

Too young to protest myself, I absolutely rejoiced and reveled in the exploits of Brock Yates and his Cannonball Baker Sea to Shining Sea Memorial Trophy Dash. A lot of name for such a simple idea: drive across this country as fast as you can "without so much as messing up anyone's hair."

Much is made about the flouting of the law in this questionable exercise, but the people that think that's what it's all about are the same people that think racing fans enjoy watching accidents. How fast is too fast? Any answer is hopelessly arbitrary.

Why do we drive so slowly here in the land of the free where everyone is supposedly so pressed for time that vacations are minimal? My personal opinion

176

is that speed limits (and driving standards) are kept so ridiculously low so that the hapless American motorist can remain an endless source of revenue to be used for anything other than supporting your right to go wherever the hell you want, whenever you want, and often to projects aimed precisely against those rights.

We toil in a world that wants to make sure that everyone and everything lives forever as it also deliberately works to deprive us of any joy that could possibly make that life worth living. We are sanitized, pasteurized, processed, surveyed, droned, and surveilled. We have "trigger words" now, the entire concept implying that a person having heard one has no power over his response to it. Everyone needs a "safe space." Young people are told that they can't possibly have any control over what becomes of their individual lives while simultaneously being taught that they are somehow in control of the weather. And the poor things seem to readily accept both.

Nurse Ratched is here with your pills! Yum yum! Down the hatch. You little darlings all be good, now. No wonder they are so miserable. We have actually allowed our breath to be classified as a "regulatable pollutant." The bumper stickers that used to say "Question authority!" now sheepishly plead for hope and some spare change. People act as if second-hand smoke from a car window four lengths ahead of them is poisoning them to the marrow while thinking nothing of subjecting themselves to an evening of debauchery that would have made Caligula wretch.

The leader of our ostensibly-still-free world somehow thought that it was ok to be seen riding a bicycle in one of those ridiculous foam rubber safety hats! What the hell was he thinking would happen after the world saw that?

I can't believe how much this decade is feeling like the 1970s. Our betters tell us that lackluster is the "new normal" but as I write this we see daily changes in this attitude. It seems that radical chic is chic again. The children of the sixties have even managed to bring back the street riots that they always seemed to feel so sentimental about. I'm feeling sentimental, too. There's a new Cannonball record!

I don't remember the exact date or time I heard about the Cannonball record being shattered by Ed, Dave, and Dan; but it wasn't long afterwards. I can only report accurately my reaction to it. Please excuse my (by now you can tell...) irrational exuberance, but I was just reveling in a tsunami of positive emotion.

I felt younger. I felt vindicated. A cosmic wrong seemed to have been righted. Some larger part of our, or at least my universe was vibrating at a sweeter frequency. This was no mere rich idiot "gumball thing." These guys did a full-on Cannonball! And Hosanna in the Highest, they did the holiest of holies, the Red Ball to Portofino run! I swear I could hear the pealing of bells. The backside of this recently reincarnated cultural revolution of joyless nanny-ism had just been given a rough, unlubricated finger.

The Cannonball record, that most revered celebration of personal transportation freedom, the ultimate American road trip had been broken and set probably insurmountably high by people I really like. And best of all for me, they did it in a Mercedes-Benz! For a marque fanatic like me, that's the home team winning the championship. You always knew they were the best, and now, finally, affirmation.

For at least that moment, everything was right in my world. To have been involved, even in such an innocent and tangential way has been an endless source of delight and inspiration. Thanks for listening, to my carrying-on, and thanks to Ed, Dave, and Dan. If it couldn't have been me, I'm so glad it was them.

Chapter 13 - The Co-Driver Draft

The problem remained that I did not have anyone to go with me. Chris was still out but he was willing to help scout for us through Ohio. Adam was ready at the controls on the home front as an eye-in-the-sky and third party witness but imminent paternity still kept him out of the car. Forrest got called away to blow things up in Arizona for the government. Taylor remained neck deep in work with the new job. It was September and it was definitely now or next year. It may have been now or never.

It was time to move on to plan G or whatever letter I was on at that point. I had met a guy named Doug Demuro a few years prior. He went to Emory University, very close to Georgia Tech, and was a serious car enthusiast. He shared a bond with me and with most of my customers where we spend an absolutely absurd portion of our income on four wheeled pursuits. He had owned multiple interesting sports cars and was never bashful about using them in interesting ways.

At the time Doug had a fantastically rare Mercedes Benz E63 AMG Wagon. He came along with us on a couple of our spirited North Georgia Mountain drives. On one recent drive he had said without solicitation, "I almost didn't come today. I was trying to get someone to come up to New York with me, buy a BMW 335i at Carmax, drive it to LA, break Alex Roy's record, and then return the BMW at a Carmax out there under their five day test drive policy."

Blank stare.

"Funny you should mention that. We need to have a conversation this week." Doug had worked for Porsche previously but was now carving a successful path as a pseudo-freelance automotive journalist. His wit, experiences, and intellect were carving out a great space with several online publishers.

Ed, meet Ed taking a slightly different path in life.

I called him later in the week and filled him in on where I was with the project. He was impressed. In his mind the overkill prepping strategy had been unnecessary but the more we talked, the more, "Yeah I guess you do need that," responses he gave. I told him that I thought my co-driver was going to flake out and I would like him to go with me. His initial response was very positive. He said that he needed to clear it with the main journalistic outlets he worked for because he was concerned they might not be able to list him on their policies if he became known for having done this. Such a misfortune would keep him from being able to do his job testing the cars and writing pun filled anecdotes about them. I probably should have heard that and checked to see if I would have the same issue but I didn't. If I am truly honest with myself, losing my job was on the table of acceptable sacrifices to make this work.

We also talked about how it read from his perspective. It is rare that people who pursue this as a dream are listed in the same breath as their co-driver. Dan Gurney came in at the last minute to co-drive with Yates. In all other attempts Yates struggled to find people he considered acceptable co-drivers or passengers that were willing to take part. Diem &

Turner were the most compatible team that I recall reading about. Alex Roy and Richard Rawlings are the most outspoken of their teams and more responsible for the planning than their counterparts so they have basked in most of whatever glory can be gained from this type of endeavor. In Roy's case, that is in spite of the fact that his co-driver, Dave Maher, maintained cruising averages that were 10-20 mph faster than his own. Dennis Collins was the money behind their drive but received far less attention.

I did not use that understanding to pursue a particular co-driver but it was some consolation as those who had more of a hand in planning (and deserving of the associated praise) proved unavailable. There is an inescapable level of narcissism that comes with trying to break any world record and it appears this one in particular caters more to an individual rather than a team. My interest in the pursuit was not primarily attention seeking but I don't wish to pretend it wasn't a factor.

For Doug, and the same would have been true for me if the roles had been reversed, this was something that he wanted to do himself. It had not occupied his consciousness for the greater part of a decade prior but it was a chapter of Automotive Americana that he loved and wanted to associate himself with one day. While I cannot imagine being able to say "no" to this trip on any level, this would have been the only grounds where I could consider it. I give Doug a lot of credit for being able to say no to an arrive and drive program. Not sure I could have done that.

Doug still wants to try it. I don't think he would

mind not breaking the record but he finds the history similarly compelling to the way I look at it. He believes that there are still secrets out there that will unlock minutes and maybe hours from the existing times. He wants to do it on his terms, using his strategy, and for his own reasons. It would be hard for me personally to find a greater reason to respect someone.

I started going through my contacts trying to find anyone I felt was a competent enough driver to co-pilot and someone else whose presence was tolerable enough to ride in the back seat, much less be useful. This was presenting an unexpected barrier to my plans I had not anticipated. If you ask anyone close to me, they all knew at some point an attempt was going to happen. I cannot imagine that the odds cast for my success were ever very high. It had made for some interesting dinner conversations over the years. Most people had very positive perceptions of the idea in theory. I am sure they thought the execution would eventually fail in some interesting way.

People had always been quick to say they would be happy to go with me on the trip. They still are to this day. When faced with driving 130-150 mph for more than a day with no real protection from jail or incident, they find something else they have to do that weekend. It may be pawned off on work, family, scheduling, an emergency annual physical, or a difficult to reschedule haircut but it is really just fear. This is an unknowable experience until you are in it and most of the people around me were simply smart enough to realize that this is fundamentally just a bad idea.

I was coming to terms with the idea that the people in the car with me were probably not going to be the group of people who had planned and contemplated this idea with me for all of these years. I realized they probably would not be fully aware of all of the risks involved. That posed a few risks in itself. They could back out at any time and they might not react as I would hope in a worst case scenario. That meant it was time for another call to the naive insurance man. $2 million general liability umbrella - check!

Over the years Kevin, Chris, Forrest and I had spent a lot of time talking about ruses, disguises, and ploys that might be useful in the trip. Getting pulled over in a car outfitted like this was going to raise a few questions and it seemed responsible to have some answers. Rawlings did not have much in that regard but Alex had put some serious time and planning into it.

He had outfitted the car with a few extra things to create the appearance of being a storm chaser. He found that the list of required gadgets for barreling into the center of a tornado is eerily similar to what you might pack to go out and try to break a cross country outlaw record. He had stickers and shirts made along with special labels for all of his equipment with weather related names. Alex Roy is the Brick Tamland of outlaw cross country street racers.

Of course the holy grail of Cannonball ruses was the fake ambulance employed by the team of Brock Yates and Hal Needham in 1979. This was not practical based on the direction that we were headed in automobile selection. When my preparation had heated up in 2008, I had phoned up a local pig slaughterhouse and procured two now-frozen pig hearts. I did some light graphics design work and came up with a sweet *TransCon TransPlant TransPort* Logo and was going to fab up some paperwork explaining why this transplant heart had to be moved by car. Threat of cyst eruption seemed appropriate.

We had talked about smoke screens, blinding LED rear facing lights, and lots of other stuff. One Gumball participant used to evade police by throwing grocery bags filled with five hundred one dollar bills out of the top of his Ferrari F50. People would stop their cars and try to grab the money, congesting the roads for pursuit. Less highway than surface street practicality but interesting nonetheless.

I had looked at color transforming options. The image of the construction workers rinsing the temporary white paint off of the Countach in *Cannonball Run II* was clearly running through my brain. I thought of a few possibilities. One was to change the color of half of the car with a line diagonally from the front right corner to the back left. That way the car would appear to be a different color when seen from the front than from the back. Another was to use low adhesive or static cling vinyl in black that could be removed on the side of the road to reveal the stock paint color. The Plasti-Dip sprayable vinyl products were also coming onto the scene and those were worth exploring. Ultimately I ended up not using any of those ideas due to cost and timing but they were a lot of fun to contemplate.

185

Around the same time as my interest in the Cannonball was piqued, I learned a fact in a social studies class that was fairly interesting. I was as an 18 year old sitting in an Advanced Placement American Government Class. My teacher was breezing through the US Constitution as it pertained the Article that governed treatment and privileges of senators and congressmen. It said in Article 1 Section 6 that:

> "*The Senators and Representatives shall receive a compensation for their services, to be ascertained by law, and paid out of the treasury of the United States. They shall in all cases, except treason, felony and breach of the peace, be privileged from arrest during their attendance at the session of their respective Houses, and in going to and returning from the same; and for any speech or debate in either House, they shall not be questioned in any other place.*"

Privileged from arrest? That sounded amazing. Knowing how hard diplomatic plates and privileges were to get, this seemed within the realm of feasibility. If I could get elected to state or federal Congressional seat and find a reason to be in Los Angeles, theoretically I would not face any consequences for speeding if pulled over. That hinged on the cop knowing the US Constitution and on them not finding some way to raise the stakes into felony endangerment or evasion. Fun as it might be, that idea got scratched.

Years earlier I had a friend with government connections in Nigeria get me a Nigerian Driver's License with an accompanying International Driving Permit. I figured that if I had to surrender it the penalties might be less severe and the documentation might not make its way back to Georgia. The friends of mine that continued on to law school helped to enlighten me as to what a bad idea using it was.

Police impersonation is a popular ruse in discussion. Like attention/performance enhancing drugs I considered guising the car as a cop car to be outside of the spirit of the exercise. There had not been any fake police vehicles in Cannonball or US Express and it felt like a direction that I did not want to go in. Alex had dressed the M5 up in various law enforcement liveries for Gumball and other events but he too decided against using even the strobe lights on his drive.

With a team that was unlikely to hold up a transplant ruse and a budget already tapped, it was time to proceed with the novel plan of simply not getting caught. Alex had spent a lot of time pouring over the laws and penalties of speeding in each jurisdiction that the route takes you through. I knew that speeding was frowned upon and I knew that you could end up going to jail for it. That being said, the reality of getting caught going 150 and 110 is generally the same so there was not much else to think about. Without a recon run to go from, my plan was to drive as fast I could everywhere and see where it got me. I had the equipment to make it as safe from the consequence of arrest as I felt I could.

Most of the people who knew enough about the record to understand the difficulty, myself included, doubted the possibility of breaking it on the first attempt. I am sure many of them were eagerly anticipating the opportunity to go next time and to profit from the lessons learned in the first failure. I know it was Tom Park's excuse. I certainly cannot blame him. Earlier that year when my schedule had gotten too full I had thought of trying to get someone else to do the first recon run to test out the car and tell me how things were working. Clearly that would never have worked.

Forrest and the Bacon Blocker were a package deal due to control functionality. He was close to having it ready but it was not ready for use in 2013. It became pseudo-operational about 4 weeks after we got back from the trip, complete with "Mercedes Benz Active Cruise Control and Accident Avoidance System PROTOTYPE" screen printed on the control board. To our knowledge it is the most advanced active radar jammer for police radar frequencies in civilian existence today.

Alex Roy had broken the record on Columbus Day which was the traditional date for the US Express in the early 1980's. That happened to fall on my birthday in 2013 and it was unclear if the car would be ready by then. Also, spending my 28th birthday in jail sounded bad. I did not want to attempt it on the last weekend of the month due to the increased patrolling of highways as different quotas were trying to be met.

The 19-21st became the target date. The dates are always a three day window due to the time change and the fact that you do not want to arrive in LA at any time other than the middle of the night.

I would leave Manhattan at 10 PM and hope to arrive in Redondo Beach by 1 AM local time for a 30 hour elapsed time. This gave me a nice margin of failure that still constituted success. I needed to get there before 2:04 AM to break the record. I prayed it would not be a close call in either direction. If I only beat it by a couple of minutes I had to assume that it would cause quite a fight over accuracy of measurement. I knew I could win such an argument but I hoped to avoid it. Disputes and accusations of dishonesty feel like they cheapen the pursuit. If I was a few minutes slower but stuck to the actual route I would feel like I deserved to claim the record even with a longer time. The car was finished in service and CarTunes was doing some last minute tinkering with the CB and Scanner.

I called Alex a few weeks before we left. I knew that in order to avoid some of the statutes of limitation, Alex had waited a year to come forward and claim the record. I assumed that if someone else had broken the record recently they would have called him even if they were not going to claim it publicly. He said that he was not aware of anyone else trying to break the record at the time. I told him I was planning on trying it soon and he cautioned me about running out of weekends. It was unseasonably warm in New York but that was bound to change at any time.

He did bring up an interesting point, someone had recently done me the favor of testing the national response to publicly breaking traffic laws. Adam Tang, going by the name AfroDuck, had recently broken a record that Alex had held several years prior - the lap around Manhattan.

It did not go well. It may have been twelve years since 9/11 but the appetite for demonstrating an ability to beat a government system in New York City without being contained by the existing defense protocols was not the black eye that NYPD wanted. The public outcry had been intense and law enforcement had gone to some unbelievably extreme lengths to find him and arrest him. This was somewhat different with no real positive historical precedent to cling to or any redemptive social value in that drive. Pot Kettle issues understood.

At least there was no image of two beautiful girls stepping out of a Countach wearing spandex racing suits spraypainting across a sign in Manhattan saying No Right on Red. Then who could resist proving the system wrong? That Cannonball Countach image was as forever emblazoned in my memory as it was for the recipient of my next phone call.

It was Wednesday, October 16, 2013.

I got into work and decided it was time. I called Laid Back Dave Black. I reminded him of our conversation a few weeks prior, an area in which his memory required precious little jostling. It was clear he thought I was about to ask him to fly to New York, rent a car, and lead us out Manhattan. He was backpedaling on his original offer as his mental personal accounting arithmetic started kicking in. Dave was still unemployed and working on some web development projects. It was hard enough to rationalize his monthly Lamborghini payment, much less spending $1,000 on an up and back trip to aid and abet.

"I want you to be my co-driver." I told him.

"[expletive] yes. I am in." He responded as a reflex. a few seconds later his brain began to process the request.

I told him to meet me the next evening at my house so we could pack up some things and plan for the trip. We were leaving Friday morning.

As soon as he hung up the phone I got a text message. "I should probably ask Lisa."

There goes the neighborhood. Fortunately, Dave knew nothing about the record other than Burt Reynolds and *32 Hours 7 Minutes*. Lisa, his wife, knew even less. Neither had read Alex's book, they didn't know about Rawlings, and had never heard of Brock Yates.

Dave was a good driver. He could hang with me in the mountains and we had done some Lamborghini track events together. He is extremely intelligent but he over-thinks most things. Having worked for Apple, he was extremely tech savvy and he processes information very quickly. Despite theoretical criteria and outward appearances, he was a great candidate to be a co-driver.

I had spent my day off earlier that week shopping for supplies, packing my toothbrush, and going through the systems on the car for functionality. I went to Bass Pro Shops to buy two pairs of the best [returnable] binoculars that they had and made sure to keep the receipt.

Their sales guy asked me, "How can I help

you?"

"I am looking for a couple sets of binoculars for a trip."

"Oh yeah, where are you headed?" He asked.

I answered. "Kind of all over the place. I need to spots bears. Probably from 1,000-1,500 yards. And out of a moving vehicle."

"That is pretty tough without stabilization. We don't sell those." He was not optimistic. He indicated that two of the designs were good. I told him I would try them both out and see how they worked. I checked the lunar phase for the coming weekend and it was going to be a nearly full moon which meant nighttime visibility should be excellent.

I am 6'5". Dave is 6'2". That meant that there was no relief for anyone sitting behind either of us. On the Thursday before we left I was getting desperate, calling people I had not spoken to in years and asking them to ride with me. I was close to getting Megan to go but I was still sane enough to know that was a bad idea. My younger brother was a short flight away but I *Saving-Private-Ryan*-ed him out of consideration before our parents would have done the same.

I thought of Dan Huang. He was small, smart, and liked cars. I didn't even have his cell phone number though. I sent him a message through Facebook. "Do you have any plans this weekend? Give me a call." I left him my phone number.

He called a couple of hours later. The conversation was brief. He agreed to go. It was a quick enough response that I was not sure he understood what we were doing. I felt the need to clarify the nature of the request but the salesman in me knew well enough to stop while I was ahead.

Dan is a couple of years younger than I am, properly sized for back seat CL riding, Chinese, extremely tech competent, and easy to get along with. Come to find out he was also very good at keeping up calm outward appearances when he was pretty freaked out on the inside. Dan had bounced around from startup to startup since exiting Georgia Tech and offered the advantage of looking at the world in a very similar manner to Dave and I. Our relocated spare tire which now rested behind the driver's seat would be in good company.

The pursuance of this record was a very entrepreneurial exercise. It had every element of a startup business just without the eventual potential for profitability. I get asked this often and I know that Alex has as well - How do you make money from holding the record?

You don't. Richard has done well with the renewal and continuation of *Fast & Loud* but that is due to his personality and the marketing of the Discovery Channel. The tattoo on his arm reading 31:59 has helped with the backstory but it is not the real reason for his success.

I had to define our goal/market, figure out what capital expenses were required, manage costs, solve problems, manage negative outcomes, build a useful team, and execute. The business planning of Great White Reptiles, Supercar Rentals, and building the Lamborghini owner database had served me well. Whatever formula for success could exist, I felt like we had it.

I made a last grocery run before the trip. I bought water, Red Bull, Gatorade, Nutrition Bars, Dried Fruits, Candy Bars, chewable vitamins (C, Multi, Zinc, B12), facial cleaning cloths, hand sanitizer, paper products, urinal bottles, bedpans, wire ties, every kind of tape, flashlights, etc.

Finally I had our driving team. On Thursday night we all met at my house. Dave and Dan showed up. Adam came as well. This was the first time that they had all seen the car in its finished state and each other. I would have loved to fully understand what was going through their heads at that point. They were both clearly nervous and the mood was one of intense confusion.

I have to assume that they were expecting a fairly casual road trip. It was a reasonable deduction based on the way that I had solicited their assistance. How would someone be taking this seriously and need to ask two people completely unrelated to the project to come on at the last possible moment?

Adam had come over to see everyone. Adam is every inch of 6'10". When Dave showed up next, he looked at Adam and assumed he was our third. The piling on concern was simultaneously amusing and telling. He was clearly on edge. Adam was growing less and less regretful on the opportunity that he was forgoing.

Dan pulled up. Dave sighed in relief. Adam hadn't looked like a Huang. "You must be Dan?" Dave said.

"Yeah, Dave?" Dan asked to confirm.

"Yes. I offered. This is Adam. He will be using

the tracking device to monitor progress and check on weather." Introductions with suspense are better.

The car changed the conversation from casual to intense. My orange LP640 had never been more overlooked since it had left the factory in Sant A'gata. When they looked inside the CL and saw all of the equipment that had been installed and came to appreciate the investment that I had made in the idea, it started to become more serious. The holes in the dash, gas tanks in the trunk, wires run everywhere, and toilet facilities on board - it was clear I meant business.

Chapter 14 - You're Leaking Gas

Some of the logistics remained open ended. The departure time posed a bit of an issue. Dave and Dan were not of a mindset or position to argue with anything I was proposing. I had decided the best time to leave was between 9 and 11 PM on a Saturday night. That meant we would get through the Midwest before people started waking up to go to church on Sunday. Sunday was inevitably going to be the lowest traffic day so we wanted to maximize the Sunday driving.

Leaving Manhattan at 10 PM after getting some real rest the day of departure was tough. I had planned to drive from Atlanta to Washington, DC on Friday, stay the night, go into New York City by noon on Saturday and then get a hotel to get about five hours of sleep before heading over to the Red Ball.

That was easier said than done. Check out was at 11 everywhere in Manhattan and check in was no earlier than 4. I would have to get the room for the night before and the night after, availability was low and cost was prohibitively high.

Ash Majid was a friend of mine who had recently moved from Atlanta to Manhattan and his apartment happened to be directly across from the parking garage where we were starting from. I sent him the first few turns as we were planning the route out of the city and he responded, "I think that might actually be right across the street from me."

He had agreed to see us off on Saturday night and gave us some advice on where to stay. The Manhattan hotels all had parking available but it was all underground valet lots that felt risky. It was impossible to remove all of the equipment from the car and a theft of any of it, albeit unlikely, was not an acceptable risk to take. Replacement was possible. Getting there again to try after re-purchase and re-installation was not. Ash told us to look at staying in Jersey City. It would be cheaper, easier, and the parking availability was much better.

Dave, Dan, and I had a discussion where they pretty much just nodded their heads and blankly stared in shock and fear at what they weren't sure they had gotten themselves into. We decided the best logistical arrangement was to make the entire drive up the first day and to get into Jersey City late Friday night or early on Saturday morning. That way we could sleep until noon or so and then go do some recon work on the best exit path out of the city. We agreed to forgo the stop in DC and make the entire drive up into New Jersey on Friday. The plan was to reconvene at my house around 9 AM on Friday morning to head out after morning rush hour traffic died down in Atlanta.

I did not sleep much Thursday night and I doubt the other guys did either. Lamborghini had scheduled a dealer meeting at Fontana Speedway in California for the coming weekend so Brandon, our GM, went instead of me. Everyone asked where I was and they were quite excited to hear what the better offer had been. The idea of Cannonball never fails to elicit a pretty strong emotional response from a group of car guys. The huge appeal of this goal to the people I hang around every day was a great thing.

You cannot love cars and not love Cannonball. Long distance exotic car road trips rest near the top of most petrolhead bucket lists. The highest rated *Top Gear* episodes were always their epic road trips.

The staff of *Top Gear* Magazine actually made a Cannonball attempt around 2006. They took 2 Jaguars on a trip from New York to Los Angeles but stopped at night to rest, stopping the clock as they did. They were arrested near the Eastern California border for speeding although their average moving speeds were no better than those of the top Cannonball and US Express times. The reader comments were critical of their half-hearted stopping strategy and they quickly took the article down from their web site.

As I continued to examine and evaluate my own motivation for doing this, the targeted marketing aspect of the reveal was always a major pro. I have never been any good at separating work from my personal life. Each defines the other. That has been easy because every job I have held revolved around a personal interest. I never needed to stop working and start playing because the demarcation was never clear. The working was a bit less fulfilling and the playing was a lot more expensive but to an outside observer I would imagine it is a tough distinction to make.

Most of the people at the dealership were not privy to what I was doing. Most of my friends were not aware of what I was doing. In fact, pretty much my immediate family, a couple people from work who I needed to clear the time off with, and the growing list of active confederates it took to pull it off were the only ones who knew what was going on that weekend.

I felt like keeping the circle close to the chest was important. It only took one person who knew someone that knew a cop along the route that could get wind of one of the biggest catches of his life coming through town to really throw a wrench into the plan. It also felt emotionally safer for me to have a smaller group of people to explain this all to in the event I failed on this attempt.

I knew I was more prepared to do this than anyone ever had been. We had the unbelievable benefit of having two teams publicly break the record in the previous decade. I had read and re-read Alex's book, Brock Yates's book, and all of the stories about Rawlings's trip. The car was ready, running well, and it looked like the uncontrollable variables were under control. As long as we didn't hit any major traffic we had a chance. I estimated our chances of breaking the record at 30% and our chances of finishing around 70%. I felt that those were higher than anyone had ever had since Yates did the recon run in May of 1971.

Assuming you are a capable driver and you have a sufficiently prepared car to reliably carry you across the country, most of it is out of your hands after you get to New York. I have used the metaphor of a Hot Wheels Track like we used to play with as children. Once you let a car go from the top of the track, it is out of your control.

You idle in front of the Red Ball and you pull the lever on a massive all-knowing slot machine. The first wheel reveals the weather, the second unveils construction and road closures, the third police activity, a fourth shows you the traffic, and still a fifth exists there as a boogeyman. It could be a deer, a pothole, a meteor. There are just too many possibilities to foresee. You just know you can't control them. Two 7's might get you under 34 hours. Three might get you in shouting distance of 31. Four puts 30 in your sights. No one knew or had felt what it would be like for all five to turn up 7's.

I spent a lot of time in prayer that evening. I do not see law breaking cross country records as a God thing but I do believe in his ability to protect me even when I do some stupid things. Prayer is valuable to me in its capacity to help me put my own concerns and problems into perspective and to recognize where preparation invariably meets a margin that is outside of our control. That is how the week had felt. Who would have guessed the most difficult part of this entire process was going to be finding someone to buckle into the seat belt next to you?

This was one of those moments where I got to stare at the ceiling and think about what was going on in my life. I realized this dream, however farcical and preposterous it might be, was an enormous privilege. People spend their entire lives trying and never get a chance to chase something this hard. I had gotten to the point of truly doing whatever it took to make this a reality.

There was not a point in my life that I could recall wanting something so badly and going to such lengths to achieve it. It was certainly lofty to believe I was capable. I could say that my preparation was on par with those who had come before me. I had no reason to believe I was less capable than they were as drivers. I did, however, realize what portion of my success was outside of my control and I recognized that I was trying to do something that hundreds if not thousands of people had been trying to accomplish for over forty years. It was amazing company to be in but I could not shake the feeling that I might not belong there.

I eventually dozed off, still curious what this all must feel like from the perspective of Dave and Dan. I came to find out later, in his own nervousness about the immensity of the undertaking, Dave had told his wife that he would drive with me to New York and if it didn't feel right, he would abandon the trip and fly home. Dan's position was very similar.

The idea begs questions about the dynamic and the diversions inside the car. What did you play on the radio? How was the small talk? Was there a lot of I Spy?

The actual drive was all business. The drive to New York was all education. As Dave and Dan had no real idea of what to expect, there was a necessary acclimation and experimentation phase that was required. We needed to develop communication methods, protocols, and learn what to expect from each other to make the drive work. Dave was extremely helpful in this regard. Much of his work at IHG was in customer interfaces and experiences. He talked a lot about zen mental focus jargon and other things that might have normally warranted a punch in the face but without someone else on deck I endured the psycho-philosophical mumbo jumbo about hierarchies of needs and idea flows.

We repositioned some of the phones, iPads, and other devices to make them more usable. We tested the communication devices and tried to figure out how to make the next two days of our lives as comfortable as they could be. I also spent a good deal of time explaining to them what we were doing - Cannonball 101 if you will.

I told them the history of Cannonball. We talked about what was realistic out of the movies and what was enhanced. We talked about our own driving experiences and about what I had learned from the stories of past competitors. I filled them in on how long I had spent working on this and and tried to get them to understand just what it meant to me. They asked a lot of questions that started with "Why...?"

I explained to them the choice of the car. They were doubtful of the qualification of a 2004 CL55 AMG but I went through the logic. High power for top speed. Diesels would not have cut it. Forced induction for altitude and fuel economy. The color was halfway between blue and gray which created ambiguity. If someone were to call the cops they could report it as either. When a cop was looking for the car he could interpret it as either.

Keeping the powertrain stock was for reliability and not sacrificing fuel economy. Dave was very proud of the few seconds that he had spent above 175 mph in his Performante, and questioned why I had not removed the stock electronic limiter on the ECU at 155 mph. The easy answer was because the ECU flashes cost you fuel economy because they come with more power we didn't need. The more valid answer was fatigue. As fun as it is to chase 200 mph in a street car it is very difficult to process as a driver. The mental decompression time required after spending 5-30 seconds above 150 is long.

We would have been hitting 175 mph for 30 seconds and then spending the next two minutes at 90 feeling proud of ourselves and letting our brains recover. We could have spent that same 150 seconds traveling at 130 and felt fine. In the first scenario you travel 4.46 miles in 2.5 minutes. In the second you go 5.41 miles. It not exactly a tortoise-hare phenomena but more of a hare versus smarter hare strategy.

Extra fuel meant extra weight that changed as we burned through it. This beget the need for an active suspension. The Mercedes Active Body Control system measured and leveled each corner of the car multiple times per second and was the best option in the business regardless of cost. It was known to be the achilles heel of reliability so it accounted for a significant portion of the recent maintenance expense. As Dave had been enjoying the warranty status of his Gallardo that was just a few months old, the idea of an $8,800 expense in maintenance on a working car was dumbfounding. Nevermind the percentage of the car's value that bill represented.

The tricked out interior with all of the toys was very interesting to my tech savvy compatriots. Admittedly, I had done very little testing of the systems. The CB and Scanner were not picking up much but there was not much trucker traffic around us so it seemed excusable. I had not programmed the frequencies for the Eastern Seaboard states into the active scanner bank so testing it was not possible. I wanted to spend some time testing out the fuel system on the drive up. They were keen to see how it worked as well.

We had two additional 22 gallon fuel cells mounted in the trunk. Each additional tank had a pump with an output line that y-ed together and fed into a 180 degree turn under the fuel filler cover and down into the filler neck through a modified cap. The flow rate was intentionally fairly slow to avoid potential backups, pressure related leaks, or timing issues. Charles had calculated it to be approximately a gallon every 90 seconds. We were sending the fuel into a 23 gallon main tank. The stock fuel gauge still worked and there was a gauge for each of the two tanks mounted to the dash. They were accurate only on a very basic level.

The plan was to transfer approximately ten gallons between the tanks four times and for that to occupy the space between 1/4 tank and 3/4 on the factory gauge. Each transfer should take fifteen minutes by Charles's math. On our way up through North Carolina we tried this for the first time.

The switch to control the fuel pumps was on a custom panel CarTunes had fabricated to replace the former ashtray on the center console. It also had a switch to kill all of the rear lights, the activation button for the MiRT, the power controls for the Laser Interceptor, and the control panel for the Passport system.

Around the time our transfer timer got to fourteen minutes a car behind us began flashing its lights and trying to pull up next to us. An angry motorist was not a terribly new or unexpected phenomena so I just expected him to get mad at us for passing too close, going too fast, or just being Ed.

As he pulled alongside us he motioned to roll the window down. Dave was driving so I obliged him from the passenger seat. He yelled, "You're leaking gas!"

Our collective mental image immediately went to a mushroom cloud of flames imminently erupting from the back of our speeding car. Dave started freaking out and I told him to find the next exit or open shoulder so that we could investigate. We cut the transfer pumps and all of a sudden the fuel gauge went from half all the way to the upper limit of its reportable range. There was clearly some latency in its ability to measure.

During transfer there was a very strong smell of gas outside of the car. It did not really permeate the cabin while driving but due to the way the vents work it is clear to an outside observer there is something strange going on behind the scenes. The trunk smelled very strongly of gasoline and that was where the little luggage that we had packed was. We had wrapped it in trash bags to help but I knew any overflowed fuel would have likely run over and through our bags on its way out of the car and onto this good Samaritan's windshield.

We immediately exited and found a gas station and Dan had figured out how to remove the safety tab from the fire extinguisher wedged inside of the spare wheel occupying the seat behind Dave. We jumped out of the car and opened the trunk. There was fuel dripping through the fender liner and it smelled of the preeminence of a Derek Zoolander incident but there was no fire to quell. It had not filled the rest of the trunk space with gasoline so we were still equipped with a usable change of clothes. We could not tell exactly how much fuel had leaked but it was at least five gallons. We deduced that our actual transfer rate was a bit over one gallon per minute.

After the tension finally left our nerves we got back in the car. Dan put the fire extinguisher back in its place and we all stared at each other trying to believe we were not as out of our depth as the past five minutes might have indicated. Each lesson in Cannonball 101 I had taught to Dave and Dan on the way up was a Jenga block. Experiences like this fuel crisis were removing blocks row by row and threatening our stability as a team. I just hoped that we would be able to keep the tower standing long enough to get to Redondo Beach.

We discussed the route and how I had arrived at the navigational strategy. I had spent a lot of time in Google Maps looking at a balance between the mathematically shortest path and a theoretical fastest route while balancing the clear preference for highway driving and minimizing the number of turns. Every navigational instruction was an opportunity to get lost and that was something I was truly afraid of.

Dave was a huge proponent of Waze. Waze is a social media navigational application that uses the travel data from other users to modify directional instructions and speed up commute times. It also allows users to report traffic issues, police activity, and other hindrances to progress. He believed this could be all you need to break this record. With enough users ahead it could feed us all of the information that we could need. Of course, the goal of the departure strategy was to minimize interaction with other road users so we were circularly handicapping the usability of this tool. More Waze users equals more traffic. Unfortunately the inevitable trucker traffic has been slow to adopt Waze, clinging to the social interaction and trash talking opportunity of the citizens band radio.

There would clearly be times when the Waze, Google, and Garmin navigational models would differ and we needed to create a protocol for dealing with those instances. Google and Garmin used licensed cell phone data from AT&T to define traffic patterns. Waze was much more advanced (this was prior to the Google acquisition). If it told you there was traffic ahead it was more likely to be correct. That being said, none of the nav systems were configured to understand the way that we were driving. Zig zagging through an industrial park may work well in downtown Atlanta to get around a gas main break but in this style of drive, the anxiety of having no idea where you are headed might end up hurting more than helping.

During the drive North to the start, we had a chance to test this. Waze said there was traffic up ahead while we were in Virginia. Users were going 7-12 mph. It advised us to take an exit, go through a small surface street, make a bunch of turns, run along an access road parallel to the highway for a bit, and then re-enter the highway.

We did. It was crazy. We couldn't see to turn, the other nav systems were screaming "Recalculating" constantly, and the roads were terrible to speed on. Dave agreed it was best not to accept those types of instructions. Minimizing stress and anxiety was worth a couple of minutes sitting in traffic rather than struggling to find a new way around it. The "keep it simple, stupid" mantra was coming into play.

In addition to spending the days prior to departure lining up people to be in the car with me, I had spent a great deal of time working on something else I thought truly could give us a competitive advantage. I had arranged for a number of people throughout the route to drive ahead of us by 75 to 150 miles. They would be able to give us real time information on weather, traffic, accidents, speed traps, and other issues. The communication would also be a refreshing tie to the world outside of the car. To my knowledge, this was something neither Alex Roy nor Richard Rawlings had done for any considerable portion of their runs. Alex had scouts out of NYC and Richard claimed to have hired a team of limo drivers to block intersections. Both had teammates lead them into Los Angeles. I wanted to take that to the next level.

During the drive up to New York we called the friends we knew along the route to confirm their willingness to serve as spotters for their legs of the trip. Ash Majid was going to see us off from Manhattan. We were going to stage in the temporary parking area in front of his place, use the restroom, brush our teeth, and change clothes there before leaving.

Danny Landoni would leave from the Eastern

Pennsylvania border when we left the Red Ball and lead us across the state. I did not know Danny and had only spoken with him on the phone once. He was a friend of Cody Heron who I knew through Lamborghini ownership. At the time Cody had an M5, Ferrari 458, Lamborghini Aventador, and had ordered a Huracan from me. He thought the idea was fantastic but was called away on business so he delegated the task to Danny who proved both extremely capable and excited to take part.

Chris Staschiak was going to leave from the Pennsylvania/West Virginia border and lead us through Ohio. He was still upset to not be riding shotgun but excited to be a part of the action anyway. David Wiggins was going to lead from Columbus on but he got the flu. He had purchased a Ferrari 458, Lamborghini Gallardo LP550-2 Bicolore, and a Lamborghini Murcielago LP670 SuperVeloce from me in the prior years and I was excited to fly by him for once but unfortunately he was unable to join us. Chris ended up continuing through the areas where Wiggins would have been useful.

Tom Greulich, one of the competitors from the 2004 AKA Rally, was going to lead us through Missouri beginning northeast of St Louis. Jules Doty was a friend of Dave's and would lead us through New Mexico. Nick Reid was scouting out the route into LA but was due in court later Monday morning and was unavailable during the actual arrival.

From **Nick Reid**
Scout - Los Angeles

Ed and I met on a cross-country road rally from New York City, NY to Los Angeles, CA about ten years ago. Both Ed and I used AWD turbo sedans for the journey. Over that week, Ed and I became friends. For years we continued to talk to each other about our similar interests in cars and long trips even though we lived a thousand miles apart.

Eventually Ed would go on to work for Lamborghini and I began producing aftermarket parts for Lamborghinis. We both now own nearly identical Lamborghini's. I have the only Grigio Telesto 6 speed manual Murcielago LP640 they brought to the US. Ed has the only Grigio Telesto 6 speed manual Murcielago LP640 original sent to Canada. The neat part is we both drive our cars often, and drive them long distances, which is uncommon in the exotic car community. Ed and I have a love for road trips.

I called Ed in mid-2013. At that time Ed hinted that he would be attempting the New York to California run and asked if I would be willing to help. I gladly agreed. A few weeks later Ed called and said that within a few hours he would be setting off from New York. Unfortunately I was not able to lead Ed into Los Angeles as planned, but I was able to help confirm Ed's planned route as the most efficient way to the coast and to avoid possible traffic delays.

During the time Ed was coming into Los Angeles I was hoping for the best for him. I had not heard any updates of how their progress was. However, they old saying "no news is good news" was going through my mind. Then it happened, late at night, a text came through from Ed, "we did it." I knew zero details for the run except for the fact that Ed did it on the first try. I was very excited for everyone involved because this was a great feat.

In the coming weeks details of the run were released. Ed was very appreciative of everyone that helped him achieve this great feat. While reading the list of "thank you's" sent by Ed, I noticed that there were many mutual friends from that cross-country rally we attended a decade ago on the list. Ed's dream to set the record from New York to Los Angeles was not only a great feat, but it brought friends together. Friends that have the same common love for road trips. Ed's dream brought us all together again, and unknowingly we all were part of a great record that we will never forget.

Chapter 15 - Pulled Over in NYC

We did not intend to set any records driving up to New Jersey that Friday but if we had, we would have been disappointed. Traffic was difficult, we were not communicating very well, we were scared of getting arrested, and the roads were not conducive to the types of speeds we were planning. Even without the concerted effort to average more than ninety it was pretty demoralizing to see the average plummeting well below eighty. I was doing my best not to read too much into it but I was finding myself too easily frustrated with Dave and truly concerned that the outcome of the next day would be quite the joke.

We stopped for dinner in Tyson's Corner, Virginia at a Maggiano's Italian restaurant. It was a strange mood at the table. The slow clap of progress to New York was gaining frequency and we were all trying to figure out what 24 hours from then would look like. As we had driven North, Dave and Dan had been able to deepen their understanding of what to expect but their tutelage was coming from me, someone who had no first hand idea of what to expect. The other guys were clearly trying to develop a timed bathroom routine to carry them into the next day.

As I was driving, Dave found a four star hotel on a travel discount site and booked it. It turned out to be the Hyatt in Jersey City, a great hotel beautifully overlooking the Hudson River and Freedom Tower. We got in there around 1:00 AM on Saturday. Dave was not comfortable sharing a room so he booked an extra one. Dan and I stayed in the other one. There was a street level valet. I tipped the attendant $20 and asked him to keep the car out front. That would make it easier for the next afternoon when we would be staging for departure. The valet looked at the car suspiciously and obliged.

I was truly concerned that I would get a call or text message at any moment from Alex Roy. The onset of paranoia was a strange sensation. Being a resident of Manhattan, we were on his home turf. If a car like this, clearly prepared to challenge his record, was cruising around the neighborhood surely there would be acquaintances around town who would alert him to the threat. All of the conversations that I had with Alex were entirely cordial and helpful but I had deliberately avoided telling him which dates we were planning on driving. I did not want to burden him with the moral quandary of sabotage. He, himself had told me that his lawyers forbade him from witnessing any other runs and advised me not to tell him (or anyone) exactly when we would be making the run.

I had gotten us a late checkout so we had enough time to get some rest. I told everyone to try to stay in bed until at least noon. Dan was the only one capable of this. I woke up at around 10:30 and stayed in bed until about 11. I texted Dave. He had been up since 7.

Dave and I went around the corner to a cafe to grab some breakfast. We let Dan keep sleeping. He seemed to have a low caloric intake need anyway. I had the drive plan with me. This was the first time that Dave had seen it. It generally outlined the windows for driver changes, estimated average speeds, and some checkpoint times through major cities and navigational instructions. The goal time remained 30 hours. Dave wrote down 31:04 on a napkin as he tried to visualize the goal. We nibbled at our breakfast and continued to talk about what the drive might feel like. That was the least knowable facet of the endeavor and I felt very much like a commander leading the crew into battle with only a slightly better vantage point than they enjoyed.

I picked up a couple of bottled fruit juice smoothies to drink along the way. Of course they were $5 each in this cafe/convenience store rather than $2 at home but I was happy knowing that I had at least 1,500 perishable calories to enjoy throughout the drive as I supplemented the nutrition bars I had planned.

I remembered the manifest of Brock Yates's Moon Trash Van with sandwiches, apples, and regular food. Other Cannonballers had set off laden with traditional Italian home cooking. The dichotomy between those trips and what we were about to embark on began to stand in stark contrast. It was not one-upmanship that had gotten me to this point of preparation and theory but instead it was the constantly pioneering spirit of gearheads and modern day explorers making intrepid steps to improve the time.

Given the margins of improvement through history we all agreed that there were significant gains still to be had. The uncontrollable variables clearly came into play.

1971 40:51 Smith/Williams/Yates/Yates Jr
       Dodge Sportsman Van

1971 35:54 Yates/Gurney
       Ferrari 365 GTB/4 Daytona

1975 35:53 May/Cline
       Ferrari Dino 246 GTS

1979 32:51 Heinz/Yarborough
       Jaguar XJS

1983 32:07 Diem/Turner
       Ferrari 308 GTS

2007 31:59 Rawlings/Collins
       Ferrari 550 Maranello

2006 31:04 Roy/Maher/Welles
       BMW M5

The margins of improvement had been huge. Alex blamed a short storm and traffic in New Mexico for at least a thirty-minute delay. The cross country drive contained so many individual problems to address and a contestant truly had to conquer them all to be in contention. We had the car, we had the drivers, we had the gear, but would we have the luck? The time to pull the arm of the mythical slot machine was nearing.

Dave and I walked back to the hotel and woke Dan up. We checked out of the rooms and got the supplies generally arranged in the car. I called Ash to tell him that we were headed his way. The plan was to scope out the Red Ball and evaluate the best route out of the city. Roy and Rawlings had used the Holland Tunnel. I also wanted to look at the New York Classic Car Club location that Alex Roy had left from to see how much of an advantage that seemed to be. At this point, Dave did not have an appreciation of the emotional significance of the Red Ball to the record so he was interested in the fastest way out that would give us the best chance of breaking any record.

I had driven in Manhattan four times and generally found it to flow well, stay busy but progressive, and remain fairly manageable as long as you were confident and kept moving forward in the same spirit as the taxi drivers around you. That was not the case that Saturday. It was absolutely nuts. We made it to the Red Ball to find the entire stretch of E 31st Street torn to pieces in a repaving project. Based on the signs and work patterns it looked like the road might actually be closed at the first intersection that we would have to go through. We met with Ash and talked for a few minutes about strategy. He had left his Laguna Seca Blue E46 M3 in Atlanta and used the Subway to get to work so his experience driving in area was fairly limited.

I asked the attendant at the Red Ball garage if he ever had anyone show up there mentioning Cannonball in cars looking like ours with extra screens inside and antennas mounted to the trunks. He said, "No," and looked at me like I was a proper moron.

We saddled up and made an exit. We simulated resetting all of the trip data on the car and

GPS systems. We started the timers and made our way out of the parking garage which was quite the flurry of button pressing. Following the GPS advice and the drive plan that I had previously formulated I piloted us away to a wider, theoretically faster moving, cross street. It wasn't. We sat and sat. The navigational instructions were tough to understand and Dave knee-jerked to Waze to attempt a re-route.

We finally got to the Lincoln tunnel and could see the entrance to it. Dave saw that Waze said a quick Left-Right-Right-Left would bypass the standstill ahead. Reluctantly I agreed to try it. I made the left only to hit another jam. I got to the front and made a right through the red light. That was against the rules in Manhattan and the cop who happened to be right behind me decided to bring it to my attention.

He popped on his lights and pulled me over. The road I turned onto as I obliged the arrest immediately split. The right looked like a parking lot so I chose the left. It was a one way street and I had led this cop down it going the wrong way. It would have been perilous if there were any cars coming. Fortunately, there were not and I was able to turn around and return to the proper direction of traffic flow with the surely dumbfounded cop close behind me.

Dave felt bad. I felt mad. Dan feared for his own safety. The cop was fairly baffled by the whole thing. He walked up to the car and asked for my license and insurance. You do not have to carry a valid insurance card in Georgia since all records are stored in a government accessible system based on your driver's license. That means that the one occupying my wallet happened to be a few renewal cycles expired. I offered it and he was not impressed. Somehow he managed not to ask about the wheel in the back with Dan, antennas on the decklid, and additional screens in the cockpit. I think he had already categorized us into some not-from-around-here idiots who would have been wearing aluminum foil helmets if they didn't impede our vision for driving. I did everything I could to apologetically reinforce that deduction. He agreed to let me off with a warning and gave me a lot of space to go about my way.

I expressed my displeasure with Dave and offered a stern warning that if he consulted Waze again between now and our arrival in Redondo Beach I would jettison his phone from the car. Dan was the only person with permission to use Waze for navigational purposes. Both accepted this new operational reality.

The labor pains finally ceased as we birthed ourselves from Manhattan via the Lincoln Tunnel and navigated our way through the interchanges that got us onto the Jersey Turnpike/78. Well, almost. Dave was defending his actions and I was being crass and insulting so we both managed to miss the navigational instruction for the turn. It took us thirty minutes to get back on track.

We had clearly missed the boat on this exit strategy. We went back into the city and decided we should try to find the New York Classic Car Club. There are two of them. We went to the wrong one. It was clearly not an advantage so we left and ruled that out. The one that we did not go to was the one that Alex used, further research showed. It would have been easier and likely tempting as our navigational confidence waned so it was a good thing we did not figure that out.

We thought about Times Square. It was iconic and eliminated about half of the driving distance on the island of Manhattan. If one were starting an event today that was the logical place to begin. The AKA Rally, GoldRush, and Gumball had done that in their visits to NYC.

Ultimately we resolved the original decision of the Red Ball still made the most sense. If we happened to fall short by less than twenty minutes perhaps we could beat ourselves up for it but we hoped it would not be the case. I decided if we could make it out of the city in less than twenty minutes it would be worth continuing. Anything longer and we could circle back and restart. I had never discussed the restarting strategy with anyone else but I thought it made sense. I also decided based on the fact that 31st eventually ran into the Lincoln Tunnel it would be best for us to simply endure the slower movement on that road and stay relaxed than to weave around searching for a few seconds here or there.

Upon coming to that decision I needed to get out of the city. We needed to gas up and after driving around Manhattan for two and half hours I needed to rest, decompress mentally, and be still for a little while. We drove off of the island and into New Jersey, followed the route to 78 and found an exit. It was getting into middle-of-nowhere zone so the only reasonable eating establishment we could find was a TGI Fridays.

In the normal course of our lives, none of us might ever have darkened the doors of a TGI Fridays again but in this circumstance it somehow made perfect sense. Simple menu, easy parking, no mental strain in ordering. After a tenser day than any of us had wanted it to be, this was perfect. It was interesting to see what constituted comfort food on such an occasion - nothing interesting, nothing new. Just whatever got us fed without making us exert any mental energy on anything other than what the next day and a half was going to entail.

I let Dave and Dan walk inside and get us a table. Before parting I told Dan that if I had to kill Dave tomorrow and bury him in the desert that he could never speak a word of it. He nodded his head and looked at me with exactly the right amount of uncertainty regarding my seriousness at the moment.

I called Megan. I was exhausted, broken, and disheartened. I doubted Dave's ability to help navigate and our capacity to operate as a team. The teamwork required to legitimately challenge this record seemed far beyond us.

I told her there was no way we were going to break it. She could hear in my voice how crushed I was and it was the only time she ever said that I should plan on trying it again. Her advice was perfect, to treat it as an exercise and to make the next one better. It calmed me down and I was able to go back inside with some semblance of a smile. I still assumed that we would get into Illinois or Missouri, realize how far off pace we were, and ask the nav systems to simply take us home with our tails between our legs. I was already thinking of the defeatist text I might draft to Alex Roy. Regardless of dwindling confidence, we had come too far to stop trying now.

Each of us ate bland food and some vegetables. It was a calm meal where we were all clearly trying to reduce our blood pressure and heart rates from the anxiety. Afterwards we looked for a place around us to go spend an hour relaxing and stretching our legs a bit. There happened to be a Target with a Starbucks inside of it just a few miles away in Watchung, NJ. We went that way.

There is a point in the *32 hours 7 minutes* documentary where Alex Roy is speaking with his friend and co-driver in his first real attempt to break the record (he tried four times). He discusses preparing his Last Will and Testament before the drive. He talks with one of his co-drivers about the idea that he is prepared to die in doing this and then they spend some time discussing the significance of that idea.

I would not say I was willing to die to do this. That is moreso a rationale for decision making within a challenge than a recognition prior to undertaking a mission. I did, however, recognize that this was the most dangerous activity I had ever undertaken. Trying to exceed 200 mph on public roads, reading a text on the way home from work, eating beef tartare, and hair raising college stunts paled in comparison to the risk I felt in this activity. I knew we had taken as many steps as we could to increase the safety of the trip and I thought we had minimized the risk. It still existed to an extent approaching my threshold of tolerability. Anyone who knows me or has read this far can appreciate my risk tolerance is foolishly high.

This recognition continued to remind me just how fortunate I was to be in that moment. Regardless of whether or not it could be rationally justified by even one other person on Earth, I was pushing full steam ahead into the storm of a challenge that was continuing to define me. The privilege of getting there and finding out just how far I could push myself was something I knew most people never got to see and feel. As unknowable as things were, my eyes were wide open and I was ready to go. Hundreds of people in the forty years prior had taken the same risks trying to lasso the same unicorn I was hunting. Only seven had held the record.

When we got to the Target we began pulling the trash, empty bottles, wrappers, and general road trip shrapnel out of the car. We got rid of the food and hydration supplies that we had over packed. There were a few things that each of us recognized that we had forgotten so we went in to grab them. I needed some lubricating eye drops. I have been nearsighted with a slight astigmatism since Middle School and I knew that I would need to switch between contacts and glasses a couple of times through the drive in order to keep my vision functional.

I had seriously considered getting a Lasik procedure done before the trip but one of the most common side effects is a halo glare around lights when driving at night. This risk was less acceptable than the inconvenience of switching between contacts and glasses. I ended up getting it done a few months after we got home and it has been fantastic. I now have vision somewhere between 20-10 and 20-15. The night glare lasted about a month and now it is better than ever. In hindsight it would have been very nice to have dealt with prior to the drive.

Over the course of about six months, I developed a trigger like colonic response to espresso using the Lamborghini Dealership corporate identity coffee machine that occupied the center of our showroom. A couple shots by themselves or as the contents of a milk containing drink and it was happening. I walked up to the Target Starbucks counter and ordered a large/grande/whatever Cafe Mocha and sat down to let it work. Clockwork. The other guys tried in vain to manage the same without success.

The bowel trigger prep showed Dan once again what this project meant to me. I later found out he was so nervous at that point leading up to departure that he barely avoided enunciating his intention to hail a cab and find his own way to LaGuardia and back home. Fortunately he stayed. We browsed around the store for a bit and then did some final organization of the contents of the car.

We left in search of some gas. At 8 PM it was way past the waking hours of Wherever, New Jersey we were. We did manage to find a station. We pulled up to their air compressor and leveled out all of the tires. Apart from the ability to change a wheel I had no onboard ability to re-inflate a tire. That would be the last they were checked before California so we spent time attempting precision.

News to us: you can't pump your own gas in the state of New Jersey. We pulled up to the pump and opened our trunk. The arrangement that I had allowed us to fill the two tanks in the trunk with the near side nozzle of a two sided pump and then pull the opposite side nozzle around and fill into the main tank simultaneously. That was quite perplexing to the attendant at this Exxon station. After some strange stares and negotiation he agreed to go back inside and let us pump our own gas.

I let Dave drive back to the starting line. I got in the back of the CL to close my eyes for a bit and rest before departure. Ash invited us to come up to his condo to change clothes for the last time, brush our teeth, and get ready for liftoff.

The feeling was that of being on a high diving board. You don't know how high it is. You can't tell if the pool is full. It could just as easily be filled with Jell-o as water. You have only heard about people doing it but you can't see anyone in any direction. Climbing up was a blur and you have no idea what to expect on the way down. All you know is...you are about to jump.

From **Dan Huang**
Navigator & Support Passenger

       It was slow Thursday afternoon. I was over at my girlfriend's place when I received the Facebook message from Ed. It simply went along these lines: "Hey man. Give me a call at (770) 633-XXXX when you get a chance. I couldn't find your number." I was curious and before you know it, we were on the phone. I was expecting to hear that he had a car in inventory that I might be interested in. At the time, I was considering an Evora, that is until I found out how terrible they actually are. Instead, the conversation asked about my plans for the next couple of days, which seemed strange to me. Finally, he tells me his grand plan - extending an invitation for me to partake in it.

       The only problem? We were going to leave tomorrow morning. I had less than twelve hours to decide. If I were interested, I would drop by his house to check out the car that night. I didn't have enough time to process the risk or gauge what I was getting myself into. After getting off the phone, I asked my girlfriend for guidance: "What do I do?" I asked, while going over all the dreadful possibilities that could happen.

       I vividly remember her answer, "I know if you don't do this, you will regret it." She said it in a way that only a supportive significant others could have - by having my selfish desires in mind while her eyes filled with worry. After hearing her answer, I texted Ed that I'll be by tonight to check out the car.

It was my first time visiting Ed's place. The moment I saw the CL, I didn't care about the stunning Orange LP640 Roadster that was its stablemate. I glanced over all the preparation and hard work that went into the car. The cockpit looked like mission control. It had all these devices that I had little to no idea how to operate. Ed reassured me that it was simple to utilize and that we'd get familiar with it on our way up. I still had my doubts though. After doing some test fitting and familiarization, I agreed to arrive Friday morning for our journey up, still unaware of the dangers. I just thought it would be a fun and interesting way to spend the weekend.

My first real scare (which questioned what I was doing) happened with the fuel leak. When the car pulled up next to us yelling "You're leaking gas!" everyone in the car (including me) went into a controlled panic mode. We had to get off the interstate and fast. Everyone was assigned a task when the car would stop. Luckily it was undramatic when we inspected what happened.

While still traveling up to NJ, I was able to watch at least half of *32:07* on the iPad, which felt like I was cramming for a test. I didn't know the history and significance of the Cannonball Run, US Express, etc. so I learned as much as I could as we headed for the start line. Seeing how much prep past Cannonballers did made me realize how insane this endeavour was.

When we got to NJ, we stayed at an awesome hotel right on the Hudson. It was surreal to walk out at night and see the NYC cityscape when ATL suburbs was the last thing I remembered seeing. It was a strange feeling to think that we were so close to NYC only to leave it the next day. This trip didn't feel like a vacation anymore - it became a mission.

After all the practice runs attempting to leave the city we had been up for ten hours already. Drained from the frustrations of how the streets of New York City had treated us and the qualms of our navigation abilities, I had no idea how we were going to manage the 30+ hour marathon ahead of us. Our morale was low. I remember Ed stepping out of TGIF to make a phone call to his wife, surely to explain how terrible the trip had been going.

When we got to the Target, things weren't much better. At this point, I realized that all my possessions were in a simple backpack and I could just Uber my way to the airport in order to wait for the next flight to ATL. However, since we made it this far, despite all our setbacks, I should at least give it a shot. This was the lowest part of the trip for me, because the desire to bail was greatest. Still, just as things would begin to unravel, they always seemed to compose themselves just enough to allow us to maintain forward progress.

I found it to be a great relief to hang out with Ash and his friends before starting our epic journey. They were really hospitable and gave us a boost of confidence moments before departure. All the worry I had built up faded after spending a few minutes in their company and lovely apartment.

Since I'm so used to working from home,

227

restroom usage was never a problem. However, when you are in a car for 30+ hours, you need to stay hydrated and you can't use the restroom any time you want. I rationed my water intake so I didn't use more than I needed or use the restroom as frequently. I tried to use the restroom on the shoulder once, but I guess i'm too shy to make it happen on the side of the freeway.

An unnamed shipping company's 18-wheeler almost ran us off the road. As we were about to make our pass on the left, the truck started moving into our lane. Ed performed admirably even when two of the CL's wheels were kissing unpaved road. All of this happened at speeds my Volkswagen GTI would top out at. I honestly thought it was over at that point, and not just the race.

Many times when I was tempted to close my eyes. I wondered if I would ever open them again.

Chapter 16 - Down the Hot Wheels Track

At 9:55 PM on Saturday, October 19, 2013 Dave Black, Dan Huang and I left from the entrance to the Red Ball Parking Garage at 142 E 31st Street and headed West. I was driving. The odometer of the 2004 Mercedes Benz CL55 AMG that we were in read just over 115k miles and the car was filled with every anti-police gadget that we could muster. We had sixty-seven gallons of fuel on board along with all of the food and supplies we expected to need for the next day and a half. There was no intention of stopping anytime soon.

Our goal was to pay tribute to the classic Cannonball Run route. That would minimize potential objection to the record and feel more legitimate to us. Dave actually downloaded Yates's book on his Kindle App as we were scouting around Manhattan earlier that day and read the first few pages. He had been leaning towards voting Times Square before but he immediately and wholeheartedly shifted his preference to the Red Ball. Of course I had to stop him from trying to read the entire book in the couple of hours we had left before leaving. I was comfortable with his exact level of misunderstanding of what the night and next day might look like. There was no benefit in making it any clearer at this point.

Around the same time that we left the Red Ball, Danny Landoni left the eastern border of Pennsylvania. This put him approximately seventy miles ahead of us and he began feeding us status reports by phone call and text. The Garmin navigation system would not process the entire route all the way to the Portofino so we had planned on programming in incremental checkpoints around the rendezvous points with the lead cars. Of course that only covered twenty percent of the trip. The navigation for this drive did not require many turns and I had each instruction broken down clearly in the drive plan spreadsheets prepared months prior.

We left and immediately found ourselves in gridlocked Manhattan traffic. As difficult as it was, we had all agreed to remain calm in the face of such a circumstance. It worked. We looked around at all of the timers, trip computers, and nav screens counting and continued the never-ending process of acclimating ourselves to the attitude of the drive.

We exited the Lincoln Tunnel in fifteen minutes. That was ahead of our twenty minute "turn around and restart" time threshold. We navigated through two toll interchanges using our EZ Pass and got onto 78. Seventy miles into the trip we were into Pennsylvania. That first stretch had taken us one hour and four minutes bringing our average nearly to the speed limit barely into the journey. The roads were rough and traffic was dense but we were threading needles through it with relative ease and little drama. I had worried about how long it might take to get our average up to a level permitting optimism but this felt amazing.

With the Danny-reported coast being clear, I pushed through Pennsylvania hard. The section through the Allegheny Mountains was a complete roller coaster. It was clearly marked but the road snaked through the terrain like an amusement park ride. The few other road users were mostly logging and transport trucks.

It is tough to describe the excitement of actually being at speed on a real attempt. Even though my nerves were still firing somewhat unpredictably, the cathartic rush of traction toward the nicely paved PA roads as well as my decade of dreaming was incredible. The massive elevation changes, long tunnels, and overlook views were probably beautiful.

We were not paying attention to those views and it was dark other than the excellent quantity of reflectors on the road. A few minutes into the state I was cruising consistently at over 140 miles per hour and Dan said his first words of the trip. "Are you serious? This is really how we are going to drive?" He said that 130 was the fastest that he had ever been in a car. That was changing. It was also not true.

Apparently, Dan had blocked out the last time that he had ridden in a car with me. Years prior I had a routine of meeting a group of customers at the dealership early on Sunday mornings for a group departure to our monthly cars and coffee gathering. We would scream onto State Route 400 headed North to the venue. It is a commuter highway so on the weekend mornings it is typically empty. One week Dan had asked if he could tag along and ride with me to the upcoming show. I obliged him and he joined me in a black 2008 Lamborghini Gallardo Spyder that we had for sale at the dealership. This must have been in late 2010 because it was before I bought the blue Gallardo from Kimmi the prostitute.

When we merged onto 400 it was a ghost town. I accelerated and found no reasons to let off.

When I looked down at the speedometer just before letting off the throttle we were doing an indicated 180 mph. That look on Dan's face in the rear view mirror of the CL as we tore through Pennsylvania was not entirely new to me.

There are very few similarities between how we drove on this trip and any regular driving on a daily basis. That is the crux of incongruence between the critical public perception of safety and the reality of being in the car. Strangely, this is some of the safest feeling driving I have ever done. When I go on a road trip with Megan, she is on her phone, playing with the radio, plotting the next ten years of our lives, or doing a hundred other things to distract me from the road. When I drive on my way to work I am still groggy, tempted to get to the dozen text messages that come in, and mindlessly proceeding through a route I could drive in my sleep.

This was not like that at all. It was just past midnight and we could not have been more alert. Further, my focus was completely on controlling the vehicle. The incoming data, phone conversations with Danny, interpretation of road conditions, and even checks on my personal well being were being done by Dave and Dan. We were our own mission control, dissecting every possible aspect of automobile operation in hopes of just making it through the next bend a bit quicker.

There was very little traffic on the road. We were passing a car every 5-10 minutes and there was plenty of space. We would slow to 100-125 depending on the radius of a turn but progress was great. The attitude in the car was much calmer than I had anticipated and the objective oriented discussion was extremely efficient.

There were times when it was clear that we were all sort of amazed with the speeds. I remember moving my hands along the steering wheel and noticing that I was gripping it so hard my palms were abrading the leather it was wrapped in. It was a good reminder to breathe, relax, and adjust my seating position. My med school friends had advised me that every fifteen to thirty minutes we should pump our legs and move our torsos in order to stimulate blood flow and minimize the risks of blood clots. The layers of unique problems to solve in this challenge never ceased to amaze.

It was 322 curvy miles across Pennsylvania and I averaged just over 100.6 mph. That was an average of 35 to 45 mph over the posted limits in the state. We were all surprised. There was nothing on the scanner, nothing on the CB to slow us down. Waze had no users ahead, Trapster reported nothing. Danny was right. Other than some early sprinkling rain we made it through the Turnpike exchange onto 470 and then to 70 without any reason to lift. Without the presentation of the endlessly possible reasons to slow down, none of us could really imagine any way to go any faster than we had been. The Pennsylvania roads were far from straight. How fast could we expect to go once the roads actually started to flatten out?

When we buzzed past Danny in his Volkswagen I had no idea the magnitude of what he had just done for us. We were literally going 20-30 miles per hour faster than I was expecting to on the high side and even though we actually dropped into the high 80's and low 90's when passing a few cars and navigating some of the harrier bends, it felt like we must have been averaging 150.

From **Danny Landoni**
Scout Driver - Pennsylvania

Who doesn't love a Cannonball Run? When I got a call from one of my most frequent partners in automotive crime that he needed me to fill in as a scout for a NY to LA record attempt it did not take long to answer in the affirmative. I didn't need to know who it was. It didn't matter how late it would be. I was there.

I spoke to Ed on the phone for about five minutes the Tuesday night before the run and he explained what he was looking for. Drive the speed limit or however fast I cared to and let him him know if I saw any cops, bad weather, traffic, or construction. We would stay on the phone and my goal was to make him press the throttle just a little bit harder. What better game could you ask for?

There was a little bit of drizzling rain early on but the drive was uneventful. Well once you get past the AMG Merc barreling through our fine state at such ungodly speeds. I was actually on the phone with Dave for most of the trip and the numbers that he was relaying from their mission control hardly made sense. I sped up a bit to maximize the window of my own utility for them but when they stormed by it was utterly surreal.

The strangest part was driving home. I am never one to shy away from whimsy of any sort. Spontaneous road trips will find no greater enthusiast but the experience of watching their tail lights disappear with such warp speed and for me to return to daily life was hard to wrap my head around. I wouldn't hear from Ed again until nine o'clock on Sunday when he said simply, "We did it. Thank you for all of your help."

What a weekend that was. I couldn't be any more proud to have been a part of the run and to have met Ed through the process. Learning more about him through the subsequent interviews and social media sharing has revealed that we have a lot more in common than being on that lonely stretch of the Pennsylvania Turnpike on a Saturday night in October.

I love stories like this because the illustrate the car hobby so well. It is not about speeding, although that is clearly a part of it. This idea is about solving the problems that face enthusiastic road users every day. The challenge is an exaggeration of my drive into work each day, of going to a grocery store, of going to see grandma. Ed met and conquered that challenge. I was just happy to be there to witness it.

Chapter 17 - Roadside Urination and Driver Changes

We were using the Mercedes Trip Computer's reset screen for each leg of the driving. To save my own sanity and to get a handle on what to expect I had reset it once we got out of Manhattan and up to speed. It was reading 104 mph for my first stint behind the wheel. It was too fresh to feel real. We were flying. The car was smooth, humming along and hitting 130-150 in each straight. The torque of the supercharged AMG V8 was surreal.

That set the tone. The sensation was unbelievable, particularly in America. I spend 99% of the time under the speed limit commuting around in life-sucking traffic in my 631 horsepower LP640. We forget quickly what these cars are capable of. Ze Germans would drive this way on the Autobahn every single day in a CLK320 cab because they can and the car can. Dave and Dan were particularly impressed. I think Dave made the decision to own an AMG car sometime within the first hour of the drive. I had to get him to shut down the browser on his phone and get off of Craigslist.

Some cars accelerate fast from a stop like a Chevrolet Corvette or a Lamborghini Aventador. Some handle with phenomenal composure around turns like a Porsche Boxster, V8 Ferrari or McLaren 650S. Other cars cruise comfortably at high speeds extremely well like a Rolls Royce, Bentley, or Aston Martin. This aged AMG beast was leaping from 80 to 130 with as much poise as I had ever seen out of a car and devouring every single curve. It was completely in its element and neither we, nor the car, were breathing hard. It illustrated what little margin of vehicle capability we deploy on a daily basis.

The attitude in the car was unique. It remained unlike any driving that any of us had ever done. While Dan's wide eyes had returned to their normal size there was an idle discussion around the data entering the car. A system reporting nothing was actually more valuable than it saying there was something to be afraid of. Clear meant hammer down. For the first few hundred miles of the trip that was it. We saw no cops, no traffic, no active construction, nothing. No reason to slow down, so we didn't. It was an invitation to test the limits of the car and of my driving. We accepted.

The cockpit dialogue was great.

"Nothing on the V1,
Passport clear too,
Waze clear,
road ahead bends left according the nav
        screen,
less than 30 degrees,
topography goes downhill after the next bend,
nothing on the CB,
scanner is quiet, clear ahead,
right lane empty,
move there,
slow Pontiac Sunfire in the left lane,
cut the brights to pass,
hug that shoulder and give her some extra
        space,
let's keep them from calling 911.
You are doing great.

Need any water?
Adjust your seat a bit, we don't need a blood
*   clot.*
Relax the grip on the steering wheel.
Car is under control.
You are clear to use the entire road on this
*   one, stay left.*
Get that apex.
Next straight looks like two miles or so.
Waze says there is a car stopped on the side
*   of the road but it looks stale.*
Clear on Trapster warnings for as far as I can
*   see.*
No traffic, no surprises.
Car sounds good, wow the revs are really low
*   at this speed.*
Give me five more miles per hour..."

It was fluid. It was inspiring. It was working.

We stopped for the first time in West Virginia. We pulled over to shoulder of the road, urinated there, and Dave took over the driving. There was some early stage fright on the part of the other two but my bladder was primed for eager evacuation.

My first shift was over. I had driven 394 miles in 4 hours 17 minutes for a 91.98 average. This was faster than the overall average of the Roy/Maher run. I truthfully had thought that it might take getting to New Mexico or Arizona to get the average where it needed to be to challenge the record. To have done it inside of the fourth state felt surreal. Further, if you take out the fifteen minutes that it took us to make it through the first two miles, the average was about 98

239

mph. That was strong for any leg of the trip, particularly the curviest leg with the most elevation change. Now it was time to let the road straighten out but we were entering Ohio, the strictest state in the country for speeding.

Chris Staschiak had staged at the West Virginia/Ohio border and left when we were about one hundred miles out. I put him on speakerphone for most of our interaction as a shallow way to reinforce the enviable nature of the opportunity he had given up. Regardless of the success of this drive it would edify the told-you-so conversations I might have the chance to enjoy in the coming days. It was clear as he meandered through his home state he regretted missing out on the mission the two of us had been plotting for the nine years since his first email to me. We were only in West Virginia for thirteen uneventful miles, we went through it in nine minutes including the stop. Average was 86.67 mph for the state, just fast enough for none of us to lose half of our teeth or elope with a cousin.

A 100-150 mile buffer between us and a spotter generally gave us a three hour closing time. They would go the speed limit and we would be 30-50 miles per hour over it depending on how encouraging their reports were. Watching the gaps shrink was exhilarating.

It worked well. There was certainly a risk that a hazard or speed trap could present in the gap between when the spotter would pass through an area and when we would arrive there but our efforts to build our own strategic Waze style group were proving successful. Even if we found reason to question the absolute utility of their permission to throttle up without fear of obstacle, the interaction was very useful. Knowing that this was a team effort and that there were other people investing their time into the project that day made the totality of the drive feel more substantial and exciting.

We were generally radio silent to uninvolved parties. Megan had gone to a Halloween party that night dressed as a zombie Alice in Wonderland. We exchanged a couple of text messages offering little more than, "We are ok. Progress is good. Haven't killed Dave yet." She had designated Dan as the "mom of the car" and he was supposed to keep her abreast of our progress and prioritize our well being over an unabashed strategy of winning at all costs.

She ended up spending the night with some friends. Megan knew more about what we were doing than anyone else in the equation because she had been the bystander to most of my decade of research and preparation. My interest in exotic cars and the record definitely predated her significance in my life so I suppose she had opted in. Still, I recognize that it was a challenging emotional place for her to be. Before we were dating, Megan's automotive expertise capped out at the ability to distinguish between a car and a truck. Now she was sitting by as her husband pursued one of the most infamous crowns of illegitimate motorsport. I was sure her parents were going to come around to approving of me now!

From **Chris Staschiak**
Friend throughout the planning process
Scout Driver - Ohio

Ed Bolian is one of those people that you are
proud to know, particularly if you are a motor-oil-for-
blood gearhead like I am. Put another way, Ed is out
of his f***ing mind. Normally when you get a bunch of
car guys together, the stories grow faster than
fisherman at a bar but when Ed says he is going to
get some dream car or do some crazy drive, you need
to listen. This madman will actually do it.

Like Ed, I was always consumed with the idea
of getting in a car and driving fast for a long time.
After I saw Ed on MTV in 2004 I had to get in touch
with him. The dialogue never stopped after that.

Initially we talked about plans to get together
and do some rallies. I did the Gumball 3000 in my
1973 Big Block Corvette in 2003 and 2004. In that
time I became familiar with Alex Roy, David Maher,
and Richard Rawlings - veterans of the same events.
Ed and I talked about Bullrun, Players Run, Gumball,
future iterations of the AKA Rally he had done, and
what cars we would work on. Ed was in the process of
starting his rental company and the kinds of things
that he dreamt up continued to amaze me.

Although our plans to drive in an exotic car
rally never came together, we became good friends
and spoke a couple of times per week. I will never
forget the experience of flying to Palm Beach to co-
drive back to Atlanta in the gorgeous Ferrari 360
Spider that Ed had just bought for the rental company.
I had been around supercars my entire life but this

was one of those bucket list experiences for any car guy. We blasted up the Florida Turnpike and onto 75. The best part of the trip, though, was just getting to know Ed more.

Ed and I grew up in very different ways, made different decisions, and looked at life from different perspectives. Figuring out the way that Ed Bolian thinks is like trying to tune a carbureted engine. It is elegant in its simplicity but complicated to master. I love the transparency that he uses to evaluate and explain the world. We each struggle in coping with life. His ventilation methods are a bit more off the wall than mine but I guess speeding across the country can land you in jail just as fast as me punching some loudmouth in the face.

The discussion of rallies quickly turned to breaking the New York to Los Angeles record. Ed has an infectious enthusiasm and he is the best salesman on the planet. He probably missed his calling as some cult leader or street mentalist. Speeding in big groups is pretty easy. If you are not out in the front of the pack, you are pretty safe. Generally, in my experience, these speeding efforts are in short bursts. Ed wanted to do this without a group of cars and he wanted to go very, very fast. Despite some reservations, he had me hooked.

As Ed started down the road of planning his first attempt in 2008, I was broke and busy. I let him continue to believe that if he footed the bill, I would come along. Fortunately, life got in the way for him too. I went to Atlanta to be a groomsman in his wedding and got to witness the chaos of the renter who crashed his Lamborghini and sold the Ferrari. Ed had me out hunting for the Ferrari in the valets of popular Atlanta restaurants as we would get reports of sightings but we could not find it. We were always just one step behind and Megan was growing more and more frustrated with anything about a car.

I have never seen anyone as cool under pressure as Ed. It is weird. I have talked him through some really strange and crazy life experiences and he is unbelievably level headed about it all. I suppose that is probably what lets you believe he can do such ridiculous things. Watching him try them and do them for the past ten years has made me a believer.

In 2012 when Ed decided it was really time I told him that I would go but that I was still in no position to throw in for my half of the bill. Seeing Ed accept that and push forward showed me he was in a new place with all of this. It was moving in the direction of NYC with or without me.

As the planning continued, my life got busier and it was become less likely that I would be able to get away for the time needed to make the attempt. It seemed like every time I talked to Ed he had just sold some Aventador or Gallardo. It seemed like he might have trouble finding the time too. Fall came and went. Spring 2013 came and went. Then Ed changed. He seemed to realize that it was now or never. I expect that may have had to do with a ticking clock of another sort.

I had pretty much bowed out at that point. Ed and Adam Kochanski were planning in full force and I would do anything that I could to help from my home in Ohio. I remember the call saying that they were going that weekend in October. I loaded up and got ready for a long night on the road. That feeling of a missed opportunity started to creep in. Ed still seemed to think that they were unlikely to break it on the first try so I would try to move back onto the active roster for attempt two in the spring of 2014. I still knew that you should never count this guy out. I would help as much as I could.

I left the OH/PA border when they were about 150 miles out. Their guy in Columbus had the flu so my plan was to lead them across the whole state. Dave had taken over in West Virginia and it sounded like their average was strong. Their first scout had served them well and I intended to do the same. Driving alone in the middle of the night in Ohio is boring. I can imagine their trip was not.

Ed and I stayed on the phone most of the time. There was very little to report. When they got about twenty miles behind me, they kept saying that they were getting small radar blips. I had not seen a single cop. Ed finally asked me to slow to 30-40 mph and try to let the cop catch up. They thought that the frequent blips were a sign that there was a cop between us, driving in the same direction. Eventually they seemed to figure out it was some interference between the multiple radar systems they were running and they got back on the horse.

I really can't describe the feeling of watching that car that I should have been in fly past at 140 mph. I could not be happier for Ed but I could not kick myself any more for having given up the chance to ride shotgun for that trip. I am sure that this will not be the last crazy story for Ed. I will definitely be along for the next ride!

Chapter 18 - Surely we can't keep this up

The full moon was brilliant. It was amazing how much it improved visibility. I had gone back and forth with different lighting solutions. The historic Cannonball and US Express cars looked like Group B Rally Cars with auxiliary lights mounted everywhere. Of course the halogen lights that they were supplementing had nowhere close to the capability of xenon and LED lights of modern cars.

I bought a huge 30" LED light bar that the advertisement implied could stand in for the capstone of the Luxor but we could not figure out a good way to mount it to the front bumper so I ended up returning it. It had been designed for off road use and was generally to be mounted along the top of the windscreen frame of a Land Rover Defender or Jeep Wrangler so I had also been concerned that it would have made the car more conspicuous than I wanted it to be. We opted to replace the headlights with a simple HID bulb retrofit kit and they were working great. We didn't need the high beams but we used them a lot of the time anyway.

We were not regretting our lack of a night vision system. I knew that some previous users were very proud of them but I had not been convinced that any of the available options would have permitted driving with the headlights off. None of them offered visibility beyond the headlights so it seemed like an expensive non-advantage. I also felt like if I was an unsuspecting Ohio-an and a Mercedes flew past me without its headlights on as I was headed to my bingo parlor, hair permanent salon, or Golden Corral family night, then I would be more upset than if the offender was using some illumination.

Similarly, I never had an occasion to deactivate the rear lights. The vigilance of three people meant we generally identified all of the hazards prior to passing them so visibility of the rear lights was a non-issue. The main concern that we had at the time was not missing a cop but having someone call the cops. A car in a compromised state was more likely to trigger a strange 911 recording than a car simply speeding excessively.

The duality of personality of the Mercedes AMG cars is probably the tallest feather in their caps. Even after nearly 100k miles of daily driving the cars over the years and scrutinizing the performance statistics in selecting the CL for the trip, I had no idea that it would perform with the unending ferocity the car had that night. We were tearing through the "course" with a mind blowing amount of speed.

"Surely we can't keep this up the whole time?" Dave said from behind the wheel. "Something has got to happen at some point, right?"

"Yes, but I think we are building up time fast enough that we might be able to recover from something pretty significant." Dan answered. I could see his mind moving. "Essentially, if we need a 90-95 average, we just need two minutes at 150 for every minute we are stopped. That would wash it out."

I was very proud of their newfound and already proficient Cannonballing skills. "Exactly, we just need to bank time where we can and continue to take advantage of these opportunities to go really fast. You are doing great Dave and it sounds like the course is clear." Foot to the floor.

Whatever groove can be found sustaining 130-140 mph speeds on a public road, we had it. The supportively ergonomic German seats were massaging away. The scanner and CB were quiet. The recently aligned car was carving a path through the generally deserted Ohio roads without a bit of trouble at all. Even Dan was amazed at how comfortable he was finding the space in the rear seat.

If it were any other type of drive, the back seat of the CL was unpleasant but on that occasion he had it arranged as his own mission control. He had an iPad browsing the area on Google maps, checking for the best options for our next gas stop, shooting an occasional text to Megan or Lisa Black, and offering the type of positive reinforcement to Dave that he soaked up like a reptile basking on a warm rock in summer.

Dave said, "Man, this feels incredible. It does seem like our luck can't last for 30 plus hours though. I just really hope it doesn't run out on this leg."

From **Dave Black**
Co-Outlaw

We slogged our way down 31st, passed the infamous intersection-of-misinformation, rolled down to the onramp to the Lincoln tunnel. We blasted through it, up onto I-95, and down to the exit at I-78 (the second blunder spot), merged on and then tore the fucking road up. My tactical directions (felt like it) were spot on, and Ed was setting an insane and somewhat scary pace through the light traffic. We got close to bumpers, cutting in the small gaps. I had a brief moment of "oh shit" during this time - the driving was the most aggressive I had seen during the trip. I was hoping this was just Ed trying to find his stride. I went back to calling tactics.

The drizzle of rain came as we worked our way through the New Jersey suburbs where we had been earlier. Ed kept a strong pace. Wipers off because the speed beading the water was more effective.

I kept my eye on the Garmins and on the car's trip computer to watch the average increase. The fifteen minutes in Manhattan made it take a long time to get the average up. I was waiting for the magic number "93" - this would be the moving average that we needed to maintain to beat Alex Roy's 31:04. Part of me believed that we'd slow down at that point, and even looked forward to slowing down. Once we reached 93 average, Ed kept pushing with speeds upwards of 130 mph. It felt really fast and a bit scary. Ed had the challenging task of snaking through the Alleghenies where we had fog and lots of sharp, blind curves. Whatever concerns I had before were gone

249

now. He was kicking ass.

The average kept rising to 103 before we stopped, peed, and switched positions. It was about 3 hours in and around the West Virginia border of Ohio. The driver change and pee break was a comforting experience for the fact that it was so fast, that I knew we could do many of them without even putting a dent in our time. I would never feel pressured to over-drive while fatigued.

As I sped up, I realized that driving has about a 25 mph lower perception of speed than being the co-pilot.

As we approached traffic or blind hills, we'd let off the gas and we'd cue each other to relax, and take a breath. We'd also use these moments to compliment each other's driving. For some strange reason, the compliments had an almost physical effect - like I could feel various feel-good chemicals pumping into my veins. It was strange. Ed gave great compliments but, then again, he is a car salesman.

Driving was easy and fun. I was in my happy place - behind the wheel, focused, and aware. The car was a dream to drive - solid, planted, smooth, comfortable seats with massagers. I tried to loosen my grip on the wheel, breathe and relax while apexing curves at 120 mph. My mantra was "smooooooooth." Once I hit the flat plains of Ohio, I hammered down.

Chapter 19 Continued

We had generally done a good job of identifying threats and strategically avoiding them. Generally. After the sufficiently high average I had managed through Pennsylvania, Dave was excited to take the helm. Chris was giving us great feedback through Ohio and we were breezing along I-70 at a phenomenal pace. I was on the lookout and Dan was keeping great tabs on all of the data coming into the car. The system, however recently contrived, was functioning well.

Dave was driving through Ohio near the Eastern outskirts of Columbus. The setting was starting to become more urban. He was in an excellent groove reaching and maintaining some very high speeds. I saw a car sitting in the median. It looked like a mid sized American sedan. I immediately said, "Brakes, brakes, brakes!"

"Oh yeah, I see the brake lights up there." Dave replied. The other drivers ahead were just then noticing the cop.

"No, Dave. There is a cop. Hit the brakes." I was certain that we were going to be bailing him out of an Ohio jail a couple of hours later.

He nailed them with all of the grace of a Floyd Mayweather domestic discussion. In fact, I think he warped the rotors. If not, that happened sometime soon after. He was traveling somewhere in the mid 130's when I first spoke up and I saw that he passed the cop still doing 95.

When we went by I could see the police officer looking into screen of the laptop mounted in his passenger seat, missing the spectacle of our sure-to-be glowing rotors just to his port side. I am not sure what he was looking at or what other work he was avoiding but that had been an extremely close call. We decided that "Cop" was a clear enough instruction. "Brakes" would be the understood response to such a command moving forward. I assume we owe a debt of gratitude to some newly updated pornographic web site for saving us there.

The gut reaction when you narrowly avoid going to jail is to slow down. In this case you can't do that. If you spend five minutes below 90 you need to spend ten above 100 to make up for the transgression. Dave shook it off well and got back on the throttle. Dan and I remained on high alert.

Radar detectors are fairly rudimentary devices. The best one that I have ever used is the Valentine 1 system. It uses arrows to indicate which sensor (front or rear) is getting the signal. There are certain beep patterns that you learn. Low intensity K or X band bogeys can be immediately dismissed as convenience store door sensors. An intensifying signal is moving towards you. Ka is usually a big deal and usually fixed.

VASCAR or radar mounted to a moving police car usually shows up as a very strong K band signal. Sometimes, though, you will get a rhythmic blip of signal up ahead that appears every 5-10 seconds and quickly goes away. That can persist for miles. It means you are approaching a cop a good distance ahead, moving in the same direction. Cruising through

Ohio we continued to get these. The driving protocol is to go as fast as you can to catch up and identify the threat while never cresting a hill or going around a blind turn without the ability to quickly brake down to within 10-15 miles per hour of the speed limit quickly and smoothly.

Chris had not reported anything ahead of us but I couldn't shake the feeling that we were about to blow past a cop coming onto his morning shift and trying to decide on Dunkin Donuts or Krispy Kreme for the morning freebie. I glanced back through the rear glass and I saw our second V1 mounted there. The sound had been turned off because it was visible to the driver and typically the noises were redundant. It was alternating with the windshield mounted one. They were tricking each other into thinking that the threat was there and reverberating within the car. I told Dan to turn it off and all went quiet. Frustrated with the oversight we accelerated hard to make up for 10-15 mins of taking it easy (not exceeding 100-110).

Chris was also making some great time through Ohio. I was planning on having him hand the baton to David Wiggins near Columbus but he still had some ground on us and Wiggins was still at home with the flu so we continued on.

The internet is full of clips of racing drivers doing mind blowing things in cars, stunt performers exercising car control that makes us all want to go to drifting school, and other displays of driving excellence. What Dave did in the early hours of that morning was something I had never envisioned. My afterthought of a co-driver knew so little about what we were actually doing that he wasn't even worried about the consequences. He was going through the most dangerous state in the Union for speeders so fast I thought my head was going to explode.

The police procedure changed once we got within twenty miles of Chris. f he were to come across a fixed speed trap he should pull over to the shoulder and ask the cop for directions. That way, he could be sure that the speed trap did not relocate between him passing it and us passing it. He could also distract the cop from noticing us as we breezed past with a quick, "Look, a squirrel!" Unfortunately, we never got to test that plan.

It was 227 miles across Ohio on 70. Dave averaged 108.10 miles per hour.

108! There is nothing else to say there. It was the single car street course Grand Prix of Ohio. Everything was working. Dave responded exceedingly well to both an invitation to competition and words of encouragement. I made sure to tell him when he made a smooth maneuver and to congratulate him on his great moments, of which there were many.

It didn't stop. It was 156 miles across Indiana on our route. He averaged an unthinkable 110.12 miles per hour. This brought our trip average up to 99.33 mph. The speeds were so great and so unrelenting that I honestly remember very little about the state. The periphery was a blur as the machine functioned perfectly.

Things were going well. When you look at a map of the route that we took and you see the time spent in the Southwestern United States, it is easy to guess the speeds carried in Oklahoma, New Mexico,

254

and Arizona will be the most intense. That is not the case. The midwestern states are usually highly patrolled but are great opportunities to build speed. We did.

It was upon noticing those averages when I realized that Danny Landoni, a guy I had never met in person and had only spoken to for about ten minutes prior to that night, had given me one of the most meaningful gifts I might ever receive. It was the key to this record. His comprehensive and encouraging reports of what lay ahead of us on that fateful night had been an invitation to drive as fast as I could everywhere we went. That driving challenged Dave into driving the way he had and thereby set the tone for the entire trip.

Chapter 19 - Excessive Oil Consumption

It was time for our first fuel stop. We were in Casey, Illinois - properly in the unremarkable middle of nowhere. We got out as high on adrenaline as we had ever been and admittedly it was a bit of a scramble. I gave Dan one of my credit cards to go to the far side pump and get it running while I negotiated the near side and got it into the auxiliary tanks. I think Dave had been supposed to remove the two caps on the rear tanks but the restroom became a higher priority. It did not matter to me in the slightest. He had earned it.

It was not surgical but it was efficient. The credit cards worked, the gas flowed, nothing caught fire, and we were back on the road in nine not-entirely-frantic minutes. While it remained difficult to judge how fast a three man, three tank, multi credit card, three bladder, delirious early morning pit stop was supposed to take; we were happy with the effort and result.

We made it 815 miles on approximately 64 gallons of gas. That was an average of 12.73 mpg. Going into the drive I had no idea how bad the fuel economy was going to get. Most of my short stints of high averages had been around 15 mpg but I knew that sustaining those speeds over these distances would be much worse. An average of ten or less would have required an extra fuel stop.

This was far beyond what we would need. That meant there was no reason not to press the accelerator a bit harder, if that were even possible. As the possibility of breaking the record crept in, I thought about areas where someone could have gone faster. With rare exception, we had gone as fast as our fast car would go. We encountered traffic but dealt with it handily. Very little was being left on the table. It still had the feeling of opening a Scrabble game with three seven letter words, tripling each score. Sure, it is going well but that can't possibly be sustained throughout the game.

I make no apologies about being competitive. I was not content to be so bested by Dave in this circumstance so it was hammer down when I got in the car for my second driving shift leaving the gas station in Illinois. The plan was to have my younger brother, Jeremy, lead us through the Illinois section. He had moved there a couple of years prior for a job with a consulting firm in Evanston. As it so happened his wife was out of town with their gasoline powered car, leaving him with their second car - a free-to-lease-after-tax-break Nissan Leaf. In addition to being my brother, Jeremy is my carbon offset. His fully charged 89 mile range was not of great use to us that night so he offered only emotional support.

Even without a spotter leading us, I was pressing hard. I was driving very fast but it was smooth and comfortable. We had elected to forgo considerable video during the trip. It had obviously been the focus of Alex Roy's drive as he was planning the documentary with Cory Welles but I decided against it on three grounds.

First - we did not need it as proof. We would have the traditional trifecta of toll receipts, gas receipts, and photos at the start and finish. We had cellular meta data for most of those photos, an evidentiary artifact unavailable just a few years prior. We had third party witnesses throughout the route and we had the easily digested third party tracking data. It also occurred to us that if were to be trying to fake the run, it would be easy for the employees of Waze, AT&T, or Trapster to check our accounts and find out we were lying.

Second - the risk of being pulled over, arrested, and having the car impounded was extremely high. Having accessible documentation of how fast we had gone along with when and where that had happened would be an invitation to take turns serving jail sentences in each of the jurisdictions we had passed through. The existence of such evidence felt scary even if we retained the Fifth Amendment privilege of not incriminating ourselves.

Third, I didn't want anyone trying to look good, spend time and energy telling a camera what was going on, and doing anything other than devoting attention to the road. When Lee and I had spent the 2004 New York to Los Angeles drive filming for MTV, that was the game. That was where our minds were. Get this shot, check the tape, is the sound working well, do you think they got that, oh there's the helicopter - do something crazy! It was too much. It was a distraction we did not need with this drive's intensity already turned up to eleven. We have a good number of short phone videos we can mince together into a bit of a highlight reel but I felt that was all that would be necessary.

I was going fast. The first 85 miles of my leg went by in just 44 minutes. That is a 115.91 average.

It was our fastest leg of the trip. We were impressed with each other and pleased that we were demonstrating ourselves to be the caliber of drivers to be competitive in this hallowed space. While we were up for it though, the car began to struggle.

We were a little over nine hours into the trip. Just after 6 AM local Central time, 7 AM Eastern. The car gave me an alert to add oil at the next fuel stop. Of course the car did not know that the next fuel stop was 700 of the hardest miles of its life away. I had driven cars with this 5.4 liter supercharged V8 over 50,000 miles in the course of the previous six years. I had never had one burn a drop of oil. This one was at the point of begging for some which must have meant that we were two or three liters low. I had only packed two.

We had kept the car running through the first fuel stop. The intention was to keep the engine and ignition on until we pulled into the parking lot of the Portofino the next day. The purpose of this was to keep the Mercedes on-board computer calculating as an additional form of verification. The tracking device was our end-all-be-all of evidence but it was very challenging to read due to the quantity of data it would record. It was useful in service as solid proof but the more photographable screens made for more compelling articles. The navigation system trip calculations and the on board computers would tell the story in a quick and digestible way.

The oil requirement threatened to foil that. The oil cap and filler neck go through the driver's side valve cover. I had no idea if I could open the cap with the car running. I assumed that it might spew oil everywhere. I called Charles, our Lambo tech. I called Brian, our service manager. I called my advisor from the Mercedes dealership. No one answered. We were 9 hours 4 minutes and 900 miles into a very intense drive and I did not want to risk the engine detonating in the middle of Illinois.

Dan grabbed the paper towels. I pulled over and electronically opened the trunk before shutting off the car. I set about releasing the cap and Dave grabbed a liter of oil. It was orchestral. As I poured the first I decided that it was probably a good idea to put a bit more in because there was no way that the threshold for an alert was just one liter. Dave grabbed the second liter we had packed. I put about a third of it in, tightened down the cap, and then we hopped back in the car.

The error message went off and all systems were go. Well, they were as much go as they were going to get. The police scanner didn't work at all. It had worked quite well when I was running it around my house but when Forrest and I had programmed it for this trip we had messed up. We went county by county for the entire route through a frequency database web site and put approximately 1,400 frequencies in. It was the most advanced civilian level scanner I could find but it simply could not get through all of them quickly enough to find and grab an active frequency before we moved away from it and the strength became useless. We needed to have separated the country into separate banks of frequencies.

The CB was not working very well either. It had enough knobs and we had enough inexperience to properly booger it up. We played with it and consulted a couple of YouTube tutorials but it did not improve much. The 90 degree flexing of the K40 Antenna was not helping at speed. It appeared based on some gurgled responses that we could broadcast fairly well but such capability did not feel very useful at the time.

We resigned ourselves to a simple idea. Messages from the CB or Scanner could only slow us down. Nothing could motivate us to go any faster. We were driving as fast as we sustainably could every single moment on the road. The occasional blip from the V1 caused a short lift but those were usually dismissed easily. We didn't see any cops set up as speed traps. I recall passing a couple going in the opposite direction where we either braked down to a less conspicuous speed or we used the cover from a tractor trailer to occlude their line of sight.

The logic says if you need an average in the low 90's and you can minimize your stops then you should be able to drive between 95 and 105 most of the time and wind up where you need to be. The idea of going balls out the whole way and only stopping for gas or cops is admittedly sexier but that was not my planned strategy. Alex and I had discussed the driving protocols that led to his time and it was generally apparent that Richard Rawlings and Dennis Collins had done something very similar, albeit with several short pulls up close to 200 mph mixed in for good measure and bragging rights. They cruised along a few miles per hour above their desired average and waited for the average to climb.

David Diem and Doug Turner had claimed to have used a 155-55-0 strategy in their drive, cruising at 155 mph the whole time, slowing to 55 to pass cops, and stopping for their five fuel stops and single ticket. In his dissection of their run, Alex Roy concluded that the fuel economy at a cruising speed that high failed to add up and resolved that they must have cruised at 95-110 the entire time. Although his final co-driver David Maher changed the strategy, initially Roy planned to rarely exceed 100 for more than a minute or two at a time. I had gone into the drive anticipating something similar.

The execution of our strategy had taken a turn due to the confidence imparted by some initial success and optimistic reports of what was ahead. We were pushing as hard as we could but it carried with it the looming feeling that it was on borrowed time. I knew that Alex had carried a high 90's average into the first Oklahoma toll plaza when he had a fuel system failure and I had heard that Rawlings was set to break 30 hours until he got caught in some miserable traffic in New Mexico. Would one of the slot machine wheels finally catch up to us and sideline our journey?

Dave had taken over driving once we added the oil and I got in touch with Tom Greulich who was going to lead us through Missouri. We left I-70 and took 255 around St Louis. We gave up the chance to see the iconic arch but we missed a lot of construction based on the instructions from Tom. He was extremely excited to be helping and loved the idea of the record. It seems like just about everyone who has been a car guy in the past forty years has at least contemplated the trip.

It was 172 miles through Illinois. Including the

two minute stop for oil, we did it in 1 hour 44 minutes at an average of 99.23 mph. Into Missouri we hopped onto 44 and continued along. Tom was feeding us great info but ultimately there was not much to report.

The Cannonball accounts and the US Express documentation talked a lot about the sensation of seeing the sunrise over St Louis. There were some wonderful aged videos in the Cory Welles documentary that beautifully illustrated the emotions that you feel coming out of the first night of driving. It is difficult to describe the confusingly demoralizing refreshment of not being in jail, the car still running, being on schedule, finally being able to see well, coming across a lot more traffic on the road, and still having about 1,700 miles to go. You want to be able to look at each other as you relish in the victory of getting there with a resounding "You ain't seen nothin' yet!" but in reality you just want to get some sleep and have a shower.

During the time that Tom was serving as our scout car I got an email. Since Dave was driving I looked down to see what it was. It happened to be a Facebook alert. That seemed like an appropriately mindless distraction from the day's work. It wasn't.

The email said that a friend had just tagged me in a post. Tom Greulich had a new status update - "Up early this morning helping a friend break some records - with Ed Bolian." I texted him immediately asking him to take it down. I knew that the risk was low but the last thing I needed was for one of his friends to know a cop and to put two and two together. If you browse through either of our profiles it becomes pretty easy to glean from a post like that we might be up to no good in a car. He obliged and we continued on our merry way.

Whatever pace the US Express guys were talking about when seeing the sun coming up in St Louis was far behind ours because it was still pitch black. I had never liked night driving. The visibility is worse and hazards are harder to see. In Atlanta there is traffic generally twenty four hours a day. My midnight runs around 285 in college were rarely in as much solitude as I would have liked. Our speeds during the course of the previous night had actually harkened me back to one of the first group drives that I organized at the dealership.

I called ten customers and told them that we were meeting at a restaurant near the start of a less trafficked state highway at 11 PM. We ate quickly and snapped some pictures of the rainbow of assembled Lamborghinis. We had a newly released Aventador, two Twin Turbo Gallardos with over 1,000 hp, and a handful of regular Gallardos there including my blue ex-Kimmi-the-prostitute mobile standing tall in the company of cars with indistinguishably less sordid pasts.

We started a conference call and everyone was using Bluetooth. We sent a guy in a BMW M3 out ahead and all hung back. We spent the next two hours taking turns getting about 2-3 miles worth of clearance and blasting off for as long as we felt like holding the accelerator down. I hit 185 mph with a measly 492 hp. Interestingly the stock horsepower output of a 2004-2005 Lamborghini Gallardo is exactly one less than my CL55 AMG. The guys with more hp were tickling 200 and shooting flames all over the place on each shift and lift. It was an amazing night where no one got hurt, no cars were injured in the making of the production, and no one who could have gotten upset ever knew about it.

That was the way that Brock Yates and Dan Gurney had described their success in the 1972 Cannonball Baker Sea to Shining Sea Memorial Trophy Dash. Apart from the one ticket Gurney received, they claimed they blasted across the country at speeds up to 172 mph and that no one even knew about it. They said they broke all of these laws that they were protesting against and no one was the wiser, certainly no one had been hurt.

Either they were lying or we were doing things a bit differently. As the sun eventually came up and the roads become more congested, we had to maneuver the car more to maintain pace. Dave and I had some lengthy discussions about the posture of the car and strategies to minimize the risk of having the bystanding motorists call the police. I am sure that despite my best efforts there were a lot of interesting 911 calls as we also set the record for getting flicked off the most times in a 24 hour period. We said that an improvement we would have made was the addition of a scrolling digital message across the rear right section of the bumper with some sincere sounding apologies. Admittedly, reading something on a car at a 50 mph differential is difficult regardless of how upset you are.

Perhaps Yates had been correct and this was just a way the changing landscape of motor vehicle traffic in America was manifesting itself. They simply spent more time with no one around. Of all the interesting statistics that show how different 1970 was from 2013, one that I think it most interesting is the number of households. In 1970 the US Census reported that there were 63.5 million households. In 2010 there were over 114 million. They were not all in urban high-rises so the geographic distribution of Americans was much more expansive. I think the longest we went without seeing a car was less than five minutes. For the 70's crowd it could have been an hour.

I tried to make sure that there was no steering input as we would pass a car, the same way that you would treat a slalom cone. That meant there would be minimal suspension lean perceivable outside of the car which would trigger less anxiety from the people we were passing. It seemed to work.

Dave continued to drive through Missouri after picking up in the stop for my stint that had been abbreviated by the oil top off. The system was working. I was constantly giving him feedback that he was doing well, the coast was clear, and it was safe for him to stay on it. The most useful instruction that I recall giving him was that "Dave, I am going to make you drive 10 mph faster everywhere." It was imperative for the passenger to take ownership of how fast the driver could go. When I did that and took the onus of making more frequent instructions and in essence clearing him for acceleration more often, he responded beautifully.

I had left Adam Kochanski with the login information for the GeoForce tracking device. When morning came back in Atlanta I got a text from him.

266

He said, "You guys are really flying. You just need to average 90 and you will break it. It is actually a little bit below that but I am not going to tell you what that is. Keep it up!" There was no bad weather to report and the construction monitoring sites he could check were still clear.

In 2 hours 31 minutes of driving, Dave averaged 105.30 mph on his 265 mile shift. About 11 and a half hours into the drive we stopped to change drivers near Springfield, Missouri. I took over to finish out that tank of gas. I continued out of Missouri and into Oklahoma along the Will Rogers Turnpike and got onto 40. Although the strain of navigation had not been difficult, it was quite a relief to have made it to the road where we would spend the lion's share of the trip mileage. As ridiculous as it sounds, it was like navigating the twisty bits of a race track and finally making your way onto the front straight. However hard you have been pushing, it had to be tempered by not wanting to overrun a turn. Now it was hammer down to an even greater extent.

There was a lot of anxiety at the first toll plaza. Dave pointed out the shoulder where he had seen the blue BMW M5 pulled over in the film. I had ordered toll passes for all areas we would pass through (stupidly in my personal name) so we did not have to stop. We breezed through the toll plazas maintaining a reasonable speed. Many states issue average speed tickets by mail when you pass through toll plazas in less time than you ought to. Fortunately none ever showed up.

Megan had slept in after the Halloween party

and did not make it to church that Sunday morning. I got a text message from the guy that taught our newly married Sunday School class with me asking if I was going to be there to help. It occurred to me that I had not told him I was going to be otherwise indisposed that morning. I was driving and we were not responding to most of the text messages, emails, and calls so I let him figure that out on his own.

I was worried about Oklahoma and Texas. The last time I had driven through there in this way was on the 2004 rally and I had gotten five tickets. I eventually got them disposed of but they don't like speeders from other states in Texas. I think they don't like people of any kind that aren't from Texas. I had generally familiarized myself with the speeding and reckless driving laws around the country but had not dwelt on them too heavily. The monster under your bed is a lot less scary if you never think about what he actually looks like.

The five ticket day had been exceptional for me. I don't speed often in routine driving. I was pulled over near my house the other day for going 66 in a 45 that I had always thought was a 55. When the officer approached and revealed my misunderstanding about the speed limit, I asked for some consideration of the fact that I had not had a ticket in about seven years. When he returned to the car he said, "You know, nines times out of ten, when someone tells me that it is a lie but it has actually been ten years since your last ticket. You have a nice day now." He let me go.

As I actually thought about it, the last ticket I had received was driving to see Megan at the University of Georgia to go out to dinner on the three month anniversary of our first date and it had been a decade since then. The irony abounds.

I do get pulled over a lot but it is frequently just for a police officer to see whatever car I happen to be driving. Getting pulled over in a sports car is fun. There are some easy answers to the normal barrage of cop questions.

"Sir, do you know how fast you were going?"

"Not really officer, I really wasn't trying to speed though."

"I clocked you at 105."

"Well for whatever it is worth, I was not trying to go that fast. If I were, it goes way faster than that. The car is nuts. Would you like to drive it?" Most cops are car guys but they aren't allowed to drive civilian cars while on duty.

"Oh, I can't do that. Besides my belt and gun would hurt those pretty leather seats."

"I am not worried about it, I will be happy to hold your gun." This usually generates quite a good laugh.

"Not today son."

"Well here is my business card, call me sometime and we can go for a ride when you are off duty." An invitation to pick this conversation up at a later and non-prosecutorial date.

I have engaged in that exact exchange many times and always gotten off with a warning. Only one has ever taken me up on the return trip for a ride. I was giving press rides at The Master's Golf Tournament in Augusta, Georgia in a rear wheel drive Grigio Telesto Gallardo LP550 Bicolore. I was sliding around turns on residential streets and generally misbehaving. Before long every cop in Richmond County showed up and I began my routine exchange. After being dismissed and asked to keep it down, one deputy returned a few hours later for his ride. He told me that he knew a road that we could get some speed on and it was just around the corner.

That corner was about twenty five minutes away and I obliged him although my reluctance increased as the trip lengthened. He told me he had been 180 mph in a Corvette ZR1 there. That was interesting. Chevrolet brought the ZR1 badging back in 2009 with a supercharged version of the C6 body cars. They were very quick but I fancied my Italian Bull to be up to besting it. As we drove I asked the cop how the surface of this road was. He told me that it had been awhile since he had been there so he wasn't sure. This was in 2011 so that struck me as being strange. I said, "Really, what year was the ZR1?"

"1991." He said calmly.

"You mean you haven't been to this road in twenty years? How far from here is it?"

"Oh, it was 95 or 6. It is just around this bend." This time he was telling the truth. As I rounded the next bend in the Southeast Georgia road, I saw it.

"That is a bridge. Bridges are very bad places to speed. They have crosswinds."

"Oh we will be fine, let's see what it can do!"

"That is also a long bridge. We might be able to go fast but that bridge goes into South Carolina and I have a feeling that whatever jurisdiction you enjoy while wearing your work clothes ends halfway along it."

"Oh yeah, but if we need to run I know all of the good places to hide," he offered reassuringly.

"That is not a contingency I was planning on while going top speed hunting with a police officer riding shotgun." I had voiced my concerns and given the little bit of traffic that was on the bridge time to clear. Despite many reasons not to, I took the cop on a ride out onto the bridge. We clipped along to about 160. The air was stable and the surface was fine. I turned the car around and stopped in the street as the single oncoming car made its way into Frank Underwood nation.

I floored the Lamborghini and spun the rear wheels into third gear with the traction control on but limited. I pushed on, redline shifting, and perceiving the childish ear to ear grin of the portly, middle-aged Sheriff's deputy. We ran out of bridge before I could hit 200 but I know we hit the happy side of 190 on the Gallardo's difficult to read speedo. He was thrilled.

I drove him to his house on the outskirts of Augusta where his wife and young daughter were waiting to photograph him getting out of the car. As I climbed out of the cockpit to greet them, his wife said, "Sir, you have made his life. I bet once a week he says something about that black Lamborghini that those purty gals drove in the *Cannonball Run* movie. Is that what this is?"

"Yes ma'am it is."

Why not roll with it?

Texas and Oklahoma both have a rolling statute of limitations. That meant that while I would generally be free from being subject to arrest in those states one year from the time of incident, that one year had to be spent in each state for it to expire. I had no intention of spending that amount of time in either so it was a sobering reality to think that I might be subject to arrest in each state for the rest of my life. Hopefully that was longer than the rest of this day.

Oklahoma was the only state where we encountered any real construction. There were three areas where the highway bottlenecked down to a single lane and we had to drive 50-60 mph behind a tractor trailer for 3-5 miles at a time. Fortunately the general traffic level was low enough that there was not a buildup of congestion in the merging areas. The times of being forced to go slow were a great chance to grab some water, loosen the grip on the steering wheel, and adjust your seat a bit to avoid cramping. It did seem, though, that I found myself in the driver's seat for every single frustrating leg we faced.

The thought that many people seem to have when they imagine what it is like to drive this fast for so long is an eventual numbness to it. It is true when you drive 130-150 mph and slow down to 100 it feels like you could get out and walk faster. That being said, the perception that we were grossly exceeding the speed limit never left me. The fear of arrest did. The recognition that the outcome of getting pulled over going 100 or 150 was likely the same actually served as some solace in keeping your foot in the pedal for a bit longer and pushing a bit harder. When conditions permitted, and they usually did, we were still flying. The sensation of continuously flipping a coin and it landing on heads every single time never left either. Surely there was a tails coming.

Hygiene was an issue. I had purchased some Neutrogena grapefruit scented facial cleansing cloths. The gods have never felt something so amazing. "Pass me a grapefruit" was a popular and exciting request to make. Halitosis was also an issue. The following scenario happened more than once.

"Dave, would you like a piece of gum?"

"No, I am good." He would reply casually.

"Dave, I would like you to have a piece of gum."

I drove 305 miles. It was the longest driving stint that either of us took for the trip. Due to the traffic and construction it was actually the least challenging leg while being the most frustrating. We stopped around Yukon, Oklahoma and Dave took over. My average for the leg was 94.82, respectable for the amount of traffic and the daylight hour driving. Our averages were consistently ten miles per hour slower during the day than we had seen the previous night.

Our roadside potty break took less than ninety seconds. We praised the decision to make side of the road pit stops and driver changes rather than staying in the same position for the entire tank of gas. I had always planned on it but then I would start looking at the math of being stopped for 2-3 minutes at a time and would question the idea. Doing it again I would stop every 2 hours/200 miles regardless of condition.

Dave took over and got us to our second gas stop.

From **Adam Kochanski**
Eye in the sky, GPS Witness

Ed Bolian is a bit of an enigma. You never quite know what to make of him or the things he talks about. I met Ed a few years ago through some mutual friends at the car shows that we both frequented. The cars that he drove added to the somewhat larger than life persona. We could never really tell if he was driving cars he owned or if they were from the dealership but Ed was always building his brand around the outrageousness of Lamborghini and the exotic car driving lifestyle.

Despite the anticipated hip hop artist, gold chain, white blazer, womanizing, pet alligator persona; Ed was different. He always left the car shows on Sunday mornings early to go to church. Our wives were very much alike and got along well. Ed went out of his way to invite me and many other guys to all of his events. He welcomed us into the dealership to drive cars and enjoy them alongside him. Ed was and is invested in improving the landscape of local car culture in Atlanta.

One of the first conversations that Ed and I had about cars was about his interest in Cannonball. I had seen Alex Roy at a local stop on his book tour and actually have a signed copy of his book somewhere. I knew of the idea and had seen the old movies. What car enthusiast hasn't fallen in love with the idea of taking a special car out and opening it up on a long deserted interstate?

Car guy conversations are full of people claiming that they are just about to go out and buy some crazy car, how fast they drove the night before, or what their grandiose plans were with their next project. You always need a serious grain of salt to endure the fluff. Ed seemed different. The first time he came over to our house for dinner, he and Megan were driving a blue Gallardo that was a bit rough around the edges but was still loud enough to make all of our neighbors ask what was going on the next time our paths crossed. When he talked about the NY to LA drive, it was not the tone of someone dreaming. It was the tone of someone planning.

Ed insinuated that his co-driver, a guy named Chris, was likely going to back out. He asked if I was interested in coming along. It was a strange request, one I was enthusiastic to receive, but a strange proposal based on the amount of time I had known Ed. I told him that I would talk to my wife about it.

Ed is overly trusting. It might come from the need to treat everyone as a buyer in the car business. It might be because he is a very trustworthy person himself. It might be from an optimism in humanity that most people people have grown cynical of. I say that Ed is trusting because he takes pretty much everything I say at face value. The skepticism that is usually necessary in car guy exchanges never seemed present in him. It is probably because Ed truly makes it seem like anything you want to do, any car you want to buy, any ridiculous financing arrangement - is possible. Normal driving seems to be a fairly mindless task for Ed. He calls me on his way to work at least a few times per week and I try to answer. Every time we hang up, though, I feel like I am on the cusp of renewing my home equity credit line and buying a Ferrari F430 Scuderia.

Ed had not purchased the CL when I met him. He was daily-ing the Gallardo. When he got into hardcore planning mode in 2012, we looked at every possible car option. I liked some of the Audis - the 03 RS6 and 10+ S4s were great on fuel, had reached a nice price point, and made good power. There was a ton of aftermarket options for them and it seemed good. Ed kept coming back to the AMG cars but even with Ed footing the bills, I was terrified at the cost of maintenance. I am a BMW and Porsche guy. The Panamera Turbo was too much and the M5 was out. The M3s I loved were too small and the newer ones were too much money to tear up. Ed started to get aspirational and look at Bentleys but then the orange Murcielago came along and that was over. Ed quickly bought an AMG car and started sending me links to Amazon shopping carts.

My wife and I had been trying to get pregnant for a while so I knew that wild card loomed. When it happened, I knew that I was going to have to let Ed down easily. I really didn't. He took it very well. He seemed used to having people back out of this pursuit. There were no hard feelings and he was as welcoming as ever for me to stay involved.

As the final team came together, I went over to Ed's house on the Thursday night before they left. I had met Dave Black at our local events and Ed had described his character to me well. I met Dan Huang for the first time that evening. It was a motley crew for sure. It was also the strangest emotional environment I think I may have ever stumbled into. No one seemed to know what to expect.

276

When they set off, Ed gave me the login credentials for the GeoForce Tracking Site. As they set off I checked in on the feed. It took them a few minutes to get out of the city and into New Jersey but once they did, it was all business. Ed was behind the wheel and was reaching 140-145 in each straight and barely slowing down for the turns. In his typical foot-in-the-door negotiation that we all love, Ed had said that he did not expect the driving strategy to dictate many excursions beyond 110. With the goal of a 93-95 mph overall average to beat Alex Roy's time of 31:04, that seemed like all that would be necessary. Clearly that approach had been thrown at the window somewhere in the Lincoln Tunnel.

I texted Ed to let him know that the signal was good and the updates were frequent. It was feeding data every minute or two. There would be occasional signal gaps of 3-4 minutes but with each ping it seemed like they were going faster and faster. It was some very impressive pace. Eventually I dozed off to sleep with my ipad set to the web address for GeoForce on the nightstand next to me.

When I woke up around 8:30 AM on Sunday morning, I refreshed the site. They were already in Missouri. The data from the tracking software showed that they were cruising along at 136 mph. They had been on the road for ten and a half hours. I plugged in the coordinates from the plotted point on the map. I set that as the destination with the Red Ball starting point in Google Maps. They had traveled 1,055 miles and were in a town that the tracking software said was Rolla, Missouri. 1055/10.5 meant that they had a

100.48 mph average. I did that math a few times because it just seemed impossible. A 100 mile per hour average! That seemed possible for an hour or two, but for 10 hours?

I reversed the calculation with the starting point where they were and the destination, the Portofino. They had 1,756 miles to go. 31:04 minus 10:30 meant they had 20.56 hours to finish. That meant that they only needed to average 85.38 miles per hour to break the record.

I texted Ed that they were doing great. I sandbagged it a bit and told them that they only needed to average 90 to break it. I was amazed, bummed to not be there by his side to continue on to what was sure to be an epic accomplishment, but amazed nonetheless. I spent the next day routinely checking in and doing some math to see how the trip was going. They didn't slow down. They didn't miss a beat. I really can't explain the thrill of seeing it happen one dot at a time.

I do a lot of track days in my cars. Each time, you show up, go through a drivers meeting, and see some new guy fresh out of the showroom in his new M3 or 911. They are dressed head to toe in the latest Alpinestars Stig suit, gloves in hand. They go out on the first lap and spin the car. More balls than skill. More talk than delivery. Ours is a world of careful social media glimpses into daily life, well manicured images of our diversions and recreations painted for the world, and an existence designed to be inoffensive while still self praising. This wasn't that at all.

This was real Coke. Nothing diet, nothing zero

calories. It wasn't watered down. It wasn't tempered for the masses. He didn't go out and buy a new Ferrari or BMW F10 M5 sledgehammer for the job. He did it by himself with the rest of us wondering if he was actually serious about it. He chose as much of an underdog car as could be imagined for the drive. He made no excuses and took no prisoners - just two guys who I had seen just a few days prior with absolutely no idea what they were in for.

What a trip.

Chapter 20 - Beating the AMEX Algorithm

We stopped for gas the second time in Groom, Texas. We had driven 1,667 miles in 16 hours and 47 minutes. Our overall average was 99.32 miles per hour. That tank of fuel had taken us a preposterous 852 miles. We were only 7.83 miles behind a 100 mph overall average. The moving average was certainly dropping as we continued through the day. The prolonged 130+ jaunts were proving more challenging and without scout cars after we had left Tom in St Louis. We had left Oklahoma with an in-state average of 94.78 mph meaning that Dave had maintained almost the exact pace that I had in his most recent 260 mile stint.

Before the run I had been concerned that there would be a glaring disparity between the pace of my driving and Dave's. I was pleased to be proven so wrong. I do not think either of us thought we could have done any better than the other at any moment. I will say, and I believe that Dave would agree, that we went faster on some of the legs when he was driving and I was navigating than when the roles were reversed. We would also agree that the reason for the slight discrepancy was the stream of instruction coming from the passenger seat. When Dave had finished his sessions he needed to rest. I am sure that I needed to rest more than I realized but he made a better point to do it. That meant I found myself doing my own cop spotting a bit more often. For that reason I was happy to be taking some of the more heavily trafficked and technically difficult sections.

Our first stop had been nine minutes of nearly

perfect execution. This second one was not that. Dave and Dan immediately scattered to the restrooms, both appearing fairly delirious. When I opened the trunk I could see a few errant drops of gasoline accumulated around the line coming out of the pump for the passenger side tank. When I swiped my credit card it was declined. Darn it.

I ran inside and told them both to get outside to help. Dan grabbed the duct tape from the rear tire storage seat and went to work on the fuel line. I was swiping every card in my wallet trying to get them to take. A MasterCard that I seldom used finally did the trick - priceless. I told Dave to swipe his on the opposite side of the pump. I saw the slight hesitation as he pondered the cost so I punched him very hard in the face [in my head]. I don't remember why I walked behind the building and peed on a dumpster in the parking lot but I did. There was probably a line or something.

That stop took twelve minutes. It was our longest time stationary by a considerable margin. When we got situated in the car I had two emails, one pertaining to each of the two American Express cards that I carry. Fraudulent charges were suspected. My cell phone rang. It was AMEX. The representative reminded me they had rejected two charges in Groom, Texas on my cards. They had seen the previous charge in Illinois just eight hours prior. There is a fairly advanced, but not quite advanced enough, algorithm that they use. It told them since neither charge was near an airport and the distance traveled was done too quickly to have been done by car they automatically declined the charges.

I did not offer any explanation as to why these were in fact legitimate charges but I reassured her that my cards were not going to leave my possession for the next twenty four hours and asked that she approve any and all charges made to the account. "If I order every single as-seen-on-tv product on the shopping network from a telephone in Mongolia just assume I needed that rainbow of Snuggies and many, many expandable hoses. Let them send them on!"

As we went through Texas it was starting to become clear just how tired we both were. I had dozed off for about fifteen minutes during an off shift the first night and the adrenal high was starting to peter out. I tried to rest as Dave drove earlier but we were monumentally faster when I was on alert offering him advice on where, when, and how to pass. This was a team sport and you never got to stop rowing for very long.

The panhandle of Texas was uneventful except for a sport bike that tried to stay with us for a little while. This added an element of conspicuousness and danger I did not want. The last thing we needed was for me to bump into a motorcycle changing lanes. It also made it look like we were racing, a much more unpleasant offense than speeding. We came upon a red compact car that took offense to the motorcycle and made an aggressive swing at it. This enraged the motorcycle who sped off. The driver made the same move at me as I passed but we proceeded away without issue.

I had packed the binoculars but they had been particularly useless. The stories of stabilized scopes were intriguing but our line of sight was unlikely to be radically different than that of a static police officer so the visual strain and the distraction from all of the other data sources sounded like quite the tradeoff. They were also really expensive and I wanted to keep a few aces in the hole in case I simply wasn't anywhere in the ballpark of the record on this first attempt and needed to add to the arsenal.

I bought the returnable binoculars to have on hand if needed but when I looked through them it was a beer goggles experience. I had assumed that would be the case, hence the beautifully preserved Bass Pro Shops original packaging and receipt back at home on my office desk. I had not anticipated the visual acuity of Dan Huang. I generally have a savant level ability to identify cars based on shapes, lights, and other visual cues and although this was the pre-Lasik Ed, my corrected vision was very good.

He was on an entirely different level. I was flabbergasted at his ability to see and read this stuff. I could barely tell what color a vehicle was by the time he was reading us the license plate and clearing it as being civilian rather than police. Phenomenal stuff. I was told by an eccentric high school teacher once that there was a job pertaining to the farming of chicken eggs that was only staffed by Asians. It involved focusing on a spot on each egg to determine fertility. He said white people were incapable of doing it. I am not sure if that is true and I am not sure if it is racist but I was starting to believe it based on Dan's performance.

Dave's wife, Lisa had been fairly radio silent throughout the trip. Megan had texted a bit to Dan reminding him to take care of me. Dave's phone rang in Oklahoma and it was Lisa. It interrupted one of the applications that we were using and it was in one of the passenger side mounts so I answered it. She knew enough to have a "see no evil/hear no evil" mentality about it so she simply asked how things were going. I told her that they were going well and that we were cautiously optimistic. She said, "Do I want to know how fast you guys are going?"

"I doubt that but let me say that we are very proud of your husband and his speeds are sufficient." That felt like the right word.

There was a moment in Oklahoma where Dave as driving. I looked down at the Garmin screen which had been estimating our arrival time based on its projection that we would average the speed limit for the rest of the trip. It read 2:04 AM. In my head we had left at the 10 PM target. That meant that after the time change, if we had simply averaged the speed limit for the rest of the drive we would match the Roy/Maher time of 31 hours 4 minutes.

It was an unreal sensation, one I had been entirely unprepared to experience. Getting the average over 90 mph had felt good. This felt euphoric. We had a shot. Now we just needed to not get arrested or break the car.

Our speeds were continuing to be about 10 mph slower during the day. It had nothing to do with testicular fortitude, fear of incarceration, or capability; it was traffic. There were just a lot of cars and trucks on the road. Each interaction with one was a time when we had to slow down. We had generally stopped caring how fast we passed people. If the lane was clear we did not slow down.

I had not been sure how we would get home. Since I had seriously felt that there was a great chance we would get through the midwest and pull out the white flag I had not made any prior arrangements. If we made it all the way to Redondo Beach, shipping the car home would be expensive, as would three last minute flights to Atlanta. We decided that if we broke the record, a treat to ourselves would be to ship the car home and fly. If we failed, we would have to endure two more days of each other's' company in the confinement of the CL. At this point, as business oriented as the drive had been, our patience was worn fairly thin.

Dave had enlisted a friend to assist us at the last minute to lead us through New Mexico. Jules Doty drove a gorgeous white Porsche 964 and provided us some excellent insight as to what we could expect. Dave and Dan were feeding me great intel from the on board equipment and we were making excellent time. We had seen very few cops up to this point but there was a fairly intense window of police activity coming up. The spotter's advice was "Ignore the cops on the left side of the road...it's a drug bust...they won't even notice you."

As we drove past he was clearly right and the local police force seemed interested in seeing what the suspect's car would look like with the interior completely removed. While it felt like we had generally blended in through the early part of the trip, I believe that our car and Jules's Porsche were the only non-American cars in the state of New Mexico.

As we had gotten away from the more

285

populated areas of Texas and New Mexico I had started to get a few chances to air out the car more aggressively. Earlier in the drive Dan and I had spent some time resetting the on board computer data and watching it calculate the fuel economy at 100, 110, 120, 130, 140, and 150. It got down to 11 on the higher end of that spectrum but we calculated that we could not go fast enough to get bad enough fuel economy for it to matter.

I was accelerating as hard as we had into clearings throughout the trip. The car's five speed automatic is extremely robust, in fact it was the same one that made its way into the much more powerful Mercedes McLaren SLR between 2005 and 2009. It's control unit interpreted the stronger throttle inputs as a request to downshift more readily, hold the gears longer and execute the shifts a bit more violently. It made Dan and Dave a bit nervous. They reminded me that even if it did not foil our fuel economy for the trip trying to spend that much time above 140 mph would not do us any good if the car did not get us there. I agreed to slow the acceleration and give the car some time to rest.

I drove 260 miles which got us into New Mexico. My leg took 2 hours 42 minutes at an average of 96.30 mph. We were finding some less populated areas of the southwest and were moving through at just over the pace required to avoid getting addicted to crystal meth. I gave up the reins near Encino, NM and Dave was ready to go.

He fatigued quickly. No one could blame him as we had been on the road for about 20 hours. We cut his trip short at about 210 miles in a completely mutual decision. The average for that leg was Dave's slowest at 92.65, still phenomenal given the circumstance and higher than the average of any other cross country drive ever. Even with the sub 100 averages we were seeing in shorter shifts during the day, we were still carrying a moving average that was well over 100. It was a testament to how fast the first night had been.

The biggest symptom of Dave's fatigue was not slowing down or dozing off - it was frustration. Every time a truck or another driver would pull out in front of our car Dave would respond with a torrent of expletives and a clearly confounding level of anger. I told him on several occasions that we would go faster for longer if he would relax. His response was always that he actually was relaxed but I begged to differ. Your mouth and brain cannot be that disconnected. It was a constant struggle but he began to improve over time. He completed his driving shift, Dan had dozed off in the back, and I took over. Dave was ready for some time to rest.

I do not enjoy the use of profanity. I feel that Jerry Seinfeld said it best when he said that "Profanity is a great shortcut of comedy and the reason I don't use it is that I am concerned about the joke quality suffering." I feel the same way about daily speech. If I can't make my point using acceptable and un-ambiguous language then I feel the need to try again in my head. Deliberate and thoughtful speech also makes people seem like they are more confident in what they are doing. That serves me well professionally.

Dave's reaction to a Buick Lesabre pulling out

in front of him was not offensive to me in the least. It simply revealed to me that he was less composed in that moment at the helm of the Mercedes than I would have liked him to be. At that stage of the drive we were both much more fatigued than we let ourselves admit. Cues like this were worth noting because we needed to help each other relax and stay focused. It was easy to see times when that attention was wavering.

The I-40/Route 66 portion in New Mexico had been under construction for almost a decade. Jules had made a point of saying the construction was over and the people responsible seemed pretty excited about it as well. There were signs every few miles thanking the New Mexicans for their patience. It felt like the rainbow God sent to Noah saying, "I had to do that, sorry, but I won't do it again." Knowing how much it had held up Alex and Richard I was eternally grateful.

The "how are we getting away with this?" sensation had not faded. There must have been dozens of cops that had been alerted to this and were pursuing us in some way. It has to catch up with you eventually. We were scanning the air for planes or helicopters. There was no way to tell how many people were negatively aware of what we were doing. We had no real choice but to press on but things couldn't keep going that well forever, right?

Rather than an intense and dramatic race from sea to shining sea this was turning into a fairly boring but quick drive by three people who shared some very strange connections prior to the trip. There were no high speed police chases, no hairy maneuvers, no near death experiences, and nothing that would have been very entertaining to watch if we had been getting it all on video. The drama was all in getting the car, the team, and our mindsets where they needed to be in New York. The rest had really been going down the Hot Wheels track. I had expected the outcome to be half based on the uncontrollable variables and half on us. The half that was us, I guessed was 30% based on preparation and 70% on execution. That was reversed and perhaps even more askew. I had done all that I could to get us to the starting line with a chance. It looked like that might be all that we needed on this unexpectedly glorious day.

It had seemed crazy to make a reservation at the Portofino before we left so I didn't. There were simply too many obstacles between New York and Redondo Beach to justify a non-refundable hotel room. Riding through New Mexico we were less than 1000 miles out. It was time to make the call. I called them and booked two rooms for us. It did not sound like the hotel was highly trafficked that time of year.

I took over in Gallup, NM not knowing what I was in store for. Dave was exhausted enough that he stumbled badly getting out of the car. As we entered Arizona the Garmin ETA was 1 AM. That meant a speed limit average for the rest of the trip would have gotten us a 30 hour time. The evolution of the terrain was difficult to appreciate at speed but eerie when we realized how different the landscape was as we traveled along. One man's vacation destination is another's cross-country speeding obstacle.

America is a great country that offers a wide variety of landscapes. There were plenty of small towns spread hundreds of miles from anything remotely interesting. I remember the feeling, "What has to go wrong in your life to end up living here? Surely they can't all be in witness protection, right?" The diversity of our country is what makes it great. Strangely, it was the common interest among three very different people that was making this team function effectively.

The only area where we saw a lot of police activity, both fixed and moving, was just into Arizona. The Sanders - Chambers area felt like cop alley. Lots of quick decelerations stand out on the GPS data in that segment. Fortunately there was usually sufficient warning either from the countermeasure devices or from Dan's laser Asian vision. The wide open desert left few opportunities for effective hiding spots. It appeared that these highway patrolmen were far more interested in finding vacationers creeping into the 90s or drug runners than cross country outlaw road racers.

One car really threw us. It seems like every car out West is an American truck or SUV. If you see a very clean, white, late model Tahoe though, you need to slow down. There was one up ahead and it had some stickers. I couldn't see any lights but it was generally adhering to the speed limit, suspicious. Dan could tell that the tag was governmental but he couldn't make out any of the other identifying characteristics.

A cop moving in the opposite direction is easy. A speed trap is generally detectable. Theoretically we had seven semi-redundant implements to warn us of those - Waze, Trapster, V1, Passport, Scanner, CB,

Dan/Binoculars. The third possibility that is almost impossible to overcome is a cop in front of you moving in the same direction. The procedure is to leapfrog your way up to him by using the shade of other vehicles and curves to obstruct his line of sight until you are right behind him. Then you have to pass the cop at a very slight 2-3 mph differential while still less than 10 mph over the speed limit. This happened to us twice.

In the situation here, I was driving and the car up ahead turned out to be a Department of Homeland Security Tahoe. After that was discovered I passed him very quickly. He tried to keep up for a bit to see what was going on but that was not happening. I lost him quickly.

The second time was actually earlier in the drive. Dave was in Oklahoma and the cop that he happened upon was an Indian Reservation cop. Now in addition to smoking Peyote and taking twenty-five cents at a time from bus tours of senior citizens via shiny slot machines, native Americans get to police their own land. It is a bad place to get pulled over. You would have thought that I was asking Dave to sing karaoke to an audience of every girl that he had ever had a crush on. He could not have been less comfortable passing a police officer. I thought I was going to have to call 911 and report an accident behind us in the eastbound lane to get the dispatcher to get this guy to jump the median.

Fortunately, Dave eventually made it by him so I didn't have to commit another crime that day.

The drive down from Winslow, Arizona was the

worst leg of the trip. I was driving straight into the sun. It should have been obvious that when you drive due West through an entire day you are going to have to spend some time driving straight into the setting sun. It should have also been foreseeable that when you drive 100 mph into the sun it actually prolongs the sunset you get to experience. I had not thought about it. It would not have changed the fact that we had to negotiate through the hazard but it would have been nice to mentally prepare for it.

When racing drivers know that they will be looking into the sun at a certain point on each lap they place a piece of tape on the section of the windshield that obstructs their view of the sun. Supposedly it works wonders. I learned that after the fact from Charles. With our arsenal of every type of tape we had the means to deploy this solution.

The car was filthy but that hadn't mattered until then. Every bug and speck of dirt on the windshield glared to make visibility impossible. Dave described it well. "It looked as if we had driven through an apocalyptic storm of locusts whose entrails were filled with super-glue." When you hit a well-fed insect going 150 mph it leaves a streak of goo on your windshield more than a foot long. Washer fluid was no match for it and we were left to press on.

It was miserable. The dark voids in the blinding light were the trucks which couldn't see either. I had on dark polarized sunglasses and I was wedging my head against the roof of the car to use the top of the windshield frame as a makeshift sun visor. I am too tall to use regular sun visors. They block the entire road from a vantage point already near the headliner of most cars. This was a part of the trip where in normal circumstances a driver would have pulled over, grabbed a bite to eat, and waited for the sun to set. We had to keep driving and we needed to keep going fast.

At one point I was approaching two large trucks, one behind the other. The back truck was a FedEx truck who decided to pass the front. I was approaching fast, around 135 mph. I flashed my lights at the trucker and braked hard for a few seconds before lifting to shift the car's weight and restore the ability to steer. I honked my horn and ended up passing the truck with two of my tires off of the road in the left rocky median.

It was loud and startling to Dave and Dan but I was able to recover smoothly. The truck driver likely would not have been able to see in his mirror due to the contrast between looking forward and backwards in those light conditions. It was as close a call as we had. The only casualties of the off-road excursion were a shattered lower left fog light that the car still wears proudly and the dislodging of one of the four laser jamming heads. I honestly cannot believe we never broke the windshield.

The CB functionality had not improved. The Cobra 29 I bought was hugely adjustable and we were too inexperienced with it to really dial it in. I should have gone with a simple Radio Shack version like I had used previously. Idiot-proof was a salient attribute for our equipment to have.

We ended up only being able to hear occasional mumbled exclamations from the truckers that we passed. Most of what we did hear was their gurgled negative remarks about the silver Mercedes four wheeler that was going very fast. We did use the CB to get past some truckers. I would impersonate the truck on the left which was blocking us with a passing maneuver and ask the trucker on the right to tap his brakes so that I could come past. Then I would pretend to be the trucker on the right inviting the trucker on the left to come on over, telling him the coast was clear.

The safety discussion about the pursuance of this record remains unwinnable. There is, however, a surface level concern and then a deeper understanding of the safety implications that is more interesting to consider.

We drove across the country in less than a day and a half. Think about all of the drama that you have experienced in a car for the last three thousand miles, which on average in America is four to five months of driving. Think of the number of people texting, cutting you off, merging without looking, painting their toenails, crying for no apparent reason, eating, drinking, sleeping, reading, and doing everything except driving. We saw all of that ridiculousness in under two days.

Driving three thousand miles was more dangerous than the speed. We had one close call with the law and one with a truck but we made it safely because all three of us were wholly engaged in the task of driving. I maintain it is actually some of the safest feeling time I have spent behind the wheel. I don't expect that to carry any weight with people who will find this offensive but I am not surprised in the least that this went off without incident.

It was fortunate that all three of us remained devoted to unapologetically policing each other for fatigue. We were ready to step up when anyone else needed a break. After the sunset I was in the mountains in Western Arizona. It was terribly curvy and I got pretty delirious. I was going as fast as I could but getting very tired. I remember seeing a set of tail lights ahead of me and feeling like it was impossible to catch them. My eyes simply could not acclimate from the intensity of the sunset earlier. I told Dan to find us the next gas station and to not stop talking to me until we got there.

This was our slowest section. I recall the on board computer read about 95 mph for the leg. It normally read a little higher than was actually true, probably due to us resetting it if we had a slow stretch in order to boost our confidence. The actual pace from our tracking software was 89.43 mph for 237 miles.

This was our last gas stop. It was in Seligman, AZ. We had driven 2,390 miles in 24 hours and 24 minutes. That tank had only taken us 723 miles but with under 500 to go we were more than fine with an incomplete refuel. The stop took seven minutes and we were certainly not in our best form.

I remember looking at the distance to destination during that last leg and it being 650 miles. We had been driving for nearly an entire day and we felt like we were close but we still had a trip to Miami from Atlanta to go. It was disheartening but our pace was still strong. The overall average at that point had actually dropped down to 97.95 mph but it was getting dark and the roads were clearing up of other users. It was refreshing to know that we each only had one more driving stint, we did not have a chance to botch a refuel, and that it was finally dark.

We crossed the Arizona border in Needles. We had averaged 93.25 mph across Arizona, quite a feat given the month long feel of the last two hours of our lives. The context of average speeds on well prepared cross country drives was limited. With the fastest time ever in Cannonball competition, Dave Heinz & Dave Yarborough had averaged 86.9 mph onto a time of 32:51 in '79. David Diem and Doug Turner averaged 89.4 mph to achieve 32:07, the fastest time of the US Express competitions. The Rawlings/Collins Ferrari time in 2007 was 31:59 with an overall average of 87.9. Road improvements and route differences made the lower average and faster time possible. Alex Roy and Dave Maher had been the only pair to average over 90. Their 90.5 average had brought them in at just over 31 hours.

The slowest and most impossible feeling leg of our trip was still on par with each of these. Having their chronicled experiences available to build on could not have been any more valuable. Our machine was getting tired but we were soldiering on. We were not out of the woods just yet though.

During the trip I slept twice for 15-20 minutes each time. Dave slept three times around thirty minutes each time. I woke up while Dave was driving in Eastern California. We were absolutely flying by some trucks. I couldn't believe it but I was pleased that he had kept the pace up. The lights were streaking in a warp speed pattern. We were South of the Vegas to LA return traffic and the only other road users were trucks. The visual up ahead was surreal. There was an endless line of trucks just a few feet off of each others' bumpers and a completely empty lane to the left. I had never seen a circumstance so densely packed with no overtaking happening. Normally it seems like truck drivers all want to travel one or two miles per hour faster or slower than the ones next to them so there is a constant passing and jockeying for position. Here they might as well have been a pack of trunk-to-tail elephants in a dust storm, never getting out of line. It was faith in that status quo that allowed Dave to barrel past them all. I wiped the drool from my cheek and started to prepare myself for the final leg.

When the truck route diverted, I remember looking at the stars. There was almost no other light visible apart from our headlights and the moon was casting an eerie glow across the desert. They were so bright and you could see every single one of them. The spectacle was truly beautiful and it offered an unexpected perspective on the undertaking at hand. We were close enough to achieving my decade long dream that I truly felt like I could taste the salty air blowing inland from the Pacific Ocean. In this big experience though, I get a chance to see just how small we are in the eternal vastness of creation. We all need significance. We all strive for greatness, excellence at a task we are qualified for. Had we found it?

I think it was Dave that alerted me that I sounded like someone enjoying a psychotropic substance while watching Fantasia. I was deliriously tired.

The first question that people ask when you talk about doing something like this is, "What about the cops?" We actually only saw four or five police parked near the road and only passed ten to fifteen police cars moving in either direction. It was a non-issue. Our detection devices worked well and the visual diligence of having three people in the car was hugely effective. Even as the police loom as the scariest boogeyman seeking to foil such a trip, they had to be treated as a simple variable in a cold and emotionless equation. The further we got into the trip, the more numb and detached that calculation became. The hard science of preparation helped save us in the trying moments. As we fatigued and found ourselves less capable of decision making, we fell back on structured procedure and established regimen to proceed.

I took over in San Bernardino. Dave had driven 214 miles and we had about 209 to go. His average for that leg was 95.82 miles per hour. It was a gargantuan effort. An average like that against the exhaustion we felt made Dave seem like Sampson, hair cut off, eyes gouged out, beaten within an inch of his life but still ready and able to tear the entire house down. He had.

I was glad to have the final leg. It felt right. Dave and Dan were all for it as well.

Chapter 21 - The Final Push

As we entered the LA Basin we knew that we were probably going to break the record as long as the car didn't break and I didn't get arrested. We voted on whether to take it easy and cruise in with a mid 29s time or to push it with the chance to break into the 28s.

The latter obviously carried a much higher risk of accident, getting lost, or me getting arrested. Dan was pretty content to take it easy but Dave was 100% go. His decisiveness was new. A short day before he was so very along for the ride that he would hardly voice a preference of fast food establishment. 2,500 miles into the craziest game of highway Russian Roulette we had all ever played, he was ready to keep pulling the trigger!

He claimed that this all-out strategy was now the only way he knew how to operate. Sorry Lisa. I was leaning towards slowing down mostly due to the fact that I had not spent any time pondering the implications of decimating the records by more than two hours. Despite that, I agreed to push as long as the other two would stay vigilant. We pushed and I averaged around 100 through the dense Los Angeles metropolis. The traffic in LA had been an unpredictable elephant in every strategy session. There is no time where you can plan with confidence on it being easy, even in the middle of the night.

I said an out loud prayer for continued safety and to get us there without getting arrested. Dan and Dave obliged in a way that was probably beyond what their typical theology would tolerate but I appreciated their camaraderie in the moment. I do doubt God cares that much about this sort of activity but I know Megan was praying fervently that I wouldn't have to do it again. He listens to her.

Dave did say, "You are not going to close your eyes are you?"

The route was generally down the 15, onto the 210, and then the 605 to Redondo Beach. Every navigational instruction got triple repeated and no one was annoyed in the slightest. It sounded more like fingerpainting instructions to four year olds than the last instructions of the greatest outlaw drive of all time but that was the tone the car needed.

Google, Garmin, and Waze all disagreed on the best route as we snaked into Redondo Beach . A solo driver would have to pick one. A pair of drivers might be able to weigh two against each other. Having a third person in the car meant we could look at them all and objectively decide what was best. We ended up using parts of the Google and Garmin routes but it was very chaotic. We were tired, it was dark, and we had no experience on the roads. Dan had truly come into his own in the most ridiculous role I am sure he will ever fill in his life, riding from sea to shining sea with no control and the most ambiguous set of expectations anyone could pose.

He compiled all of the data, processed the pros and cons, and seamlessly presented navigational instructions for Dave to confirm and me to execute. Late in the game, with it all still on the line, we hit a true symphonic crescendo of teamwork.

The only red light we sat at after New York was

crossing the street into the parking lot for the Portofino Hotel and Marina. I forgot to use the traffic light changer and we let it cycle. The next morning I checked it when we left the parking area and it worked perfectly. Sorry Forrest.

We entered the parking lot to the Portofino at 11:46 PM PDT on Saturday, October 20th, 2013. We stopped the timers and put the car into park. Each of us grabbed our cameras and began taking pictures of everything - the Garmin screens, the stopwatches, the other phones, maps, and screens.

Our family pet growing up was a 232 pound English Mastiff named Caesar. He is the laziest, goofiest, drooliest, most gentle dog ever and his favorite thing in the world was chasing cats. One day I was out with him and he was running around. After not seeing him for a few minutes I heard a faint panicked meowing. I turned a corner to see Caesar's eyes as big as they could get and a very confused look on his face. He had caught something he had been chasing all of his life and now he had no idea what to do next. I walked over and pried his enormous jaws open, liberating the petrified but completely unharmed kitten.

For a moment we just sat in the car looking at each other in the same way that Caesar had looked at me that day. We had chased it so hard and we actually did it. What was literally the next movement that our bodies needed to make?

The trip had taken us 28 hours 50 minutes and 26 seconds. We drove 2,813.7 miles at an average of

97.55 mph. Our moving average discounting the 46 minutes of stops was 100.22 mph. Our three fuel stops had taken 9, 12, and 7 minutes respectively. That accounted for 28 minutes of the stopping time. The other 18 minutes had been the side of the road stops for oil, driver changes, and urination.

We traveled through 13 states, 93 counties, passed 5 speed traps and 12 moving police cars using 34 devices and countermeasures installed in a 9 year old car with over 115,000 miles. We were never pulled over and received no tickets during or after the trip. We averaged 13.2 mpg and the top speed reached was 158 mph. It required the work of 29 people in various capacities.

We parked in front of the hotel and asked the Valet to take a picture of us in front of the car. I am sure that three stinky, tired guys and a car covered in bugs having its own stench of fuel was a unique sight to him. He was by no means a wizard of digital SLR functionality but you can tell we are there. We shut the car off.

I called Megan. The emotion was overwhelming. We had the nav computers and multiple stopwatches displaying the time but I still could not believe it. We had beaten the existing record by 2 hours 14 minutes.

How had that been possible? It was just before 3 AM in Atlanta but she answered the phone on the first ring. Tears were streaming down my face and I could barely manage the words, "We did it." She was more relieved than happy or congratulatory. She asked if I was ok and I tried to reassure her even if the composure of my voice didn't. I was too scared that the time was somehow miscalculated to tell her what it was. Dave, Dan, and I had agreed not to tell anyone the exact time until we dealt with a press release. That boundary did not apply to her but I still couldn't form the words.

I managed to tell her that we had beaten it by over two hours. "What?" she yelled. "Are you kidding? How?"

"I know sweetheart. I still can't believe it. We just went really, really fast. Get some sleep and I will call you when I am up in the morning. I love you."

We went to check into the hotel and dropped the bags in the rooms. I asked the receptionist if she had ever had anyone coming in during the middle of the night talking about Cannonball. She said that she had only worked there for a couple of months and had never heard of it. The valet had not either.

I fired them both but Dave said I did not have the authority to do that. I thought I had just earned the privilege but I guess not. One day I will have to go back there and host a quiz show competition on Cannonball Trivia.

I honestly couldn't believe the time. The lack of fanfare at the finish made it a bit anticlimactic but I was definitely a bit sanguine about the whole thing. We had just beaten a world record that had been pursued for over forty years by a margin of over ten percent. I knew it would be unbelievable to the people I wanted to believe me. I knew that we had proof but the idea of having to prove this kind of a time felt unbelievably daunting.

I texted Adam, my parents, Chris, Ash, Danny, Tom, Jules, Nick, Charles, Forrest, and the rest of the team to let them know that we had done it. I told them that we had agreed not to tell anyone the exact time until we got home, compiled the proof, and arranged the release. We told them all we made it and we were safe. I thanked them all for coming with me on this journey in whatever way they had.

Of course they were all able to figure out that we had shattered the record by the timing of those texts.

We were as hungry as we were tired. Dan looked for nearby restaurants that were open at midnight and found a Denny's. The irony of getting back into a car after that drive was not lost on us. I am not superstitious but it almost seemed morbidly appropriate for us to be involved in some horrific crash on the way to eat an omelet after breaking nearly every traffic law in the United States the day before.

The large Samoan gentleman that was waiting on all two of the occupied tables in the Redondo Beach Denny's was not worried about us being secret shoppers. Dave was not thinking too well which added to the hilarity of each exchange. He put together an order of eggs, bacon, and some hash browns. The expressionless face of the waiter was difficult to read but there was a clearly condescending, "why is this idiot messing with me" guise as he pointed to the menu and said, "That's a Grand Slam." The most popular item on their menu.

I had an omelet. I think Dan had fried chicken fingers for the eighth time in three days but I could be wrong. We ate and headed back to the hotel.

The Portofino Hotel offers earplugs to help you sleep through the moans of the indigenous sea lions. We didn't need them.

The next morning I woke up around nine and signed onto the hotel wifi. I went to the tracking device web site and logged in. I tried to export the data for the prior two days and the site locked up. I called their support line and asked them to perform the same export. The technician sent me the file and it was missing half of the data including the start and finish of the run.

There was not a good way to tell if the device was reporting during the drive so we never knew how accurate it was. I called them back and they confirmed that they had a server issue but assured me that it was there and that they could get it. He emailed me the full file a few excruciatingly long hours later. It clearly shows when we left, when we arrived, and how far we drove.

As I said, I was truly concerned that even with as much proof as we had, people who had any experience in this event would not believe us. If we did not have a complete set of the GPS data I did not think that we had a prayer. Dave and Dan knew I was nervous about it but the relief of finally getting the end-all-be-all of verification in my hands was unreal.

My favorite image remains one of the nav screens. They tell the entire story. Distance, average speed, moving time, moving average, time stopped, total time driving. The image of the stopwatch is great too. I have never understood how Roy and Rawlings could do this drive and not end up with pictures like that.

Dave and I had breakfast next to the marina. Dan slept. It was surreal to think about what we had just done. The Portofino Inn is now called the Portofino Hotel and Marina and has been recently remodeled. It is a gorgeous place. I had to get back to work and I hated not having a few days to enjoy it.

We drove the car to Lamborghini Newport Beach and dropped it in their service department. I told Pietro, their GM, I would send a truck for it later that week. He was happy to let us leave the car but he never looked at it. A few days later he actually saw the CL in their parking lot and he asked me in his perfect Americanized Italian accent, "What type of crazy race is this mad Batman car built for?" I told him to watch the news in a few days and it would all make sense.

We booked some flights online, UBERed a car to LAX, and flew home. When we had a few minutes before the flight left I decided to call Alex Roy. He picked up the phone, "Ed Bolian! How does it feel?" I was caught entirely off guard by the tone and the question.

"It feels good Alex, could you feel it?"

"Well I figured you had done it after the text that you sent me last week."

"Alex, I didn't text you last week did I?" I checked through our text log. "Yeah, I haven't texted you in months."

"Sure you did, some time from a random number. 31 something, just a little bit longer than my time."

"I just finished last night Alex."

306

"Really, well what was your time?"

"Honestly I can't believe it either but I can prove it. 28:50."

"Are you kidding me? That is unbelievable. I guess you aren't the only person to do this in the last ten days."

Alex was skeptical but he knew I was telling the truth. He was and continues to be a great sportsman and competitor.

It turned out that an Ohio man named Greg Ledet had been the one who had sent Alex the time by text just a few days prior.

His claim was that he had made his fourth attempt at a New York to Los Angeles drive on Columbus Day weekend, just a week before. He claimed to have done it in 31 hours 17 minutes in a BMW 335xi sedan, leaving from the Trump Hotel and finishing at the Santa Monica pier which would make it the third fastest transcontinental driving time ever. I have gotten to know Greg very well since our drive and he has never been able to show even a circumstantial piece of evidence that he actually made the drive. As I said before, I find it emotionally useless to spend time believing that people lie about this sort of thing so I have given him the benefit of the doubt.

Right before we got on the plane I made a social media post. "For those who know what I am talking about - we did it. Thank you for all of the thoughts and prayers. More to come soon." I checked in to tag it as being at Los Angeles International Airport to offer a small clue.

Before they closed the cabin door and told us to shut our phones off I was seeing all of the congratulatory replies scroll in. People who I had not seen or talked to in years knew exactly what it was and had understood back then what it meant to me. Those who had no idea found it to be the most intriguing thing ever and begged for an explanation.

A few days later they got it.

Chapter 22 - Catharsis

Dave, Dan, and I settled into our three adjoining exit row seats on that plane bound for Atlanta. The catharsis of the record was still washing over me. There had been so many times in my life that I finished a task only to immediately feel the need to go onto the next one. This was clearly different. It seemed to be setting in for the other two as well. The emotional overload of falling into something significant at the last minute and then investing so much of themselves into it over the course of the prior two days was hitting the guys hard.

I loved how it meant something so different to each of them. They can speak for themselves but I will try to explain it from my perspective. Dan had enjoyed it as the adventure of a lifetime. He had risen to the challenge and added something to his resume that he had never been looking for. It appealed to the car guy in him but the idea of being called upon seemed to be the reward in itself. I think he took pride in being the kind of guy that you ask to do something like this. He should.

It has been three years now as I put the final touches on this book and I am still not sure that either Dave or I completely know what the experience meant to him. It was a new pearl in a string of personal reinvention. Leaving Apple, a new job, another new job, two Lamborghinis, a new circle of friends, and now the Cannonball had made him a person that I doubt the two year younger version of himself would have recognized. He should be proud of that. I am proud of him.

He had impressed himself in some ways he was clearly not anticipating. As someone who keeps a very fluid life direction, I could see Dave trying to see how much he wanted this drive to be his personal brand. As we flew home he was uncontainably curious about what the next week would look like.

The five hour flight was an interesting opportunity to debrief. Dave was desperately trying to think of any strategies that would have improved the time. I could not tell if this was purely academic or if the next weekend he wanted to be back in New York at the starting line. The part of the conversation I think I enjoyed the most was the explanation of what the odds were that anyone ever got that same chance to get the right combination of positive outcomes to each of the variables that could have foiled the trip. Could the Cannonball Slot Machine ever throw all 7's again? That served as a supplementary rationale to explain why I was so happy.

It also probably helped explain why I looked like I could not have been more relaxed if I had just spent a week getting twice daily massages in Bora Bora. If my blood pressure and pulse were any lower on that flight home I would not have been able to open my eyes. It was the level of relaxation where you can actually hear your occasional heartbeat and feel your skin start to warm up rhythmically because the blood isn't moving very quickly through your veins. It feels awesome.

Since it was a complete toss up as to whether or not the public reaction would be positive or negative, we agreed that I would be the initial face of the story. Dave and Dan still wanted to be able to pass the Google-your-name portion of a job interview and so they were very pleased not to be in the proverbial driver's seat for the next steps in the process.

I emailed Richard Rawlings and spoke with him and Dennis Collins about our time a few days after we got back. They were both excited at the prospect of such a time but very skeptical. They were very pleased that we had adhered to the most traditional Cannonball start and end points. Richard seemed incapable of wrapping his head around the idea of our time with us only achieving a 158 mph top speed. He had always been quick to say that they had reached 207 mph (nine miles per hour faster than the manufacturer stated top speed of a 1999 Ferrari 550 Maranello) on several occasions during their drive.

At the time they were headed to Jupiter, FL to film with Burt Reynolds for *Fast and Loud*. He later told me that they had discussed my time and that Burt had passed along words of congratulations. It is tough to get much cooler than that.

I called Brock Yates Jr. who now organizes the Cannonball One Lap of America event that his father started in the 1980's. I told him how much I thought of his father and how fondly I remembered the conversation I had with him nearly a decade prior. I told him that we had broken the record and our goal in all of this was to pay tribute to the legacy of Cannonball and the chapter of American automotive history it represented. Brock had Alzheimer's and did not remember anything about Cannonball but I told his son I wanted to find a chance to visit his father and stepmother (Pam) at some point soon to pay tribute to the man who had motivated me for the last ten years to accomplish this ridiculous dream.

I got back in touch with Doug Demuro, who was starting to do the majority of his journalistic writing for Jalopnik - an online car blog that had broken the story of Alex Roy breaking the record in 2007. Doug wrote and released the story on the Wednesday before Halloween. They spoke with an unnamed employee of the tracking company (in fact, the CEO) to confirm the accuracy of the tracking data. The Jalopnik editorial staff contacted Waze as well to corroborate our claims. They refused to release their files but quietly re-inforced the data. The article went viral quickly. I was told it was the most read article ever on their site.

The story was on every major network, it was the most clicked on article on CNN.com for a 24-hour period on Friday, November 1st. There were more than 500 television mentions, over 1,000 articles, countless blog and forum discussions, radio interviews, magazine remarks, etc. This drive I thought might barely matter to the American car enthusiast community became a shot heard round the world.

My pursuance of this stood in stark contrast to that of Yates and the original Cannonballers of the 1970s. On one hand, the similarities are awesome, but in reality the spirit could not have been much more different. They were mad that people were saying that they couldn't do something. They were making a case for a higher level driving license for qualified drivers and challenging a new establishment. It was a protest of an idea and it was designed to show that speed limits were unnecessary and that highway patrol agencies were inadequate.

Our goal was not that at all. I do not believe that speed limits should be abolished. I think that the metrics of success are off but I think that they do a good job. Our drivers education programs, licensing requirements, and general driving protocols are nowhere close to where they would need to be in order to have higher or no speed limits.

If you want to raise speed limits this is how you do it. You start by placing the penalties on activities that are truly dangerous. Institute $5,000 mandatory and uninsurable fines for the following - at fault accidents, DUI, texting, using the phone, and running red lights. Fines go to fund a full scale performance driving education system that can be privatized. Road and written tests must be conducted every five years. A license is immediately suspended at each offense until paid. Get three fines in one year and license is suspended for the next twelve months. Raise speed limits on controlled access highways 5 mph per year. There is zero cost of implementation and no loss in revenue for government. Police officers could never justify spending time writing $250 speeding tickets if they could be chasing $5,000 texting fish. It would not make driving a rich man's game. It would make it critical for people in no position to afford a five grand fine to be careful and follow the rules.

It would cut down on road users and create a huge demand for quality public transport. Government could step in to fill that void. This also has the added political benefit of being unobjectionable. No one can say that it is a bad idea to penalize people for causing accidents and drinking or texting while driving. Perhaps if I were not completely unelectable by the Google criteria as a politician now I could run for Senate and make that my platform.

Can I still be arrested for this? The statutes of limitation have expired everywhere but Texas and Oklahoma which continue to roll whenever I am in each state. In that first year window it would have been difficult but not impossible for a police officer to develop probable cause to get a warrant to arrest me or Dave and to open an investigation. They would need to show proof of which of us was driving in their jurisdiction and rather precisely where we sped. This could be as easy as referencing footage from traffic cameras or toll booths but we have not had any issues. Most cops are car guys and as long as you do not try to rub their noses in your speeding exploits, they tend to be fairly good sports after a safe outcome.

A crime stoppers organization sent out a lot of emails to local Georgia police precincts imploring them to find a way to arrest me. The blast included a very un-hateable picture of me with Megan from my Facebook profile. There were some internet petitions circulating encouraging various states that we drove through to find and arrest us. None received many signatures. The story was shared on Facebook more than 25,000 times from the CNN article as well as a similar number on the Jalopnik site. The CNN article had over 5,000 comments posted. CNN Television named my trip the "Best Commute of 2013."

Interestingly, I have not been contacted by anyone saying that they are seriously working on a plan to break my record. I do get asked often if I have any interest in breaking my own record. Certainly not until someone breaks it but if I am honest with myself, if I had ten attempts and $250k to throw at it, I doubt I would have all of the uncontrollable factors align to even make it possible to break the record. Once you start adding up the theoretical probabilities of the slot machine variables - of having no bad weather, no construction projects, no accidents that cause traffic jams, light rush hours where unavoidable, a full-ish moon for visibility, no issues with the car, not hitting any animals crossing the road, being able to coordinate with a team, and generally being psychologically ready to do so; it starts to get asymptotically close to impossible to recreate.

A few months following the record, I was talking to Richard Doherty. He organized the 1980-1983 US Express events after participating in Cannonball and being disappointed in the publicity circus of 1979 and the discontinuation of the event. The stories from these guys never get old to me. I don't think his head lifted off of his pillow in the decades following their last 1983 running where he didn't hope someone would call inviting him on another cross country race. I told him how in every conversation I had with someone who had done this type of drive, they all offered "well, if this hadn't happened..." scenarios where they would have gone faster. I felt like the only person to have felt like I could not go any faster. Everything that went right surely could not all go so well again.

Many commenters and friends have offered various solutions on how to improve the time. As I contemplate the possible improvements that I could have made to lower my time, this is what I have come up with:

- Pay for fuel in cash (eliminates credit card issues). Race car dump cans, fuel trucks on the side of the road or alongside the car while moving on the highway, etc. are overkill. The advantage is not worth the risks. Fuel volume on our trip was perfect. No need for more. We did need a fuel additive to cope with poor quality gas in the Western US. I had planned to take some but forgot.
- Have friends at each gas stop to help pump, clean the windshield, and manage logistics.
- We used Waze on an iPhone. It is better to use it on a 3G/4G tablet.
- A faster car - a Bentley Continental GT Supersports 2+2 ($100-130k current value) would be the best option. This would make occasional 180 mph stints possible without losing handling ability.
- Lead cars out of Manhattan to block intersections (Rawlings/Collins did this)
- Working CB and Scanner
- Slightly overfill the car with oil to begin the drive.
- At this point you can probably scrap the spare tire and jack. The time to replace it would probably make it nearly impossible to break the record and the extra space will make the drive

more comfortable. At the very least, move it to a completely out of the way location.

- Stabilize or mount the binoculars so that people other than Dan can use them.
- Find some way to apologize to the people who you pass. This could be a scrolling LCD sign along the back of the car.
- A cleaner dash would decrease stress.
- Deploy more scout cars throughout the country.

Each of these ideas would save 1-5 mins overall.

Combined they are not enough to overcome issues with any one of the variables that we had favorable outcomes with. A storm, traffic jam, accident, car issue, or ticket would likely end any chance of improving on our time.

During an interview that I did on CNN, the hosts asked what I would do next. The hosts at the *Today Show* in New York were similarly interested in what happens to someone after they spend a day and a half breaking just about every traffic law in the country. I answered that according to my wife, my next adventure to look forward to was having children. The ticking clock that was not mounted with double stick tape to the dashboard of the Mercedes had not slowed its tempo. We got pregnant the next month and found out on January 1, 2014. Graham Edward Bolian was born at 3:12 on August 20, 2014. He was 7 lbs 4 ounces, 20.5 inches long.

In the aftermath of the record announcement, I

came to find out that our one-off time trial style drives were not the only modern interpretation of the Cannonball legacy. Immediately following the announcement of the Roy/Maher/Welles record, a man from San Francisco named John Ficarra had an idea. He was disgusted by the money-no-object approach at the record pursuit and was enamored by the recently launched 24 hours of Lemons racing series (endurance track racing in $500 cars). He decided it would be interesting to blend the two and The 2904 was formed.

This is a longer story for another day but after our drive, Ficarra contacted me. He said that they had run the event six times and if they were going to do it again, they wanted to spice it up a bit. The premise was that each team could spend no more than $2,904 which was representative of the mileage of their original New York to San Francisco route. They had also done the event from New York to Los Angeles. Like Lemons rules, safety related items were not counted in the budget. He said that if I were interested in joining their merry event, it might do just that.

I told him that I would love to do it and experience the drive in a bit of a different way. It also offered me the chance to continue exploring different solutions to this problem I had been kicking around for my entire adult life. I purchased a 12 owner, 2 accident, salvage title, airbags previously deployed, frame damaged and repaired, 8 shades of white and yellow 2002 Mercedes S55 AMG on Craigslist Las Vegas for $1,500. The woman selling it had lent it to her daughter to drive to Hollywood to become a famous movie star. The car had broken down and she had never become famous. The driver's window was stuck down, the suspension was collapsed, the gauges didn't work, and the mileage was unknown.

I bought the car and had it shipped home. Dave "Klink," Chris Staschiak, and I drove the car among a field of eleven cars to win the 2015 running of the event with a time of 32 hours 5 minutes, making it the fastest time ever in a competitive New York to Los Angeles style event. This was not the only Cannonball related news story of 2015, however.

2015 marked an unexpected renaissance in the notion of competitive cross country driving. It seemed to have been fueled by the popularity of the news story about our run but it was an explosion of creative interpretation around the same idea. During the year, there were twelve new "Cannonball" related records claimed. They were:

- Solo Atlantic to Pacific Record – David Simpson – 27 hours 49 mins
- Atlantic to Pacific Record – Vic Echeverria, Bill Farmer – 26 hours 19 mins
- Shortest EV Charge Time NY to LA (Guinness officiated) – Carl Reese, Deena Mastracci, Rodney Hawk – 12 hours, 48 mins
- EV NY to LA Record – Carl Reese, Alex Roy, Deena Mastracci – 57 hours, 48 mins
- Autonomous Car NY to LA – Carl Reese, Alex Roy, Deena Mastracci – 57 hours, 48 mins
- Motorcycle NY to LA Record – Carl Reese – 38 hours 49 mins
- 3 Wheeled LA to NY Record – Alex Roy & Zach Bowman – 41 hours 49 mins

- EV Coast to Coast to Coast Record – Carl Reese, Deena Mastracci – 6 Days 6 hours 22 minutes
- Coast to Coast to Coast Record – Pierce Plam, John Ficarra, Alex Richter – 5 days 10 hours 49 mins
- Solo NY to LA Record – David Simpson – 34 hours 33 mins
- Competitive Event NY to LA Record – Ed Bolian, Chris Staschiak, Dave Klink – 32 hours 5 mins
- John Ficarra set a record of having participated in 7 competitive Cannonball-style events

It was an amazing year to be associated with this craft. Also, there was a spinoff of a spinoff created. Paying tribute to The 2904, which itself paid tribute to the Cannonball Baker; some New Zealanders created an event called the C2C Express. In addition to limiting the purchase budget at a rounder $3,000, all participating cars had to be built prior to 1980. I was asked to participate in the second running of this in September 2016 along with fellow 2904 competitor Arne Toman and Forrest Sibley. We dressed as the Blues Brothers and drove a 1974 Dodge Monaco Bluesmobile to a winning time of 34 hours 17 minutes.

2016 was also an extremely sad time for the Cannonball community. Early in the year, Richard Doherty passed away. In October, we lost Brock Yates. I had the honor of penning an obituary for my late hero for Jalopnik and it brought back all of the emotion that this chapter of my life had involved. The outpouring of love and admiration from the motorsport community was plentiful and well deserved.

I continue to receive calls of congratulations and camaraderie from various past Cannonballers, US Express guys, and even heard of other small events of this kind that have happened over the past few decades. It is an interesting fraternity of lunatics to currently be in charge of but it has been a very fun ride.

Epilogue - Now Find Yours!

The takeaway from this experience is simply how awesome God can allow our time on this planet to be. It is a story of an inspiration, identity, and a very unique challenge. Cross country record breaking will never be a mainstream goal or activity and it should not be. I want this story to serve as an illustration that there is probably an out of the box idea out there that can become your Cannonball record.

I am the luckiest guy in the world. Not for winning, not for surviving, and not for avoiding jail. At a very young age I found that "thing." I found a challenge that could preoccupy my consciousness, both demand and justify an endless string of sacrifices and incremental commitments, become an obsession, and be an intense source of pride in achievement. Through the arc of my engagement with the challenge it went from an interest, to an idea, to a goal, to a challenge, to a lifestyle, to an obsession, to something that I would do almost anything to achieve. The transformative arc revealed more about myself than it did about driving.

It was at the preparatory moment when I knew nothing was off the negotiation table when I knew I had found it. It existed in the intersection between my interests, abilities, and self image. There was nothing that could tick more resonating boxes for me.

The drive appealed to my passions, edified the image of myself I wanted the world to see, demonstrated the attributes about me I am most fond of, and helped me come to grips with the flaws within me. The Cannonball Record could hardly have been a more obscure dream but I truly believe there was nothing else on Earth that I could have accomplished that would have made me this content.

There is not a prescription to offer for how to find your "thing" and this is not meant to be a self-help book. Writing this has been a personal celebration for me to look back on how my perspective evolved with respect to this quest. The growth was the prize. I have heard a lot of motivational speakers preach ideas of working at what you love, visualizing success, and staying dedicated to your dreams.

That is all well and good but that is not what got me here. I do those things but they would never have led me to this as a goal. This happened because I let myself be exposed to it early on and I never gave any credence to the multitude of reasons it could not or should not be done. Due to my general lack of respect for rules and boundaries, that realization came fairly easily for me but it may be a challenge to some. Push through it.

The obstacles in this pursuit served to show how everything that makes me broken as a person actually made me qualified for this. The unrelenting subtle gravity pulling me toward it never let go for an entire decade. Things could stand in the way and pull me in other directions for a short time but the tidal movement was toward the reality of this happening some day.

My preference for improvisation over structure, my indignance to authority and my unique moral interpretation of the world, my love of cars, my faith in the unknowable, and even the psychopathy that desensitizes me; it all came together to make me a person who could contend.

The two people standing by my side in the Portofino parking lot are a testament to the uniqueness of this type of pursuit. Along the way, I found an endless line of people who found it interesting or fun. They offered to help, to discuss, and even to dream alongside me. When it came time to act though, it was not right. It was not their thing. At the point where procedure shifted from fun and spirited to not letting anything stand in the way, the wheat and the chaff separated.

I ended up with one guy who wanted to go on a road trip and one that just wasn't doing anything that weekend. The experience was completely different for them and I absolutely love them both for it. It truly would not have happened without them. If Dave knew all of the reasons to slow down like I did he would not have maintained and improved upon the pace. If Dan had built the car with me he would have used it all in the theory in which we intended it rather than adapting it to our immediate needs as he saw them.

When the rubber literally met the road I found the planning was the last thing I had to let go of in order to reach for victory in a final push. If I had held out for a perfectly functioning car and the team that I was expecting, I would still be dreaming while procrastinating. Whether you believe that it is God, the universe, or just random coincidence pulling you in the direction of your opus it will quickly become clear that it is not a destination that we get to drive to on our own accord. For me, this is a God thing.

Even though there were years of a gravitational pull toward pursuance, success was neither guaranteed nor likely. The wheels of the slot machine were entirely outside of my control. Dressed in priestly garb, an inebriated Dean Martin joked to Sammy Davis Jr. that God was their co-pilot in *Cannonball Run*. The astronomically improbable opportunity we had to complete our drive in such a staggering time reinforced to me God was with us in a much more serious sense. If I had tarried any longer in the rental business, married the wrong girl, pursued other selfish ambitions, given into the temptation of divorce, or refused to glorify Him through my incremental successes - I would not have done it. My God is faithful.

"For I know the plans I have for you," declares the Lord, "plans to prosper you and not to harm you, plans to give you hope and a future."
Jeremiah 29:11 (NIV)

My story is one of alternating between seasons of pushing as hard as I could with disregard for the risks and the seasons of accepting advice and yielding to the direction where I needed to go.

Basketball gave way to business
Ivy League gave way to cheap local school and disposable funds
Journalism waned and Supercar Rentals was born
I gave my own selfishness the back seat and let myself love Megan

She showed me when it was time to let
Supercar Rentals go and to go to the
dealership
Those sacrifices eventually created the resolve
to chase a dream that had always been there
in a stronger but more responsible way
A balanced life finally gave way to the
permissive trigger to do whatever it takes to
make the last push
And even then, my team and my ideas had to
yield to the people that God put in my path at
just the right time.

It is my choice to view it in that way. I could
take ownership and say that I meant for it all to
happen just as it did but that would be a lie.
Masculinity tells us to beat our chests, own the
victory, and claim the spoils but that is not what is
merited here. God remained in control and deserves
whatever glory can come from it.

The ebb and flow of preference versus "being
along for the ride" is what made this whole thing so
useful for personal growth. At times I rowed upstream,
at times downstream. The wind was at my back and
also blowing in my face. At times the ground
crumbled, other times it was the only thing holding me
up. Somehow, though, I never stopped getting closer.

Winning was undoubtedly the icing on a long
baked cake. It was one of the life moments where the
payoff was exactly as good as you dreamt it might be.
The true reward, though, was the road that took me
there. It was a crutch when I needed to limp through
the harder times in my life. It was the hope for

something great when everything else tried to pull me down. It stayed there as a beacon up ahead just reminding me it was there while I was busy with the rest of life. Crucially, when I badly needed a win, it was still right there.

When the beauty of life comes through the challenges that we face, our job is to simply make sure that we are focused on the game and that we end up doing what we need to. The first flush after finally getting around to fixing that endlessly running toilet would never be as fulfilling if it hadn't spent so much time tormenting you in the background.

Perspective is critical. What we need to do is try as hard as we can and then let the pressure off for a moment. Let the world around settle as it will. Take a break, appreciate how far we have come. Then we can get ready to push again.

I praise my God for every step of the path that led me to Cannonball and for holding me in His hand to bring me through it. My two sincerest prayers are that my newborn son come to know and love that same God the way that I do and that one day he will find a "thing" of his own that he can strive to conquer. If one day he gets to cry the same tears of joy I did as I stood on that dock overlooking the Pacific Ocean in the middle of the night on October 20, 2013 then he will know he found it. On that fine day, there will be two happiest people in the world.

Now go find yours!

Supercar Rentals Fleet (Ferrari 360 Spider, Lamborghini
Gallardo, 612 Scaglietti)

The Prostitute Gallardo

Lamborghini Murcielago LP640 Roadster purchased the same
week as the record-setting CL55

Electronics installation

Cockpit setup

Custom switch panel

Two additional 22 gallon fuel cells

Team photo prior to departure from Atlanta to New York

Checking for gas leak on
the way to New York

View from our hotel in
New Jersey

Staging at the Red Ball Parking Garage the day of the run

Photo of our departure by Ash Majid

Cockpit at night

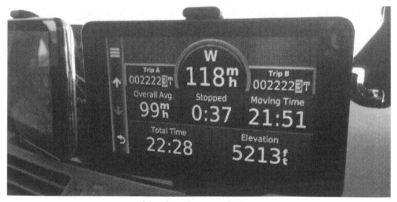
Navigation updates

Fatigue

Bug splatter

Driving into the sun

Navigation screen trip data

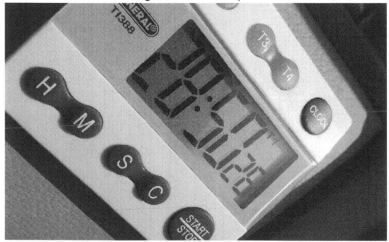

Stopwatch

Arrival at the Portofino

Bugs, dirt, and a broken fog light

At the Today Show with Megan

Graham – born August 20, 2014

30146203R00197

Printed in Great Britain
by Amazon